Drawing on recent work in critical theory, feminism, and social history, this book traces the lines of tension shot through Victorian culture by the fear that the social world was being reduced to a display window behind which people, their actions, and their convictions were exhibited for the economic appetites of others. Affecting the most basic elements of Victorian life – the vagaries of desire, the rationalization of social life, the gendering of subjectivity, the power of nostalgia, the fear of mortality, the cyclical routines of the household – the ambivalence generated by commodity culture organizes the thematic concerns of these novels and the society they represent. Taking the commodity as their point of departure, chapters on Thackeray, Gaskell, Dickens, Eliot, Trollope, and the Great Exhibition of 1851 suggest that Victorian novels provide us with graphic and enduring images of the power of commodities to affect the varied activities and beliefs of individual and social experience.

*Literature, Culture, Theory 17*

# Novels behind glass

## Literature, Culture, Theory 17

❖❖❖❖❖❖❖❖❖❖❖❖❖❖❖❖❖❖❖❖❖❖❖❖❖❖❖❖❖❖❖❖❖❖❖❖❖❖❖❖❖❖❖❖❖❖❖

*General editors*

RICHARD MACKSEY, *The Johns Hopkins University*
and MICHAEL SPRINKER, *State University of New York at Stony Brook*

The Cambridge *Literature, Culture, Theory* series is dedicated to theoretical studies in the human sciences that have literature and culture as their object of enquiry. Acknowledging the contemporary expansion of cultural studies and the redefinitions of literature that this has entailed, the series includes not only original works of literary theory but also monographs and essay collections on topics and seminal figures from the long history of theoretical speculation on the arts and human communication generally. The concept of theory embraced in the series is broad, including not only the classical disciplines of poetics and rhetoric, but also those of aesthetics, linguistics, psychoanalysis, semiotics, and other cognate sciences that have inflected the systematic study of literature during the past half century.

# Novels behind glass

## Commodity culture and Victorian narrative

❖❖❖❖❖❖❖❖❖❖❖❖❖❖❖❖❖❖❖❖❖❖❖❖❖❖❖❖❖❖❖❖❖❖❖❖❖❖❖

**ANDREW H. MILLER**

*Indiana University*

CAMBRIDGE
UNIVERSITY PRESS

Published by the Press Syndicate of the University of Cambridge
The Pitt Building, Trumpington Street, Cambridge CB2 1RP
40 West 20th Street, New York, NY 10011-4211, USA
10 Stamford Road, Oakleigh, Melbourne 3166, Australia

First published 1995

Printed in Great Britain at the University Press, Cambridge

*A catalogue record for this book is available from the British Library*

*Library of Congress cataloguing in publication data*

Miller, Andrew H., 1964–
Novels behind glass: commodity culture and Victorian narrative / Andrew H. Miller.
p.   cm. – (Literature, culture, theory)
Includes bibliographical references and index.
ISBN 0 521 47133 8 (hardback)
1. English fiction – 19th century – History and criticism – Theory, etc.
2. Fiction – Economic aspects – Great Britain – History – 19th century.
3. Literature and society – Great Britain – History – 19th century.
4. Great Britain – Social life and customs – 19th century.
5. Commercial products in literature.   6. Culture – History – 19th century.
7. Narration (Rhetoric).   I. Title.   II. Series.
PR878.E37M55   1995
823'.809355–dc20   95-44402

ISBN 0 521 47133 8 hardback

TAG

*To Lou Horton and William Lee Miller*

# Contents

# Illustrations

# Acknowledgements

Many people have read the following book and improved the arguments I make in it; I'm glad to have the opportunity now to thank them. Aileen Douglas, Uli Kneopflmacher, George Levine, and Elaine Showalter provided both encouragement and important criticism during the early stages of research and writing. At Indiana, my colleagues Pat Brantlinger, Mary Burgan, Mary Favret, Don Gray, and Susan Gubar have read and commented on the entire manuscript, in some cases more than once. Conversations with other friends and colleagues have helped me think through the other issues with which I engage here; I'm especially grateful to Jim Adams, Andrew Barnaby, Don Cameron, Fraser Easton, Lou Horton, Jean Kowaleski, John Kucich, Michael Lucey, William Lee Miller, Jim Naremore, Steve Pulsford, and Lisa Schnell. Michael Sprinker has been an ideal editor and Adrienne Munich a very sharp, helpful reader for Cambridge University Press.

Portions of this book have been published in different form. An early version of chapter 1 appeared in *PMLA* (October 1990); an early version of chapter 3 appeared in *Genre* 25 (Spring 1992), pp. 91–111; passages from chapter 2 appeared in *Yale Journal of Criticism* 7.2 (1994), pp. 131–49. Finally, a fellowship from the Andrew Mellon Foundation allowed me to concentrate my energies on this project when it most required them.

# Introduction

By the absolute emphasis on its exhibition value, the work of art becomes a creation with entirely new functions, among which the one we are conscious of, the artistic function, later may be recognized as incidental.     Walter Benjamin, *Illuminations*, p. 225

In the mid-1830s, new glass-making technology was introduced into England, technology which allowed the mass production of glass sheets of unprecedented size. With the repeal of the excise tax in the forties, the market for these glass sheets expanded considerably, and by the early fifties panes of up to four feet in length were being made fairly regularly. Health-reformers and construction firms encouraged the use of the new sheets in domestic architecture, but the most immediate and visible beneficiaries of these technological developments were retailers who used the glass for their display windows. These windows radically transfigured the experience of walking through commercial sections of London, fashioning the streets into gas-lit spaces of utopian splendor. "When we arrive at St. Paul's Churchyard," wrote one observer in 1851, "we come to a very world of show. Here we find a shop whose front presents an uninterrupted mass of glass from the ceiling to the ground."[1] This "world of show" became the occasion for elaborate fantasies of consumption, sensuous experiences of imagined acquisition, and almost immediately these sheets of glass and the fantasies they encouraged were used as evidence displaying the material progress of the nation and its capitol, uniting observers in admiration:

---

1 George Dodd, "London Shops and Bazaars," in Charles Knight, ed., *London* (London, Henry G. Bohn, 1851), p. 392.

By what steps the shops of the metropolis have arrived at their present positions – how the heavy shapeless window yielded to the light bow window, and the latter to the modern flat window; how small squares of glass have given way to later ones, crown glass to plate glass, clumsy wooden sash-bars to light brass ones, how the once lowly shop has reared its head so as to include even the next higher floor within its compass – must have been noticed by all who are familiar with the huge metropolis.[2]

In this passage, as elsewhere, the windows themselves cease to be transparent media for display and become items of display themselves, worthy of study and admiration. "Twenty years ago," George Dodd writes, "most of the bakers' shops had small flat windows, and were very modestly lighted in the evening by a lamp or two ... But now the window displays its large squares of plate-glass, its brightly-blazing gas-jets, and its long array of neat trays filled with biscuits."[3] The window "displays" its glass and gas-jets along with its biscuits, the glass of as much interest as the goods it frames. This wonder and pride in the technologies of display indicate a larger movement towards the pleasures of consuming spectacles. Dodd's essay, written on "London Shops and Bazaars," spends little time lingering on the goods available for sale in these shops, on their uses, histories, production, or aesthetic qualities. Instead we are simply told what the shops and particularly their windows look like; we are sedentary flaneurs, invited to consume the commercial exhibits of the city.[4]

In 1857, six years after Dodd's essay was published, Charles Manby Smith wrote that the old gloomy streets of London, "in which a few blinking oil-lamps just sufficed to render the dark-

---

2 Dodd, "London Shops," p. 389.
3 Dodd, "London Shops," p. 391.
4 A writer for *Sharpe's London Magazine* similarly attends to the display value of windows rather than the goods behind them when, in the course of an article on the subject, he or she remarks that some shops "exhibit *walls* of plate glass," 4 (17 July 1847) p. 188. Thomas Richards' *The Commodity Culture of Victorian England: Advertising and Spectacle, 1851–1914* (Stanford University Press, 1990) provides the most incisive history of Victorian commodity culture and its dependence on spectacles and advertisement; in *Advertising Fictions: Literature, Advertisement, and Social Reading* (New York, Columbia University Press, 1988), Jennifer Wicke has studied Victorian advertisements as a mass literature the emergence of which was dialectically related to that of the modern novel. On Victorian material culture more generally, see Asa Briggs' *Victorian Things* (University of Chicago Press, 1989).

Plate 1. "The World of Show" in St. Paul's Churchyard, 1847: Allan and Son Drapers

ness visible" and in which goods were displayed in "the narrow shop-window, with its panes of bulging glass, twenty inches by twelve, lighted by a couple of tallow candles or an argand-lamp," had been banished.

*Now*, the departure of the day is the herald of a light such as the sun never darts into the nooks and crannies of traffic: broad streams of gas flash like meteors into every corner of the wealth-crammed mart – from which it may be but one invisible wall of solid crystal separates the passenger, who might easily walk through it but for the burnished metal guard which meets him breast high.[5]

This nocturnal world of show, illuminated by newly available, relatively safe gas lights, improving on the natural but mundane experience of daytime life, presents the commodity fetish in all its glory, easily available to the admiring eye if not to the acquisitive hand. "Behind these crystal walls," writes Smith, stand men "whose sole purpose in life it is to gratify ... wishes."[6]

As Richard Sennett has written, however, plate glass is a "material which lets [one] see everything inaccessible to desire."[7] Restrained by the invisible wall of crystal, if not by the burnished metal guard, you can look but you cannot touch, desire but not possess. Making goods "look better than they really are," windows simultaneously confer upon them an aura of shining inaccessibility.[8] From this vantage Victorians like Smith saw the windows of pawnshops as paradigmatic, displaying the inaccessibility of commodities with particular clarity:

In dim, yet dazzling confusion, the inharmonious collection floats before the vision, and will not be disembarrassed of the living forms and faces with which imagination connects each single item in the endless catalogue. Let us invite from the mass one or two forlorn specimens, and listen to their oracular voices. They will speak nothing but the truth now, though they may have helped to spread many a delusion in days that are gone. May we be the wiser for the revelations they impart.[9]

---

5  Charles Manby Smith, *The Little World Of London* (London, Arthur Hall, Virtue, and Co., 1857), pp. 324–5.
6  Smith, *Little World*, p. 325.
7  Richard Sennett, "Plate Glass," *Raritan* 6: 4 (1987), p. 1.
8  Georg Hirth, quoted in Wolfgang Schivelbusch, *Disenchanted Light: The Industrialization of Light in the Nineteenth Century* (Berkeley, University of California Press, 1988), p. 147.
9  Smith, *Little World*, p. 332.

Although these goods are unavailable to those who once possessed them, the relationship of owner and object nonetheless can be recuperated through the imaginative labors of fiction. Having created tales for several of the hocked goods, Smith tells us that each of the other items "of itself might yield the groundwork of a romance, all the more touching and instructive in that the details are drawn from the reality of our social life."[10] The "truth" of the commodity stands out from the falsehood which normally shrouds it and is spoken, in oracular tones, through poignant, instructive narratives.

While transforming the experience of walking through London streets, the technological development of plate-glass windows in shops of all kinds also came to be an emblem of the increasing pretensions, impersonality and mobility of social and commercial life. Writing three years after Smith imagined his utopian space of gratification, George Eliot recalled that her fictional town of St. Ogg's had

> no plate-glass in shop windows ... The shop windows were small and unpretending; for the farmers' wives and daughters who came to do their shopping on market days were not to be withdrawn from their regular, well-known shops; and the tradesmen had no wares intended for customers who would go on their way and be seen no more.[11]

In Eliot's nostalgic vision the shops of St. Ogg's provide a social space not for "passengers" but for familiar figures, women in particular, who know each other and the shopkeepers who regularly sell them their goods. Distancing consumers from the goods they desire while simultaneously heightening that desire, the invisible wall of solid crystal was also seen to encourage an increasing distance between people.

The display windows in this nation of shopkeepers thus served as emblems of an economic dynamic which was also and simultaneously libidinal (producing desire and disenchantment), epistemological (concerning the representation of falsehood and truth), and social (marking individual isolation and the possibilities of communal relations). Organizing my reflections on these dynamics and their implications in the following pages will be

---

10  Smith, *Little World*, p. 338.
11  George Eliot, *The Mill on the Floss* (New York, Oxford University Press, 1980), pp. 117–18.

the specifically aesthetic development of the "exhibition value" of goods. Also marked by the wide-spread installation of plate-glass windows, this aesthetic development is most commonly associated with the emergence of new visual technologies, photography and film most particularly.[12] And we will see, in Chapter 2 below, that these new plates of glass were important elements of a comprehensive institutional change, part of a complex of developments in museums, department stores, exhibitions and galleries. What follows, however, will attend most fully to impact of this increased exhibition value on the realistic novel; read in isolation away from the crowd, dependant on signs more linguistic than visual, novels too slipped behind the "barrier of glass."[13]

## II

The idea that propels the following book can be stated in a deceptively simple fashion: among the dominant concerns motivating mid-Victorian novelists was a penetrating anxiety, most graphically displayed in Thackeray's *Vanity Fair*, that their social and moral world was being reduced to a warehouse of goods and commodities, a display window in which people, their actions, and their convictions were exhibited for the economic appetites of others. While this fear was stated both by novelists and by contemporary cultural critics, the lines of tension which it sends through novels, the narrative difficulties and affective ambivalences it produces, have not been exactly or thoroughly traced. From the gendering of subjectivity and the vagaries of desire to the atomization and rationalization of social life, from the endurance of memory and the power of nostalgia to anxieties concerning legacies left to the future, from the trajectories of public careers to the cyclical routines of the household, from the

12  See Walter Benjamin's comments on the ability of photography to create new objects for economic display in "Paris, Capital of the Nineteenth Century," in *Reflections: Essays, Aphorisms, Autobiographical Writings*, trans. Edmund Jephcott (New York, Schocken, 1986), pp. 146–62, as well as his more extended remarks in "The Work of Art in the Age of Mechanical Reproduction," in *Illuminations*, trans. Harry Zohn (New York, Schocken, 1969), pp. 217–52.
13  Dodd, "London Shops," p. 386.

enjoyment of particular pleasures to the frustrations of mortality, from the metaphoric and conceptual power of "ownership" to the consequences of theft and loss, the ambivalences generated by commodity culture organize the thematic concerns of these novels and the society they represent. Following Marx in this regard, each of the following chapters will take the commodity as its point of departure; considered together, the chapters will suggest that the Victorian novel provides us with the most graphic and enduring images of the power of commodities to affect the varied activities and attitudes of individual and social experience.[14]

In tracing out each of these concerns and others, the following pages will analyze the implicit and explicit attitudes writers adopt towards the commodification of their own literary products; indeed, I will argue that it is in these attitudes that the effects of Victorian commodity culture are most profoundly present. Adopting a moral stance against the commodification of the world, novelists simultaneously understood that literary work itself was increasingly commodified; they were, as a result, required to negotiate between their moral condemnation and their implication in what they opposed. In order to study this complex and awkward negotiation, I take up the formal characteristics of, as well as the representation of commodities within, a range of novels. In the narrative form of these texts one can see most clearly the complicated set of attitudes, conscious and unconscious, entertained by writers about the process of commodification – and one can also see most clearly the fundamental significance of those attitudes for our understanding of the Victorian novel.

All the texts I consider closely – *Vanity Fair*, *Cranford*, *Our Mutual Friend*, *The Eustace Diamonds*, and *Middlemarch* – were written during the triumphant moment of free-market capitalism, the quarter-century that saw, in addition to the repeal of the glass-tax (1845), the repeal of the Corn Law (1846) and

---

14 Jeff Nunokowa makes a similar claim in his recent study, *The Afterlife of Property: Domestic Security and the Victorian Novel* (Princeton University Press, 1994), p. 4. Reading that book while correcting the final manuscript of this one, I am pleased to see the degree to which our varied arguments complement each other.

the Navigation Acts (1849 and 1854), the elimination of duties on sugar (1854) and of taxes on soap (1853) and paper (1861), the legal acceptance of the limited liability corporation (1855 and 1856).[15] In literary production itself, the most basic index of free-trade ideology was found in what N. N. Feltes has designated the "commodity-text." Emerging with the early novels of Dickens, the "commodity-text" was associated with serial publication and was opposed to the petty-commodity form of the dominant three-volume novel, what Feltes calls the "commodity-book":

> the "beliefs," the ideology of the consumer of the borrowed, three-volume commodity book, were distinct from those of the consumer of the serialized or part-issue commodity-text. For whereas the commodity-text interpellated generally the individual bourgeois subject, the commodity-book was part of an apparatus which interpellated the 'middle- or upper-middle class' subscriber to Mudie's.[16]

While the commodity-text "interpellates the assumed 'normality' or classlessness of the individual bourgeois subject/reader," the commodity-book "interpellates in general the sense of an exclusive collectivity, as is implied by the 'prestige' and 'grandeur' associated with the three-decker."[17] Isolating and addressing the individual reader, the commodity-text similarly isolates the individual writer. The emergence of the serialized commodity-text, Feltes argues, marked the emergence of new professional authors who retained a greater degree of control over their work (most importantly, by controlling copyright) while, simultaneously and consequently, being more vulnerable to economic loss. George Eliot's regret, Feltes writes, "at having sold the copyright to *Adam Bede*, a petty-commodity production relation, is directly related to her desire – when she inferred that John

---

15  For the emergence of the limited liability corporation, see H. A. Shannon, "The Coming of General Limited Liability," in E. M. Carus-Wilson, ed., *Essays in Economic History*, 3 vols. (London, E. Arnold, 1954), vol. I, pp. 358–79, and my "Subjectivity Ltd.: The Discourse of Liability in the Joint-Stock Companies Act of 1856 and Gaskell's *Cranford*," *ELH* 61 (1994), pp. 139–57; in *The Afterlife of Property*, Nunokawa similarly locates his study of Dickens and Eliot within this high moment of "the age of capital."

16  N. N. Feltes, *Modes of Production of Victorian Novels* (University of Chicago Press, 1986), p. 27.

17  Feltes, *Modes of Production*, p. 27.

Blackwood saw her next book as 'a speculation attended with risk' – to change the relations of production by contracting only for the first edition of *The Mill*: 'I prefer incurring that risk myself.'"[18] This controlling yet uncertain position, adopted in various ways by each of the writers I consider, locates them as producers within a fully capitalist mode of production and makes them especially attentive to the consequences of commodity production and exchange within their novels.

Considered together, the first two chapters, on William Thackeray's *Vanity Fair* and on the Great Exhibition of 1851, introduce many of the critical themes concerning these consequences; these two "fairs" also allow me to establish much of the theoretical architecture for the succeeding pages. More than any other Victorian novel, Thackeray's book imagines the fetishistic reduction of the material environment to commodities, to a world simultaneously brilliant and tedious, in which value is produced without reference either to the needs or to the hopelessly utopian desires of characters. While Thackeray decries this reduction, his own engagement with material culture leaves him deeply invested in the processes that produce the multifarious commodities surrounding him. His desire for these goods and his expectations of utopian satisfaction to be gained from their possession fully implicate him in his economic system. This continually unsatisfied desire is frustrating, but it also allows Thackeray to sustain an image of himself as a deserving, if unrewarded subject; never attaining his desires, he never loses them either. At the largest level, Thackeray's ambivalence shapes the attitude he takes towards his own novel: like the other social products he describes, *Vanity Fair* is an inadequate vehicle for the value he wants it to carry and, as a result, Thackeray stands estranged from the product of his own labor.

Thackeray exhibits his circulating, dispiriting objects in an oddly depthless space; the physical contiguity of objects within relations of perspectival realism is rendered insignificant by the insistence with which those objects refer to unattainable levels

---

18  Feltes, *Modes of Production*, pp. 46–7. Discussing the effects of the 1842 Copyright Amendment Act, David Saunders similarly notes that it "encouraged authors not to alienate their copyright entirely or for ever." *Authorship and Copyright* (London, Routledge, 1992), p. 141.

of abstract meaning. In a similar fashion, the objects displayed at the Great Exhibition gained their significance not by their contiguity in the Crystal Palace but by their participation in a series of codes constructed through them: the congeries of goods on display was arranged by and understood through a range of relational and contingent discursive patterns concerning class, gender, and nationality. Taking up these patterns allows us to see the ways in which the formal concerns described in literary texts operate at a larger social level; the Exhibition developed the allegorical form of *Vanity Fair* into a relentlessly positive vision of utopian possibilities. But, while Thackeray's failures allowed him to maintain a satisfying, if impoverished, understanding of himself, the fetishistic structure that underlay the optimistic Exhibition inversely imports the depressing possibility of failure and frustration even as it declared its own success. A celebration of Victorian industrial strength, the Exhibition also revealed middle-class fears about that strength and the workers who were gathered to view the products of their labor at the Palace. Similarly, the Exhibition inspired several male observers to imagine the display of British women under glass, an act of sexual objectification and an attempt to manage the unsettling desires which the Exhibition inspired in the women who admired its wares. Imagining the Exhibition as a display of British technological superiority, commentators necessarily imagined it as a display with an audience – but the foreign visitors to the Palace, the women, and the workers, aroused intense anxieties about the management of the appetites that circle around the display and consumption of goods.

Together, *Vanity Fair* and the Exhibition starkly illustrate two versions of one dynamic of desire and disenchantment, a dynamic the consequences of which the novelists studied in the remaining chapters of this book attempted to escape. The resistance of these writers to the suasion of fetishized commodities took several forms, both obvious and elusive. Most obvious, perhaps, was the definition of domestic enclaves, the organization of household spaces free from the force of commodification. Chapters 3 and 4, on Gaskell's *Cranford* and Dickens' *Our Mutual Friend*, explore the development of such enclaves and the association of writing with them. Gaskell writes out of and about the routines of domestic everyday life, and the quotidian inflects both the form of her novel and, centrally, its treatment of female subjectivity. In *Vanity Fair* and the Great Exhibition, women fluctuate between being objects under the gaze of men and being agents desiring goods on their own; in *Cranford*, perhaps the period's most detailed and sympathetic novel of domestic material culture, Gaskell does not see objects as the instigators of unsettling appetites and resists notions of subjectivity defined as insular, fungible, and threatened. Instead she attempts to represent goods in her novel as the occasion for communal understanding between women whose identities are open and labile. Gaskell candidly recognizes that such identities exist uncomfortably in an economy based on rational economic calculation, but she is more ready than others to accommodate the discomfort of this relation. Indeed, she sees negotiating between an emotional and social life conducted according to the principles of rational exchange and one shaped by the economy of the gift as a central purpose of fiction.

Like the women in *Cranford*, Charles Dickens had a housekeeping heart and a "domestic nature,"[19] but, unlike them, the homes in which he lived and which he represented in his fiction did not encourage communal practices and fluid personalities; instead, the objects and people within these homes were shaped according to the dictates of Dickens' sovereign will. In *Our Mutual Friend*, more than any of his other novels, the energy with which Dickens fashions the home is heightened by its opposition to a threatening public world: the home and, along with it, the space of writing, are presented as sanctuaries from the destructive energy of London's social and material environment. Represented by Dickens as effortless, writing and domesticity appear to be free from the mystification and emotional desiccation that attends the exchange of goods: this labor is not oppressive and its products are not occlusions. That these enclaves finally collapse means not only that writing and domestic life are subject to the routinization and commodification more characteristic of public spaces, but also that subjectivity itself can find no satisfying haven.

The final chapters turn to Anthony Trollope and George Eliot, two writers closely associated with Thackeray. In *The Eustace*

19 John Forster, *The Life of Charles Dickens*, 3 vols. (London, Chapman and Hall, 1874), vol. III, p. 473.

*Diamonds*, Trollope's most Thackerayan novel, we do not see a fetishistic representation of the goods of the world; indeed, in this austerely furnished novel we do not see much of the titular diamonds themselves. But if goods are oddly invisible, the language of ownership and property saturates the novel, defining characters' moral and psychological identities as well as their relation to the material environment. Trollope understands the self in terms derived from the market: identity and its parts are owned, sold, lost, and stolen. This appreciation of subjectivity as property extends beyond *The Eustace Diamonds* to shape Trollope's representation of his own authorial identity; his concern with issues of copyright, with his reputation, with the use of his name, all are understood as issues of ownership. As the language of property spirals out to shape the self, however, the futility of possession accrues new pathos: just as the possession of commodified goods is a vexed enterprise, so the possession of the self becomes troubled; like the diamonds themselves, the self becomes fugitive. While Trollope's productive career demonstrates the enormously enabling energy provided by the routines of commodity production for those who enter into them and make them their own, it also suggests the ease with which the language of commodities returns to define the author's career and the individual living it.

Of the writers I consider, Eliot confronts the critical vision outlined in the opening chapters most directly; Thackeray was, Eliot thought, "on the whole the most powerful of living novelists," and, like him, Eliot forcibly describes the alienation possible when commodification defines the relation between people and things.[20] Unlike him, however, she attempts to find, in the form of her writing as well as in the activity of her characters, means to imbue goods with enduring significance, resisting the idea that the novel is inevitably defined by commodification. One sign of Eliot's shared concern is her use in *Middlemarch* of the same institutions and practices which figured prominently in Thackeray's narrative – auctions, pawnshops, and gambling. But Eliot's central representation of this theme comes through her depiction of female attire. Women's dress is the paradigmatic instance of

20  George Eliot, *George Eliot Letters*, ed. Gordon Haight, 9 vols. (New Haven, Yale University Press, 1954–78), vol. II, p. 349.

Introduction

material culture in *Middlemarch*, the emblem of its fundamental importance for Eliot's understanding of subjectivity and social relations: *Middlemarch* opens, after the "Prelude," with a description of Dorothea Brooke's ornamentation, its successive chapters develop this initial concern, and its climax is, remarkably, presented as a recognition of the proper attitude towards women's dress. The compromise Eliot reaches regarding dress – women should attend to it enough to effectively limit its importance – becomes homologous with her understanding of the aesthetic more generally. Attending to the commodity status of her own novel, Eliot's interest lay in managing and limiting its effects on the aesthetic interests which she promoted.

Together these six essays describe an array of responses to the possibilities and dangers of commodification – and, in particular, the possibilities and dangers of conceiving literary products as commodities – during the period when material culture was becoming a dominant cultural force. They trace a shifting matrix of uneven affiliations between material culture, social relations, and subjective practices, as those affiliations are registered in the thematic material and narrative patterns of the period's highest form of literary achievement. This matrix does not constitute a narrative history of material culture and its representation. My own sense is that such histories, when attempted, tend to flatten and occlude the unevenness of large-scale historical change, to package and wrap the ungainly object of their study. I have attempted instead to place the mid-Victorian novel on display within the material culture of the period while leaving it accessible to further speculation and reflection. Rather than close off my discussion at its end, then, I suggest, in a brief afterword, some of the continuing significance of material culture in narratives of the *fin-de siècle*.

❖❖❖❖❖❖❖❖❖❖❖❖❖❖❖❖❖❖❖❖❖❖❖❖❖❖❖❖❖❖❖❖❖❖❖❖❖❖❖❖❖❖

# Longing for sleeve buttons

❖❖❖❖❖❖❖❖❖❖❖❖❖❖❖❖❖❖❖❖❖❖❖❖❖❖❖❖❖❖❖❖❖❖❖❖❖❖❖❖❖❖

I tried in vain to convince the fine folks at Mrs. Fox's that revolution was upon us: that we were wicked in our scorn of the people. They all thought there was poverty & discomfort to be sure, but that they were pretty good in themselves; that powder & liveries were very decent & proper though certainly absurd – the footmen themselves would not give them up. William Thackeray[1]

The allegoricist with the commodity is in his element.

Walter Benjamin[2]

The translation of political revolution into domestic insurrection, understood as the desire of servants to discard the appurtenances of subjection and acquire the material possessions of their masters, is one of William Thackeray's obsessive concerns in the late 1840s. The liveried footman, whose job is to announce himself as his employer's packaged possession, adorned in clothes that he can not afford to buy but must wear to represent his master's wealth, is for Thackeray a logical extreme of a culture fashioned from commodities; and his nervous suggestion to "the fine folks at Mrs. Fox's" that these members of the "vicarious leisure class" might reject their commodification registers his anxiety over the consequences of that culture.[3] Even as the threat of revolution

1 William Thackeray, *The Letters and Private Papers of William Makepeace Thackeray*, ed. Gordon Ray, 4 vols. (Cambridge, Harvard University Press, 1945–6), vol. II, pp. 364–5.
2 Susan Buck-Morss, *The Dialectics of Seeing: Walter Benjamin and the Arcades Project* (Cambridge, MIT Press, 1989), p. 181.
3 "The vicarious leisure class is distinguished from the leisure class proper by a characteristic feature of its habitual mode of life. The leisure of the master class is, at least ostensibly, an indulgence of a proclivity for the avoidance of labor and is presumed to enhance the master's own well-being and fullness of life; but the leisure of the servant class exempt from productive labor is in

recedes, Thackeray continues to see the commodity as a rebarba-
tive form, inhuman in its blithe disregard of individuals. At the
same time, however, his fascination with footmen emerges from
his own intense engagement with these commodities; despite his
criticism of what Lukács would later call the "reified mind,"
Thackeray remains deeply invested in the processes that produce
the multifarious material objects surrounding him.[4] Desire for
these goods fully implicates him in the economic system he
simultaneously decries.

Thackeray's ambivalent attachment to goods is encouraged
both by the objective circumstances of his culture and by his own
fetishistic purchase on that culture; and because these circumstances and Thackeray's habits support each other, this attachment
stubbornly resists modification. In particular – and this is the point
at which the interconnection between Thackerayan representation
and the historical circumstances of that representation is most concretely, most empirically, manifest – the commodity form and
Thackeray's fetishism mutually sustain Thackeray's relation to his
own work. What Walter Benjamin and Theodor Adorno would, in
this context, call Thackeray's literary "technique" participates in
the commodification of the material world:

Rather than ask, "What is the *attitude* of a work to the relations of production of its time?" I should like to ask, "What is its *position* in them?"
This question directly concerns the function the work has within the literary relations of production of its time. It is concerned, in other words,
directly with the literary *technique* of works.[5]

Like the other social products Thackeray describes, novels are
inadequate vehicles for the significance he wants them to carry
and he, as a result, stands estranged from the products of his own
labor. While this condition of estrangement was shared by
Victorian writers as a feature of writing for the market, Thackeray

some sort a performance exacted from them, and is not normally or primarily
directed to their own comfort. The leisure of the servant is not his own
leisure." Thorstein Veblen, *The Theory of the Leisure Class: An Economic Study in
the Evolution of Institutions* (New York, NAL–Penguin, 1953), p. 56.
4 Georg Lukács, *History and Class Consciousness: Studies in Marxist Dialectics*,
trans. Rodney Livingstone (Cambridge, MIT Press, 1968), p. 93.
5 Benjamin, *Reflections*, p. 222. For another instance of this usage, see Theodor
Adorno, *Philosophy of Modern Music*, trans. Anne Mitchell and Wesley
Blomster (New York, The Seabury Press, 1973), pp. 34–7.

presents its consequences in the most stark fashion; his writing graphically dissects the stubborn and vexed relations between the commodity form and narrative form in Victorian novels.

# I

Complicitous with the desire of servants for their master's "movables," Thackeray's texts derive from that desire a propulsive narrative energy. The rebellious longing of Jos Sedley's servant, Isidor, is representative:

As he helped Jos through his toilsome and complicated daily toilette, this faithful servant would calculate what he should do with the very articles with which he was decorating his master's person. He would make a present of the silver-essence bottles and toilette knicknacks to a young lady of whom he was fond; and keep the English cutlery and the large ruby pin for himself. It would look very smart upon one of the fine frilled shirts, which, with the gold laced cap and the frogged frock coat, that might easily be cut down to suit his shape, and the captain's gold-headed cane, and the great double ring with the rubies, which he would have made into a pair of beautiful ear-rings, he calculated would make a perfect Adonis of himself, and render Mademoiselle Reine an easy prey. "How those sleeve-buttons will suit me," thought he, as he fixed a pair on the fat pudgy wrists of Mr. Sedley. "I long for sleeve-buttons; and the captain's boots with brass spurs, in the next room, *corbleu*, what an effect they will make in the *Allée Verte!*" So while Monsieur Isidor with bodily fingers was holding on to his master's nose, and shaving the lower part of Jos's face, his imagination was rambling along the Green Avenue, dressed out in a frogged coat and lace, and in company with Mademoiselle Reine; he was loitering in spirit on the banks, and examining the barges sailing slowly under the cool shadows of the trees by the canal, or refreshing himself with a mug of Faro at the bench of a beer-house on the road to Laeken.[6]

Isidor's desire moves metonymically from pin to coat to cane, propelling his fantasy and Thackeray's narrative towards a private paradisiacal state where objects become the accoutrements of a life of ease and assurance, where desire languishes, and where service is not required.

Thackeray emphasizes the distance between the actual, unpleasant world of economic service and Isidor's personal

6 William Thackeray, *Vanity Fair* (London, Oxford University Press, 1983), p. 375. All further references will be included parenthetically in the text.

utopia by having him hold Jos's nose and pudgy wrists while
indulging in his fantasy; but the implicit violence of the servant's
vision is firmly suggested by the presence of Isidor's razor along
his master's neck. Subjected to the force of Isidor's desire as it
drives towards his utopia of conspicuous leisure, distinctions
among objects and among people become uncertain: that Jos's
essence bottles and toilette knickknacks can be given to Mlle.
Reine testifies not only to Jos's effeminacy but to the wavering
instability of all social categories, including those of gender and
class, when seen through the heat of Thackerayan desire. In
Isidor's vision, human relationships, such as the one he imagines
with Mlle. Reine, emerge with difficulty from the clutter of commodities that his material passion arranges around him. The
gold-laced cap, frilled shirts, and sleeve-buttons which will deify
him are his primary objects, not Mlle. Reine, who exists primarily
as she appreciates this Adonis, or contributes to his effect.

The logic of this situation, in which servants acquire the objects
reserved for their masters, is clarified and extended in *Pendennis*.
There, Morgan, the valet to Major Pendennis, does not merely
desire the major's goods, he secretly purchases the house in
which he and his master live. "My servant's a capitalist, begad,"
the Major exclaims.[7] Thackeray's deep discomfort with this
domestic *coup d'état* – like that in *Vanity Fair*, where the servants
occupy the Crawleys' house (p. 692) – and the forces that propel
it emerge as Morgan's character develops: the valet becomes a
demonic figure across the course of the novel, clandestinely pursuing information with which he can blackmail his betters.
Thackeray's sense of futility in the face of this class appetite and
the circumstances in which it was, at the end of the forties, being
released is revealed by the conclusion of this particular line of the
plot. When Morgan, in the process of packing his things and leaving the Major's service, attempts to blackmail his master, the
Major calmly calls in a policeman to search Morgan's bags: "the
guilty valet remembered some fine lawn-fronted shirts – a certain
gold-headed cane – an opera glass, which he had forgotten to
bring down, and of which he had assumed the use along with
certain articles of his master's clothes, which the old dandy nei-

7 William Thackeray, *The History of Pendennis* (Harmondsworth, Penguin,
1972), p. 710.

ther wore nor asked for."[8] Again, the denouement turns on the possession of goods. But this uncharacteristic moment of drama depends on the Major's ingrained (if not innate) patrician assurance: revolutionary desires will be frustrated, the implication is, by the simple fact that society – here in the shape of the local policeman – will merely recognize and reinforce the existent set of social privileges. Morgan's threatening recognition that material culture creates social distinction is countered and defeated by the fact that social distinction also creates material culture. By the time *Pendennis* was written the fears of 1848 had largely faded and the social hierarchy, on which the Major's self-assurance depends, seemed to remain intact. But in *Vanity Fair* the revolutionary desire for objects collides with no such secure social edifice; class barriers do not absolutely prevent servants from satisfactorily possessing objects.

In that novel, however, desire does meet the opposed motion of the dialectical form of the commodities themselves. Most often, Thackeray represents this opposed motion as death: no object can be owned which does not suggest to his imagination, sometimes distantly but more often quite immediately, the ruin and death of those who own it. When we first meet Jos Sedley he is hardly visible through the clothes that Isidor later will covet:

A very stout, puffy man, in buckskins and hessian boots, with several immense neckcloths, that rose almost to his nose, with a red striped waistcoat and an apple-green coat with steel buttons almost as large as crown pieces (it was the morning costume of a dandy or blood of those days), was reading the paper by the fire when two girls entered, and bounced off his armchair. (p. 24)

By the end of the same monthly installment of the novel, Becky Sharp has staged her first performance as the arachnoid Clytemnestra and entangled Jos in the web of her green silk purse. (Each element is exact: the green, like the green of her eyes, reminds us of her shifting ambiguities; the silk suggests the spider's filament; the purse reminds us that her act is at once monetary and sexual.) The last performance of Clytemnestra, during which Jos dies, is merely a successful reprise of the first. Similarly, in *Pendennis*, the Major, whom we also first see in dandiacal morning dress and reading the paper, becomes an urbane

8 Thackeray, *Pendennis*, p. 716.

and cosmopolitan death-in-life figure, ailing and isolated but with *bon ton*. It is in Miss Crawley, however, rather than Jos or the Major, that possession and death are united most exactly. Surrounded by objects (as in the sketch, "Miss Crawley's Affectionate Relatives"), she functions in the text almost solely as a source of wealth. And she is most memorably drawn as a *memento mori*: "Picture to yourself – O fair young reader, a worldly, selfish, graceless, thankless, religionless old woman, writhing in pain and fear, and without her wig" (p. 164). The final turn of Thackeray's phrase sketches wigless Miss Crawley as a monitory skull: "The fetish is," as Adorno writes, "a faithless final image, comparable only to a death's-head."[9] The possibility of freedom initially offered by commodities, the dream-like fulfillment of desire, is thus replaced by an apparently inescapable failure. At this level of abstraction – the level at which Thackeray's prose customarily operates – commodities and the wealth which purchases them produce a familiar narrative form:

If there is an order regulating the forms of wealth, if this can buy that, if gold is worth twice as much as silver, it is not because men have comparable desires; it is not because they experience the same hunger in their bodies, or because their hearts are all swayed by the same passions; it is because they are all subjected to time, to toil, to weariness, and, in the last resort, to death itself.[10]

In the earthbound economy of *Vanity Fair*, where possession anticipates death, it is not surprising to see the auction of the household goods belonging to Jos Sedley's father figured as a travesty of the day of judgment:

If there is any exhibition in all Vanity Fair which Satire and Sentiment can visit arm-in-arm together; where you light on the strangest contrasts laughable and tearful: where you may be gentle and pathetic, or savage and cynical with perfect propriety: it is at one of those public assemblies, a crowd of which are advertised every day in the last page of the *Times* newspaper, and over which the late Mr. George Robins used to preside with so much dignity. There are very few London people, as I fancy, who have not attended at these meetings, and all with a taste for moralizing must have thought, with a sensation and interest not a little startling and queer, of the day when their turn shall come too, and Mr. Hammerdown

9 Theodor Adorno, "Letters to Walter Benjamin," trans. Harry Zohn, *New Left Review* 81 (1973), p. 58.
10 Michel Foucault, *The Order of Things* (New York, Vintage, 1973), p. 225.

Plate 2. Goods mediating human relations

will sell by the orders of Diogenes's assignees, or will be instructed by the executors, to offer to public competition, the library, furniture, plate, wardrobe, and choice cellar of wines of Epicurus deceased. (p. 200)

Mr. Hammerdown's hammer descends "like fate," but its descent marks the conclusion of a partial and worldly evaluation of John Sedley's possessions rather than a moral and divine judgment of his existence. The auction, a public institution devoted to the display and distribution of private objects, recycles not merely wealth, but significance: in this highly visible theater of competing desires, the meanings of goods are developed and reinforced as their purely monetary value is recreated and calculated anew.[11] The recycled significance thus generated is riven with ambiguities: auctions are trivial – worthy of only a notice on the last page of the *Times* – and immensely consequential; each one is unique, idiosyncratic, and topical – presided over by George Robins, a Covent Garden auctioneer who himself died immediately prior to the publication of this installment of the novel – and universal – presided over by Mr. Hammerdown; they encourage antithetical emotions, pathos, and cynicism. Most significantly, however, auctions provoke the fetishistic libidinal response I have been describing: they repel and fascinate. Auctions present to spectators the possibilities of utopia and of hell, the satisfaction of all desires, and the frustration of all needs. From the objects presented to them, the spectators at these exhibitions can assemble fantasy existences or, if wealthy and fortunate, fantastic actual existences. At the same time, however, these goods, the opulent detritus of economic failure, retain the traces of the misfortunes they have witnessed and announce the approaching misfortune of those who, in spite of their queer and startling sensations, decide to buy. Two years after this monthly installment of the novel was published, Thackeray's friend Lady Blessington was forced to auction off her goods; and Thackeray, fascinated and repelled, attended the event:

I have just come away from a dismal sight – Gore House full of Snobs looking at the furniture – foul Jews, odious bombazeen women who drove up in mysterious flies wh. they had hired, the wretches, to be fine so as to come in state to a fashionable lounge – Brutes keeping their hats on in the kind old drawing-rooms – I longed to knock some of 'em off: and say Sir be civil in a lady's room ... There was one of the servants there not a powdered one but a butler a whatdyoucallit – My heart melted towards him & I gave him a pound – Ah it was a strange sad picture of Wanaty Fair [sic].[12]

11  Jean Baudrillard's "The Art Auction" in *For a Critique of the Political Economy of the Sign* (St. Louis, Telos Press, 1981), pp. 112–23, analyzes the production of meaning in similar social settings.
12  Thackeray, *Letters*, vol. I, p. 532. Another strange, sad picture, this one in Thackeray's novel, disposes the goods of one Mr. Scape, an Anglo-Indian who

Satire and sentiment walk arm-in-arm in these strange scenes from Vanity Fair and melting hearts find emotional expression in generous tips. Thackeray and the whatdyoucallit who received his sympathy and largess together mourn sentimentally over the ruin of their friend and mistress: in a letter to the Countess in Paris the butler averred that generous Thackeray was, of the people at the spectacle, perhaps the only one truly affected by her fate.[13]

The dynamic of desire and disenchantment I have been describing finds a suitable emblem in Thackeray's representations of plate-glass windows.[14] As I noted in the introduction, the spread of these windows in the early nineteenth century marked an important development in marketing and sales, and revolutionized the experience of walking in London's streets. Although it appears as if, behind the crystal walls of the shops, there stand men whose "sole purpose in life it is to gratify ... wishes," some of these men are "unblushing tricksters," practicing "legerdemain behind sheets of plate-glass and in a blaze of gas."[15] Their windows invited one to look but not touch, desire but not pos-

---

lost his fortune in an Indian financial failure, which recalls that actually suffered by Thackeray in 1833. With no reflection on his father's similar failure, Jos Sedley takes the house, lives among the Scapes' carpets and sideboards, and admires himself in their mirrors (pp. 761–2).

13 R. R. Madden, *The Literary Life and Correspondence of the Countess of Blessington*, 2 vols. (New York, Harper and Brothers, 1855), vol. I, p. 176. "When I see the beautiful objects collected in these [curiosity] shops," Lady Blessington wrote in her "Idler in Paris," "I often think of their probable histories, and of those to whom they belonged. Each seems to identify itself with the former owner, and conjures up in my mind a little romance . . . Through how many hands may these objects have passed since death snatched away the persons for whom they were originally designed . . . 'And so will it be when I am gone,' as Moore's beautiful song says; the rare and beautiful bijouteries which I have collected with such pains, and looked on with such pleasure, will probably be scattered abroad, and find their resting-places, not in gilded salons, but in the dingy coffers of the wily *brocanteurs*, whose exorbitant demands will preclude their finding purchasers" (Quoted in Madden, *Literary Life*, vol. I, pp. 172–3).

14 Indeed, later in the century, one writer saw the shops in London and their "specious window dressing" as "auctions on a small scale." Like Thackeray, he worried that they were "sadly damaging to green lads sighing for knickknacks, gold chains, so marvelously cheap – watches, at such a low figure, the gold entirely on the surface." "Aleph," *London Scenes and London People* (London, W. H. & L. Collingridge, 1880), pp. 95–6.

15 Charles Smith, *Little World*, p. 325; "Aleph," *London Scenes*, pp. 95–6.

sess. In *Sketches and Travels in London*, a series of short pieces Thackeray wrote for *Punch* during the late forties, the ambling narrator, Spec, pauses for a moment on Lawfeldt Street:

A little further on ... is Mr. Filch's fine silversmith's shop, where a man may stand for a half-hour and gaze with ravishment at the beautiful gilt cups and tankards, the stunning waistcoat-chains, the little white cushions laid out with delightful diamond pins, gold horseshoes and splinter-bars, pearl owls, turquoise lizards and dragons, enamelled monkeys, and all sorts of agreeable monsters for your neckcloth. If I live to be a hundred, or if the girl of my heart were waiting for me at the corner of the street, I could never pass Mr. Filch's shop without having a couple of minutes' good stare at the window. I like to fancy myself dressed up in some of the jewelry. "Spec, you rogue," I say, "suppose you were to get leave to wear three or four of those rings on your fingers; to stick that opal, round which twists a brilliant serpent with a ruby head, into your blue satin neckcloth; and to sport that gold jack-chain on your waistcoat. You might walk in the Park with that black whalebone prize riding-whip, which has a head the size of a snuff-box, surmounted with a silver jockey on a silver race-horse; and what a sensation you would create, if you took that large ram's horn with the cairngorm top out of your pocket, and offered a pinch of rappee to the company round!" A little attorney's clerk is staring in at the window, in whose mind very similar ideas are passing. What would he not give to wear that gold pin next Sunday in his blue hunting neckcloth? The ball of it is almost as big as those which are painted over the side door of Mr. Filch's shop, which is down that passage which leads into Trotter's Court.[16]

The longing of Spec and the little attorney's clerk, intense and pathetic, spurs them as it spurs Isidor to fabricate from a limited number of objects a complete fantasy existence. But the balls painted over the side door in the alley, mentioned in a quiet, deflationary aside, announce that this shop is a pawnbroker's. "Amid universal fungibility," wrote Adorno, "happiness attaches without exception to the non-fungible," but the non-fungible is rare in Thackeray's world.[17] Social life is a facade, and its props are in hock: "When we read in the *Court Journal* of Lady Fitzball's head-dress of lappets and superb diamonds, it is because the jew-

16 William Thackeray, *Sketches and Travels in London*, in *The Complete Works of William Makepeace Thackeray*, 25 vols. (New York, Harper & Brothers, 1904), vol. XII, p. 549.
17 Theodor Adorno, *Minima Moralia: Reflections from Damaged Life.*, trans. E. F. N. Jephcott (London, Verso, 1978), p. 120.

els get a day rule from Filch's, and come back to his iron box as soon as the Drawing-room is over."[18]

Behind the windows of Mr. Filch's, the enamelled and carved animals create an impression of unnatural, monstrous transgression. This transgression and the extraordinary extent of Thackeray's catalogue – rings, opal, ruby, gold jack-chain, black whalebone riding whip, silver jockey on a silver race horse, ram's horn with cairngorm, gold pin – are essential to his effect.[19] Thackeray and the reader are allowed to indulge in a vicarious, transgressive consumption of the precious qualities of things, but at the same time the number and extravagance of those things – the "atmosphere of surfeit," as Orwell described it – is grotesque and cloying.[20] These animals and objects, however, remain merely a feast for the eyes; in the next of the tales in *Sketches and Travels*, "A Dinner in the City," Thackeray describes a Trimalchian feast enjoyed by the London Bellows Menders:

"Waiter, where's the turtle-fins?" – Gobble Gobble. "Hice Punch or My deary, sir?" "melts or Salmon, Jowler, my boy?" "Always take cold beef after turtle." – Hobble gobble."These year peas have no taste." Hobble-gobble-obble. "Jones, a glass of 'ock with you? Smith jine us? Waiter, three 'ocks. S., mind your manners! There's Mrs. S. a-looking at you from the gallery." – Hobble-obb-gobble-gob-gob-gob. A steam of meats, a flare of candles, a rushing to and fro of waiters, a ceaseless clinking of glass and steel, a dizzy mist of gluttony.[21]

The dinner ends with a glance into the tea room, "where gents were assembled still, drinking slops and eating buttered muffins,

18 Thackeray, *Sketches and Travels*, pp. 549–50.
19 "What museums of marvels are pawnbroker's shops! What a halo of wonderment, half smiling, half sad, consecrates each of the curiosities which, in the shape of unredeemed pledges, illustrate the window." Beyond remarking, in Thackerayan phrasing, the wistful ambivalence inspired by pawnshops, this writer for *Chambers's Journal* also demonstrates their ability to incite narrative: "Into what a sea of conjecture we do not drift. Who was the ill-fated proprietor of that handsome cruet-stand, 25s., and what was the untimely occasion that compelled its mortgage? Who was it purchased temporary alleviation of his impecuniosity by 'putting away' that solid silver soup-ladle, 13s, 6d ... " 7, 171 (11 April 1857), p. 225.
20 George Orwell, "Oysters and Brown Stout," in Sonia Orwell and Ian Angus, eds., *The Collected Essays of George Orwell*, 4 vols. (New York, Harcourt Brace Jovanovich, 1968), vol. III, p. 301.
21 Thackeray, *Sketches and Travels*, p. 559.

until the grease trickled down their faces ... Who is it that *can* want muffins after such a banquet?"[22] The implicit answer to Thackeray's question is that everyone continues to want muffins in one form or another, though the grease butters their chins. The ability to consume, whether comestibles or more lasting commodities, is without limit and, finally, repellant; when objects of use enter into a system of exchange, need is lost amid the pulsations of desire.

## II

Two biographical moments present themselves as emblematic origins for this interminable dynamic of desire and disenchantment. For three years, beginning in 1816 when he was five, Thackeray was separated from his mother, Mrs. Carmichael-Smyth, and sent from India to schools in England. Each night while in school, as John Carey notes, "he would offer up the same plea: 'Pray God I may dream of my mother.' In his loneliness, he transformed his mother into something almost divine; and he would often, later in life, speak of her as an angel."[23] Writing in 1852, Thackeray claimed, "It gives the keenest tortures of jealousy and disappointed yearning to my dearest old mother (who's as beautiful now as ever) that she can't be all in all to me, mother sister wife everything but it mayn't be ... Eh! who is happy? When I was a boy at Larkbeare, I thought her an Angel & worshiped her. I see but a woman now, O so tender so loving so cruel."[24] Thackeray explicitly associated his mother with the less daunting women in his novels and, in particular, with Amelia and Mrs. Pendennis.[25] But the representations of commodities and commodified women in his novels – Becky Sharp being the paradigmatic instance – hearken more strongly back to this originary moment of estrangement from his mother – "so tender so loving so cruel" – and to the unsatisfied desire attendant upon that estrangement. Bearing his psychological burdens, women incite Thackeray's desire while representing his alienation. On the one hand, the fetish objects he describes and desires are sub-

22  Thackeray, *Sketches and Travels*, p. 563.
23  John Carey, *Thackeray: Prodigal Genius* (London, Faber and Faber, 1977), p. 12.
24  Thackeray, *Letters*, vol. III, pp. 12–13.
25  See, for instance, Thackeray, *Letters*, vol. II, p. 394 and p. 456.

Plate 3. The limitless ability to consume

stitutes for his mother which encourage him to believe that she is not a frightening representation of the possibility of fundamental loss. On the other hand, these commodities remind Thackeray that she has, in fact, been lost to him. The dynamic of desire and disenchantment Thackeray describes thus embodies contradictory beliefs; the fetish objects he represents simultaneously suggest the possibility of plenitude and of lack. "Naturally," Freud writes, "a fetish of this kind constructed out of two opposing ideas is capable of great tenacity." The fetishistic split, by which the subject "retains this belief [in the woman having a phallus] but he also gives it up," precisely describes Thackeray's alienated position. Furthermore, as Marjorie Garbor has shown, the naturalizing of fetishism is "dependant upon an economics of display" like the process of exhibition we will see in Thackeray. Thackeray's fairs and exhibitions represent an undecidable condition of "seeming," in which there is the possibility of both possession and lack, of having and not having the phallus or any of the objects for which it is the type.[26]

This theoretical psychology should be supplemented with a later emblematic moment which extends and gives a new content to its exhibitionary and fetishistic structure. As Thackeray's letters reveal, the loss of his inheritance in 1833, when he was 21, continued to influence his activity throughout his later life, spurring him to write so that he could provide for his children as he thought he should. In an 1859 letter to his mother he comments:

> If I can work for 3 years now, I shall have put back my patrimony and a little over – after 30 years of ups and downs. I made a calculation the other day of receipts in the last 20 years and can only sum up about £32000 of moneys actually received – for w[h]. I have values or disbursements of 13000 – so that I have spent at the rate of more than 1000 a year for 20 years. The profits of the lectures figure as the greatest of the receipts £9500 – Virginians 6 – Vanity Fair only 2.3 years more please the Fates – and the girls will then have the 8 or 10000 a piece that I want for them.[27]

The years of writing and the books produced, cited by the money they brought in, appear here as Thackeray's attempt to restore his inheritance, to return to a situation of ownership and plenitude – to make him at 50, as he says in another letter, what he was at 21.[28] Occurring as he entered his maturity, the loss of his patrimony taught Thackeray about the meager endurance of possessions and supported the cycle of acquisition and loss that he obsessively repeated in the fiction.[29] Walter Bagehot wrote that, in his fiction, Thackeray amassed "petty details to prove that tenth-rate people were ever striving to be ninth-rate

---

26 Sigmund Freud, "Fetishism," *Collected Papers*, ed. James Strachey, 5 vols. (New York, Basic Books, 1959), vol. v, p. 203 and p. 200; Marjorie Garbor, *Vested Interests: Cross-dressing and Cultural Anxiety* (New York, Routledge, 1992), p. 119 and p. 121. See also Jacques Lacan, *Ecrits: A Selection*, trans. Alan Sheridan (New York, Norton, 1977), p. 289.

27 Thackeray, *Letters*, vol. IV, p. 155.

28 "When I have written two more novels, for w[h]. I shall get £5000 a piece – why, then, at 50, I shall be as I was at 21." Thackeray, *Letters*, vol. III, p. 528.

29 John Carey observes, similarly, that "the sudden loss of his fortune brought a sense both of the deceitfulness of commodities and their painful desirability." *Thackeray*, p. 69.

people."[30] But amassing petty details – meanly admiring mean things, Thackeray would say – is exactly the procedure by which the tenth-rate struggle to become ninth-rate. In this way, Thackeray's narratives repeat the desires of his characters: both aspire to greatness by accumulating minutiae.

The dispossession subsequent to this period of early maturity, the years during which he maintained an ambiguous position within the social configuration (as a poor artist in Paris and hack writer in London), reinforced his affiliation with individuals alienated from society. More precisely, it encouraged a habit of self-analysis that Bagehot clearly recognized:

> Hazlitt used to say of himself, and used to say truly, that he could not enjoy the society in a drawing-room for thinking of the opinion which the footman formed of his odd appearance as he went upstairs. Thackeray had too healthy and stable a nature to be thrown so wholly off his balance; but the footman's view of life was never out of his head.[31]

Thackeray's position on the stairs, as it were, near the servants in the hall and not yet fully ensconced within the drawing room society – "the fine folks at Mrs. Foxes" – into which he was born and to which he, during the late forties and early fifties, was reascending, allowed him a purchase at least contiguous with that of the footman and the butler. This contiguity is achieved by a kind of self-objectification, an estranged perception of his own odd appearance as he ascends, a sudden recognition of himself as something alien. And this characteristic self-objectification marks Thackeray's greatest point of imagined identity with the lower-classes, the cause of his ability to see himself from their point of view: for Thackeray, as for Lukács after him, servants are more apt than the men and women in the drawing room to look on their own social selves as constructs from which they are estranged. "It is true," Lukács writes,

> for the capitalist also there is the same doubling of personality, the same splitting up of man into an element of the movement of commodities and an (objective and impotent) observer of that movement. But for his consciousness it necessarily appears as an activity ... in which effects

30 Walter Bagehot, "Sterne and Thackeray," in Norman St. John-Stevas, ed., *The Collected Works of Walter Bagehot*, 15 vols. (Cambridge, Harvard University Press, 1965), vol. II, p. 310.
31 Bagehot, "Sterne and Thackeray," p. 304.

emanate from himself. This illusion blinds him to the true state of affairs, whereas the worker, who is denied the scope for such illusory activity, perceives the split in his [own] being.[32]

To the extent that servants can perceive their social selves, they perceive commodities. Thackeray's self-objectification, rising from his restricted position, is thus a source of his insight into the impoverished attraction of the commodity form, and distinguishes his understanding of material culture from that of other writers. The footman fascinates him – and he adopts the footman's "view of life" – because of the common estrangement he believes they share.[33]

This unhappy impotence does have its compensations. The fetishes Thackeray and his characters desire provide the satisfaction that comes with thinking of a deserving self in the midst of the inevitable, painful failures; they retroactively support an experience of essentialized subjectivity. Although Thackeray may never return to being 21, and though he will never rejoin his mother, he nonetheless maintains the sense that he deserves

---

32  Lukács, *History*, p. 166. Marx similarly rewrites Hegel's dialectic of lordship and bondage in *The Holy Family*: "The possessing class and the proletarian class represent one and the same human self-alienation. But the former feels satisfied and affirmed in this self-alienation, experiences the alienation as a sign *of its own power*, and possesses in it the *appearance* of a human existence. The latter, however, feels destroyed in this alienation, seeing in it its own impotence and the reality of an inhuman existence." Karl Marx, *The Holy Family* in *The Marx–Engels Reader*, trans. and ed. Robert Tucker (New York, W. W. Norton, 1978), p. 133.

33  This passive alienation marks the valets in Thackeray's world – and, more importantly, Thackeray himself – as cynical possessors of knowledge: servants recognize that they are alienated and commodified while capitalists do not understand this objective fact. "Cynical thinking," writes Peter Sloterdijk, "can arise only when two views of things have become possible, an official and an unofficial view, a veiled and a naked view, one from the viewpoint of heroes and one from the viewpoint of valets." Peter Sloterdijk, *Critique of Cynical Reason* (Minneapolis, University of Minnesota Press, 1987), p. 218. In Thackeray's novel without a hero the knowledge that arises from the valet's viewpoint does not lead Thackeray to change his desires or adjust his actions; he continues to act as he otherwise would, but carries with him the cynical knowledge of his own alienation. Thackeray and his servants are what Horkheimer and Adorno would call enlightened consumers, desiring the commodified products of the world even as they see through them. Max Horkheimer and Theodor Adorno, *The Dialectic of Enlightenment*, trans. John Cumming (New York, Continuum, 1988).

those utopian experiences. Indeed, because these ideal states are impossible to achieve, this essentialized subjectivity has a stable existence; the very failure of Thackeray's desires ensures the persistence of this deserving self. His memory securely remains a debt that his future continually promises to pay. Understanding this psychological situation itself as an asset to be acquired, Thackeray's friend Trollope would later write that "A huge, living, daily increasing grievance that does one no palpable harm, is the happiest possession that a man can have."[34] Although servants may have no analogous experience of actual possession, Thackeray's quietistic cynicism is inherently democratic and available to them; they too can experience an essential being which deserves the things of the world, which rightly exists on the banks of the canal. Isidor insistently desires sleeve-buttons and will never acquire them – or, if he does, he will discover a new object and cause of desire. Because this circuit of desire is self-perpetuating, Isidor's experience of an essential subjectivity which deserves the Belgian utopia held out by each commodity need never be undermined. In the next chapter, we will see this democratizing force operate with immense success on a much larger scale in the construction of the Great Exhibition.

What is finally most significant about these formative events, Thackeray's separation from his mother and the loss of his patrimony, is not their endurance in his psychology, but the extraordinary variety of experiences that the motif of material disenchantment can explain at his moment in history. Accidents in Thackeray's life became the media for his exploration of certain kinds of content – the curries, calipash, and commodified women, the riding whips and splinter bars – and of certain kinds of form – in particular the form taken by the commodity.

## III

To understand why Thackeray's experience of loss had such explanatory power, we must look at the larger economic system he describes. Objects circulate ceaselessly in that system; the pawnshop is merely a station in their progress. When Becky

---

34 Anthony Trollope, *The Eustace Diamonds*, 2 vols. (Oxford University Press, 1983), vol. I, p. 34.

Sharp's domestic establishment crashes, her maid Fifine makes off with "four richly gilt Louis Quatorze candlesticks, six gilt Albums, *Keepsakes*, and *Books of Beauty*, a gold enameled snuff-box which had once belonged to Madame du Barri, and the sweetest little inkstand and mother-of-pearl blotting book … and all the silver laid on the table," spoils enough to allow her to set up her own milliner's shop in the rue du Helder in Paris (p. 691).[35] Becky may lose her possessions, but the objects she has owned will endure and will briefly support other people as they have supported her. (Surprisingly few objects are destroyed in *Vanity Fair*; all letters should be written in disappearing ink, Thackeray tells us, but none are [p. 230].)

Society treats this circulating history of failure casually: "'I got this box at old Dives's sale,' Pincher says, handing it round, 'one of Louis XV's mistresses – pretty thing, is it not – sweet miniature'" (p. 201). The image here reproduces the larger circulatory process – things are continuously handed round in Thackeray's world – and powerfully describes the sexual circulation of diminished, commodified women. Furthermore, the mention of Louis XV and his mistresses suggests that Regency England and Louis's France are alike in their moral complacence – a parallel that may be seen to presage the personal if not the societal or political flood that follows such complacence: *après nous le déluge*. The image of "handing round" is repeated in Spec's reverie in front of Filch's shop: "what a sensation you would create," he exclaims to himself, "if you took that large ram's horn with the cairngorm top out of your pocket, and offered a pinch of rappee to the company round!" The impulse to display one's goods – to consume conspicuously and create what Bourdieu calls "distinction" – returns with gloomy irony at the larger level of impersonal social fact: objects there are handed round beyond an individual's control, and cause failure rather than sensational success. Even those characters who most successfully manipulate the exchange of commodities to produce their own social identity and surround themselves with goods finally

35 Victorian criticism of women servants who desired the goods (especially the clothes) of their mistresses was pervasive, more threatening even than that of male servants like Isidor. Mariana Valverde discusses strategies to contain this threat in "The Love of Finery: Fashion and the Fallen Woman in Nineteenth-Century Social Discourse," *Victorian Studies* 32 (Winter 1989), pp. 168–88.

suffer from circulation. Commodities "[shrug] off their private affiliations," in John Carey's phrase, as the Louis Quatorze candlesticks shrug off Becky.[36]

Mayhew's *London Labour and the London Poor* – published after *Vanity Fair* finished its serial run – includes a lengthy description of Newcut market, which, on a Saturday night, "has more of the character of a fair than a market."[37] The two closely printed columns cataloguing discrete objects in incongruous collections show Thackeray's close attention to detail:

Here, alongside the road, are some half-dozen headless tailors' dummies, dressed in Chesterfields and fustian jackets, each labelled, "Look at the prices," or "Observe the quality." After this is a butcher's shop, crimson and white with meat piled up to the first floor ... A little further on stands the clean family, begging; the father with his head down as if in shame, and a box of lucifers held forth in his hand – the boys in newly-washed pinafores, and the tidily got-up mother with a child at her breast. This stall is green and white with bunches of turnips – that red with apples, the next yellow with onions, and another purple with pickling cabbages.[38]

Mayhew concludes: "Such, indeed, is the riot, the struggle, and the scramble for a living, that the confusion and uproar of the Newcut on Saturday night have a bewildering and saddening effect upon the thoughtful mind."[39] Mayhew is writing the sociology of poverty – of life across the river from Thackeray's West End and City world – in Thackeray's terms. "A man with a reflective turn of mind, walking through an exhibition of this sort, will not be oppressed, I take it, by his own or other people's hilarity," the Manager of the Performance hopes (p. 1); but the text later asserts: "This, dear friends and companions, is my amiable object – to walk with you through the Fair, to examine the shops and the shows there: and that we should all come home after the flare, and the noise, and the gaiety, and be perfectly miserable in private" (p. 228).

As objects acquire a history in this bewildering environment, their empirical qualities recede in significance behind their function

---

36 Carey, *Thackeray*, p. 75.
37 Henry Mayhew, *London Labour and the London Poor*, 4 vols. (New York, Dover Publications, 1968), vol. I, p. 9.
38 Mayhew, *London Labour*, vol. I, p. 10.
39 Mayhew, *London Labour*, vol. I, p. 10.

in the system of exchange. This explains the paradoxical feeling one gets, when reading Thackeray's narratives, that objects are simultaneously important and insignificant. They furnish all corners of the narrative, are detailed with great attention by the narrator, invested with great significance by the characters, and even have causal importance for the plot. We are told, for instance, that a bowl of rack punch, along with the intoxicated loss of control it induces, is "the cause of all this history" (p. 66), and an appropriate index, a sign produced within a causal chain, of the limitations characters have within this narrative. That particular object, and not the intentions of any character or collectivity, propels the story. At the same time, however, the objects of the text are finally merely means to another end, the creation of wealth and status and the production of the novel's pageantry. That the candlesticks were Louis Quatorze and the blotting book mother-of-pearl matters less than that they support Fifine in her progress up the social scale; that the ram's horn was ornamented with a cairngorm rather than an amethyst is occluded, in the eyes of Spec's imaginary admirers and actual readers, by the abstract understanding that Spec is wealthy.

The material world is thus instrumental in *Vanity Fair*: commodities do not satisfy needs but do register their owners' varying degrees of wealth and status. Such instrumentality defines what Marx describes as an M-C-M' economy: money is exchanged for commodities that are again exchanged for money (money which has become capital through the addition of surplus value). Money (as capital), and not objects, is the end of exchange. In the inverse economy, a C-M-C pattern of exchange, money is instrumental and goods are enjoyed for their intrinsic uses: "consumption, the satisfaction of needs, in short use-value, is therefore [the] final goal."[40] Further distinguishing between these two, Marx writes:

The simple circulation of commodities – selling in order to buy [as in a C-M-C economy] – is a means to a final goal which lies outside circulation, namely, the appropriation of use-values, the satisfaction of needs. As against this, the circulation of money as capital [as in the M-C-M' economy of Thackeray's world] is an end in itself, for the valorization of value takes place only within this constantly renewed movement. The movement of capital is therefore limitless.[41]

40 Karl Marx, *Capital*, trans. Ben Fowkes (New York, Vintage, 1977), p. 250.
41 Marx, *Capital*, p. 253.

The psychological dynamic which supported Thackeray's construction of an essentialized subject and encouraged characters to sustain rather than satisfy their desires returns here at the level of economic abstraction. The bellows maker's insatiable desire for 'ock and turtle-fins is only an especially vivid representation of the principle of limitless movement Marx describes. Objects are valuable not as they are used, but as they are exchanged; commodities realize their full economic and psychological value only at the moment one no longer possesses them.

Money becomes both the central element of this rational economy and the image of absolute fungibility that the economy implies. As Georg Simmel and, more recently, Anthony Giddens have most forcibly pointed out, money is the primary emblem and facilitator of the circulation that Giddens, like Thackeray, calls "pass[ing] around."[42] All objects have a monetary value and all objects can be exchanged.[43] In Thackeray's world, there appear to be no goods which one might not want to have: all goods are assets, all things are available to impatient appetites; the omnivorous energy of the system – the "dizzy mist" of its gluttony – transforms everything, even money itself, into a fungible good. Thackeray spent a brief period as a bill-discounter and this occupation, one can imagine, would have neatly displayed both extremes of this process, the extremes his later work as a novelist also exhibited: the movement of money at its most abstract and detailed scenes of individual failure, the particular circumstances which forced people to sell their bills.[44]

While suggesting that any object can be exchanged for any other, this fungibility paradoxically encourages a contradictory appearance of self-enclosure and discrete isolation: a good is identical either to all other goods or only to itself. This was for Thackeray a matter of artistic principle as well as of economic observation. In response to the critic David Masson, who distinguished Thackeray's method of "truthful resemblance" from the

---

42 Anthony Giddens, *Consequences of Modernity* (Stanford University Press, 1990), p. 22.

43 The extent of money's power to create equivalences is a recurrent issue in consumer theory. Michael Walzer has a lucid and straightforward catalogue of what money cannot buy in *Spheres of Justice: A Defense of Pluralism and Equality* (New York, Basic Books, 1983).

44 Gordon Ray, *The Uses of Adversity* (New York, McGraw Hill, 1955), p. 159.

practice, associated with Dickens, of "taking the mind out of itself into a region of higher possibilities, wherein objects shall be more glorious, and modes of action more transcendent, than any we see,"[45] Thackeray wrote: "[I]n a drawing-room drama [such as a novel should be] a coat is a coat and a poker a poker; and must be nothing else according to my ethics, not an embroidered tunic, nor a great red-hot instrument like the Pantomime weapon."[46] In Thackeray's view objects have no extrinsic, transcendental meaning.

*Vanity Fair* makes this point in a more complex fashion and with greater precision. As we have seen, there *are* regions of higher possibility in the novel in which objects are "more glorious than any we see" – but Thackeray satirizes them. For Isidor the region of higher possibility lies outside a beer-house on the road to Laeken, and for Spec it is in the Park. Social discourses of (largely aristocratic) leisure – anatomized in *The Book of Snobs* as well as in *Vanity Fair* – construct images of "higher possibilities" that characters internalize and reduce into scenes of solipsistic fulfillment. Thackeray's fiction "records, with remarkable fidelity so far as physical detail goes, the ghastly social competition of the early nineteenth century, when an aristocracy which could no longer pay its way was still the arbiter of fashion and of behaviour."[47] Among the upper and middle classes, this longing is licensed and organized; the auction is only one institution that allows and is allowed by the ordering of privileged desire. Among the lower classes, this desire upsets that order and violates social relations; it causes the many napoleonic insurrections imagined and achieved on the domestic front of his novels. But whether the desire is exercised by the aristocracy and middle classes or by servants, whether its arena is the auction or the windows of a pawnshop, Thackeray mocks it by underscoring its temporary and private character.

Objects gain this lonely meaning for characters, then, through an allegorical process in which they seem to prefigure a distant realm of satisfaction. Walter Benjamin describes the production

45 David Masson, "Thackeray and Dickens," in Geoffrey Tillotson, ed., *Thackeray: The Critical Heritage* (London, Routledge & Kegan Paul, 1968), pp. 114–15.

46 Thackeray, *Letters*, vol. II, p. 773.

47 Orwell, "Oysters and Brown Stout," p. 300.

of allegorical significance in German *Trauerspiel* in terms that apply equally to the allegories of *Vanity Fair*:

Any person, any object, any relationship can mean absolutely anything else. With this possibility a destructive, but just verdict is passed on the profane world: it is characterized as a world in which the detail is of no great importance. But it will be unmistakably apparent ... that all of the things which are used to signify derive, from the very fact of their pointing to something else, a power which makes them appear no longer commensurable with profane things, which raises them onto a higher plane, and which can, indeed, sanctify them. Considered in allegorical terms, then, the profane world is both elevated and devalued.[48]

For the characters in *Vanity Fair* the profane world is not sanctified; objects acquire a libidinal content rather than a religious one and derive their "power," or significance, from being desired. But the process of elevation and devaluation is identical. Significance and desire are produced by the dialectical relationship between objects and the "higher plane" of libidinal fulfillment that the objects anticipate. As Benjamin writes, the object is "quite incapable of emanating any meaning or significance of its own; such significance as it has, it acquires from the allegorist."[49] Fact and value, object and meaning, are related subjectively in Thackeray's world, according to discourses of solipsistic pleasure.

But for Thackeray himself, as he says, objects are simply objects, and not harbingers of enduring contentment. He endorses no image of secular perfection in the novel, and his characters live, as he wrote his mother, "without God in the world," and with no fully delineated religious ideal provided for them.[50] As I have suggested, objects do anticipate for Thackeray the death of their owners, but this death is a privative category, primarily understood as simply the loss of things owned, an ontological bankruptcy: it is generally observed by an estate sale.

In Thackeray's later fiction, the utopian finds a home in the representation of mothers; unlike most of their desirable daughters, good mothers are seen as free from the ceaseless circulation of goods. In their country homes, at a distance from London (but not so far away as India) mothers are the non-

---

48 Walter Benjamin, *On the Origin of German Tragic Drama*, trans. John Osborne (London, New Left Books, 1977), p. 175.
49 Benjamin, *Origin*, p. 184.　　50 Thackeray, *Letters*, vol. II, p. 309.

commodified, utopian objects and causes of desire. The education of the hero – most obviously perhaps in *Henry Esmond* –
centers on his movement from the exciting world of commodity
desire to the stable maternal world of the country home, from
Beatrix, who is available to the highest bidder, to Rachel, the
mother who is uniquely distanced from all economics. The whole
dynamic of the fetish drops away when Thackeray turns to represent his ideal, imaginary mothers. In *Esmond* this produces a very
disturbing narrative – what George Eliot called "the most uncomfortable book you can imagine … The hero is in love with
the daughter all through the book, and marries the mother at the
end."[51]

In *Vanity Fair*, however, there is no stable maternal figure, no
home in which desire can rest, however uncomfortably, without
cost. But the notion of a higher plane or an ideal state is not simply discarded; the category of the ideal, though evacuated of specific content by his satire, nonetheless maintains power over him,
as its more showy and substantial versions hang over his characters. Indeed, it is the absence of specific content that enables this
category to house a large number of inevitably frustrated, shifting aspirations. The ideal, reduced to an empty shell, lingers to
elicit Thackeray's desire, to encourage the creation of possibilities
that will, even at the moment of their creation, only be dismissed.

Thus, Thackeray, judged by the standard of his own desires, is
defeated as a narrator by his continual, and continually unsuccessful, attempts to construct the dialectical relationship between
profane and sacred that Benjamin describes: Thackeray is an allegorist *manqué*. In his novels, and in *Vanity Fair* in particular, he
presents impoverished intensities of consumption and, encouraged by the vain, exaggerated promise of a higher plane, conveys
a significance most fully represented by death; but he neither
negotiates an understanding between the two distant realms, nor
offers any mediate possibilities. Fredric Jameson has described
the allegorical relationship between individual occasions of *jouis-
sance*, of the kind Thackeray repeatedly experiences, and the total
experience of utopia; and it is exactly the movement from
instances of pleasure to this utopia in either the religious form
that would have been familiar to him, or, certainly, Jameson's his-

51  Eliot, *Letters*, vol. II, p. 67.

torical one, that is impossible for Thackeray.[52] *Vanity Fair* achieves no dialectical whole, makes no unified understanding of the world; desire and frustration remain unsynthesized. And finally, as we will see, the later overwhelms the former.

## IV

The system Thackeray describes subjects the most private spaces of domestic and personal life to its violence. Before the sale of Mr. Sedley's goods, "old women and amateurs ... invaded the upper apartments, pinching the bed-curtains, poking into the feathers, shampooing the mattresses, and clapping the wardrobe drawers to and fro" (p. 201). Not only is the objective world transformed by commodification; the subjective realm too suffers from its invasion. In this world of commodities, even thought proceeds in terms derived from the economy. Monetary wealth determines the individual's interpretations of others, and thus a rational process of homogenization and reduction occurs, a reification of mental habits. The individual subject is isolated and cast adrift in a sea of things, commodified and bereft. Thackeray develops what Jameson terms a "textual determinant" – a form and style that supports the mode of subjectivity appropriate to the objective processes that encircle and permeate it – to complement the fragmented but densely cluttered material world.[53] Without the hope of communal identity, individuality is reduced to a perpetual solitude so deeply rooted that it rarely recognizes itself as such. Solitary individuals provide Thackeray with points of view from which to tell his story, with thoughts, impulses, desires, and actions to guide the course of his narrative; the narrator's voice, unstable, constantly shifting its position, impossible to naturalize, enters the interstices between these monadic units, comments on their behavior, and remarks that he can discover no community among them.[54] As with the construction of an unachievable,

52 Fredric Jameson, "Pleasure: A Political Issue," in *Ideologies of Theory: Essays 1971–1986*, 2 vols. (Minneapolis, University of Minnesota Press, 1988), vol. II, pp. 61–74.
53 Fredric Jameson, *The Political Unconscious: Narrative as a Socially Symbolic Act* (Ithaca, Cornell University Press, 1981), p. 154.
54 "With rare exceptions," writes A. V. Dicey, "the characters of Thackeray each stand out distinct and separate from one another. You know Ethel, and you

ideal individuality in the text, the practical impossibility of forming an ideal community allows community as a value to be maintained. By postulating ideal states (the essential subject, the model community) which are then frustrated, Thackeray allows himself to maintain those states as ideals. Experience disheartens but does not disillusion.

The resistant, enticing insularity of Thackeray's characters takes two forms, associated most fully with *Vanity Fair*'s two central women. "Our little adventuress," as Thackeray calls Becky, has a keen eye for those moments when the dominant system of commodity exchange lapses, when the strict principle of reciprocity at the center of that exchange does not function, and when something may be had for nothing. Gambling, for instance, in its pure form appears to subordinate rational calculation to chance; an economy based on calculation gives way to an economy free from calibrated fungibility, where gains can be made without expense. But in *Vanity Fair* chance does not offer freedom. Becky, carefully deploying her husband, manages to manipulate fortune so that she gains while others lose. Similarly, love ideally presents itself as liberation from a rational economy: one gives without regard to return, and receives without obligation. For love *or* money: the two are antithetical. But Becky's amorous careerism exploits erotic relationships for personal gain, profiting from the expenditure of others.[55] Indeed, her demure social profile, when she chooses to don it, parallels Rawdon's sham bad luck and incompetence: both disguise astute calculation. What appears initially as love becomes whoring; and what appears as gambling becomes, appropriately, sharping. For Becky, the other is not an other, with a particular history, an idiosyncratic set of varying predilections, talents and weaknesses. The

know Clive. You perfectly understand Becky or Sir Pitt Crawley, but you do not generally see, and Thackeray does not generally care to make you see, the exact influence say of Ethel upon Clive. You do not feel that they, acting together, are something essentially different from what either of them would have been uninfluenced by the other." A. V. Dicey, unsigned review of *Middlemarch*, available in David Carroll, *George Eliot: The Critical Heritage* (New York, Barnes & Noble, 1971), pp. 343–4.

55  U. C. Knoepflmacher aptly describes this rational and instrumental habit of thinking: "Becky thrives by disregarding sentiment. She knows that emotions are salable wares in the mart of Vanity Fair. She is logical and clear-eyed." *Laughter and Despair: Readings in Ten Novels of the Victorian Era* (Berkeley, University of California Press, 1971), p. 76.

other is an opportunity. Exercising rational calculation in even the few spheres of life generally reserved for the irrational, for chance and love, Becky represents the triumph of capitalist exchange; she expands and perfects the implicit principles of Vanity Fair. Thackeray's term for the practice of manipulating people and social procedures to get something for nothing is, of course, gaining "credit": Becky lives her life – social and erotic as well as economic – on "nothing a year."

Amelia in a very different way lives on credit, but her purchases are more purely sentimental and less material or practical than Becky's. John Kucich has analyzed the erotic pleasure Victorian characters derive from repression: like Dorothea Brooke in *Middlemarch*, many enjoy giving things up.[56] This apparent selflessness does not lead to communal activity and collective identity, as one might expect, but to a heightened interiority and perversely autoerotic isolation. By indulging in an erotic relationship with an image of George she knows (partially at least) to be false, Amelia sacrifices herself to the selfish pleasures of nostalgia and establishes a consoling line of sentimental debt. (When little Georgy becomes the objective correlative of this reminiscent eroticism, Amelia's egotism takes the form of intense maternal possessiveness – no Rachel she.) Just as Becky, in her determined attempt to establish credit and thereby enjoy the pleasures of material possessions and status, treats others as things and means, foregoing intersubjective experience for isolation, so Amelia, sustained by the nothing a year that George's memory provides, refuses all attempts by others to establish real relationships with her, and remains insular. "Amelia's love," U. C. Knoepflmacher writes, "like Becky's, thus, is self-love … Becky's cynicism leads her to deny all bonds; Amelia's love of love results in similar denials."[57]

We can illustrate these rival egotisms and the isolation they promote by noting the various ways Becky and Amelia respond to gifts. "Real giving" as Adorno remarks, "means choosing, expending time, going out of one's way, thinking of the other as a subject."[58] Gift exchange implies an understanding of the other

---

56 John Kucich, *Repression in Victorian Fiction: Charlotte Bronte, George Eliot, and Charles Dickens* (Berkeley, University of California Press, 1987).

57 Knoepflmacher, *Laughter and Despair*, p. 77.

58 Adorno, *Minima Moralia*, p. 42.

as a distinct person with her or his own history, needs, and desires; if successful, it resists an economy based on the exchange of commodities. The economy Thackeray represents subscribes to this utopian notion of giving and receiving while repeatedly describing its impossibility. In Thackeray's world, all objects are considered valuable only insofar as they signify and promote wealth and all persons take the appearance of objects; and this makes the process of giving and receiving immeasurably difficult.

From the moment Miss Jemima Pinkerton offers her a copy of Johnson's dictionary to the fatal moment Jos insures his life in order to leave her "a little present" (p. 874), Becky privately receives objects with demure gratitude (the episode with the dictionary being the exception that proves this rule) and displays them for public appreciation. She values them as they contribute to her effect. Amelia, in contrast, accepts gifts for Georgy because they support her belief in him (and through him George) and endorse her selfless devotion. But she refuses gifts for herself. When Mr. Binney offers her his hand and, as Thackeray's sketch shows, an unabashedly phallic gift, she "thank[s] him for his regard for her ... and ... her poor little boy, but [says] that she never, never could think of any but – but the husband whom she had lost" (p. 492).[59] And when Dobbin, in one of the few real acts of giving in the novel, sends Amelia the piano he purchased at Mr. Sedley's auction, she values it only so long as she thinks it came from George:

It struck her, with inexpressible pain and mortification too, that it was William who was the giver of the piano; and not George as she had fancied. It was not George's gift; the only one which she had received from her lover, as she thought – the thing she had cherished beyond all others – her dearest relic and prize ... It was not George's relic. It was valueless now. (p. 759)

Thackeray seems to be creating a space for the non-reified and human here: if George had given the piano to Amelia, or if Amelia did love Dobbin, this gift would be a vehicle for authentic, intersubjective emotion; but that possibility, already extremely distanced by the simple facts of the plot (George did

59   U. C. Knoepflmacher brought this gift to my attention.

not give her the piano; she does not love Dobbin), is made impossible by the attitude towards gifts and people produced in Amelia by the system I have described. She sees gifts as means to the self-indulgent pleasures of sentimentality, not to communal experience. "Giving in *Vanity Fair*," writes Barbara Hardy, "is corrupted, like sex and art, and even the most noble characters are not exempt from the corruption."[60] Neither Becky nor Amelia recognizes presents as an opportunity for collective union; instead objects reinforce the isolation within which each lives.

This insularity, forcibly developed as one of the novel's themes, produces serious formal instabilities. If social processes encourage retreat and isolation, how will the novelist describing society represent the subjective lives of his characters? Repeatedly, Thackeray gestures towards these spheres of existence – moral conscience, prayer, private desires – to which he has no access; and equally often he represents those spheres with apparent nonchalance. When Isidor, hovering over his master's dressing table, concludes his paradisiacal fantasy in a languid, post-orgasmic vision of the Belgian countryside, Thackeray's narrative abruptly finds itself without direction or energy. Isidor's omnivorous desire has provided it with a propulsive force; the conspicuous leisure he finally imagines leaves the novelist without an occupation. Thackeray, as a result, must abandon Isidor's consciousness, and discover another source of narrative purpose. He turns to Jos. But, in doing this, he tells the reader that such epistemological oscillation does not occur in *Vanity Fair*:

> But Mr. Joseph Sedley, luckily for his own peace, no more knew what was passing in his domestic's mind than the respected reader and I suspect what John or Mary, whose wages we pay, think of ourselves. What our servants think of us! – Did we know what our intimates and dear relations thought of us, we should live in a world that we should be glad to quit, and in a frame of mind and a constant terror, that would be perfectly unbearable. So Jos's man was marking his victim down, as you see one of Mr. Paynter's assistants in Leadenhall Street ornament an unconscious turtle with a placard on which is written, "Soup tomorrow." (p. 375)[61]

60 Barbara Hardy, *The Exposure of Luxury: Radical Themes in Thackeray* (Pittsburgh, University of Pittsburgh Press, 1972), p. 107. See also her "Objects in Novels," *Genre* 10 (Winter 1977), pp. 485–500.
61 This moment of narrative crisis, when recognition of the speaker's isolation and epistemological limitations becomes an explicit matter of moral and

The claims in Thackeray's passage are obviously and comically paradoxical: we cannot know what others think, Thackeray tells us, but he knows nonetheless that, if we did, we would be terrified – we would discover ourselves behind plate-glass windows, a placard advertising us for the appetites of others. Thackeray negotiates this tangled collection of assertions and identifications by shifting the ground of his claims: the reader and author, he now implies, share a set of circumstances and a set of attitudes towards those circumstances. Although Thackeray again is perched on the stairs and conscious of the footman's thoughts, the significant identification is with readers in the drawing-room: if "we" knew what our servants thought, "the respected reader and I" would be terrified. The frightening urgency of class revolution fades, giving way to a more innocuous argument about reading. A community is possible, this argument holds, not interior to the novel but exterior to it, between the author and reader; the scene of reading in this way appears to be constructed as space of intersubjective clarity, free from the obstructions imposed by self-centered commercial interests. Reading novels and reading the advertisements behind Leadenhall Street shop windows are opposed activities. Thus Thackeray says, in the famous passage previously quoted, "This, dear friends and companions, is my amiable object – to walk with you through the Fair, to examine the shops and the shows there; and that we should all come home after the flare, and the noise, and the gaiety, and be perfectly miserable in private" (p. 228). The melancholy knowledge that comes from reading thus

social comment, recalls lines from Pope's *Essay on Man*, which Thackeray was to quote in *The Newcombes*: "The lamb thy riot dooms to bleed today,/ Had he thy Reason, would he skip and play?/ Pleas'd to the last, he crops the flowr'y food/And licks the hand just rais'd to shed his blood" (lines 81–4). *The Poems of Alexander Pope*, ed. John Butt (New Haven, Yale University Press, 1963), p. 507. In the 115 years since Pope's *Essay*, the ontological hierarchy that invested actions like slaughtering a lamb with meaning has become less secure; in Thackeray's "world without God," the relation between God and man has been narrowed to that between Isidor and Jos. The lamb, with its iconographical resonance has been replaced by the resolutely unresonant turtle; the setting has been moved to the urban shopkeeping world of commodities on Leadenhall Street; and the innocent ignorance attributed to the lamb and to man has been replaced by an insularity caused by social forces of the economy. Most importantly, the role of "Reason" has been replaced by the social knowledge of economic practices, the unsentimental effects of greed and the invisible hatred it produces.

appears to be one of the few goods actually produced in the world of *Vanity Fair*. The reader and the author do not take part in the shops and shows but, as jaundiced *flaneurs*, they do walk together among them, and retire at the end of the day to similarly rueful solitudes: they are not elements of the movement of commodities, but objective and impotent observers of that movement.

In the late 1840s, Mary Poovey argues, social practice ideologically constructed authors and readers as autonomous members of a relationship free from both traditional associations of patronage or inherited wealth and the mechanized exchange of commodities.[62] Public debates over the "dignity of literature," over domestic and international copyright laws, and over the formation of professional literary associations, centered on the autonomy of the writer and his or her productions from commercial claims and forces. While, as I've suggested, these arguments partially defined Thackeray's work, neither its form nor its substance was finally determined by the ideology of authorial autonomy. His ambivalent nostalgia for the Regency, for the objects that serve as props in its scenes of leisure, is bound up in a conservative desire for this autonomy, for freedom from the demands of the market. That Thackeray recognized the restrictions imposed by the market is registered superficially by his various representations of himself as the Manager of the Performance, rather than, for instance, a Carlylian free and "original" author; this is a novel without a hero, and its author does not conceive of himself a Hero as Man of Letters. "In some way or other," wrote Thackeray in 1846,

for daily bread and hire, almost all men are labouring daily. Without necessity they would not work at all, or very little, probably. In some instances you reap Reputation along with Profit from your labour, but Bread, in the main, is the incentive. Do not let us try to blink this fact, or imagine that the men of the press are working for their honour and glory, or go onward impelled by an irresistible afflatus of genius.[63]

62 Mary Poovey, *Uneven Developments: The Ideological Work of Gender in Mid-Victorian England* (University of Chicago Press, 1989), pp. 101–16.
63 William Thackeray, "A Brother of the Press on the History of a Literary Man, Laman Blanchard, and the Chances of the Literary Profession," in Thackeray, *Works*, vol. XXV, pp. 467–8. Thackeray made similar comments in a letter to John Douglas Cook (Ray, ed., *Letters*, vol. II, pp. 633–4); on this issue generally, see Craig Howes, "*Pendennis* and the Controversy on the 'Dignity of Literature,'" *Nineteenth-Century Fiction* 41 (1986), pp. 269–98.

Thackeray's understanding that writing and the "trade of literature" lack autonomy and are governed by the same forces that govern the production of commodities may be seen in a more significant way if we look at the narrative form often viewed as central to his work: parody.[64]

In the late forties, Thackeray wrote a series of parodies for *Punch*, in addition to those in the first edition of *Vanity Fair*. The best of this series, "George de Barnwell," purportedly by E.L.B.L. (Bulwer-Lytton), is a tale of romance, crime, and literary life. Thackeray's intent is to parody Bulwer's idealistic prose, to mock the distance between fact and Bulwer's representation of fact, the poker and the pantomime instrument. And to do this, he chooses to set the story among the goods of a grocer's shop:

In the midst of the shop and its gorgeous contents sat one who, to judge from his appearance (though 'twas a difficult task, as, in sooth, his back was turned), had just reached that happy period of life when the Boy is expanding into the Man. O Youth, Youth! Happy and Beautiful! O fresh and roseate dawn of life … Immersed in thought or study, and indifferent to the din around him, sat the boy. A careless guardian was he of the treasures confided to him. The crowd passed in Chepe: he never marked it. The sun shone on Chepe: he only asked that it should illumine the page he read. The knave might filch his treasures: he was heedless of the knave. The customer might enter: but his book was all in all to him.[65]

The relationship between literature and reality that Thackeray is parodying is inscribed within his text. The distance between the prose and the scene E.L.B.L describes is replicated as the distance between George's idealistic reveries and the goods supposedly in his charge. George de Barnwell's mistake – and, implicitly Bulwer's as well – is to conceive of books he reads as fundamentally superior to, and different in kind from, commodities, the currants and tea and cocoa sold in the shop:

64 Thackeray, "Brother," p. 467. "Like Austen," writes George Levine in *The Realistic Imagination: English Fiction from Frankenstein to Lady Chatterley* (University of Chicago Press, 1981), "he begins with parody, but his art is always importantly parodic" (p. 132). In *Thackeray and the Form of Fiction* (Princeton University Press, 1964), John Loofbourow discusses Thackeray's parody in a similar fashion.
65 William Thackeray, *Novels by Eminent Hands*, in Thackeray, *Works*, vol. XII, p. 469.

"Figs pall; but oh! the Beautiful never does. Figs rot; but oh! the Truthful is eternal. I was born ... to grapple with the Lofty and the Ideal. My soul yearns for the Visionary. I stand behind the counter, it is true; but I ponder here upon the deeds of heroes and muse over the thoughts of sages."[66]

For Thackeray, however, books simply are objects, and are governed by the forces that govern the production of objects in the world he describes.

In this parody, as in many others, Thackeray employs conventional forms and language that he ultimately does not value, but that he uses, often with a kind of desperation, to feel and think. This is a volatile practice, and Thackeray is not always in as firm control over his material as he is in "George de Barnwell." His first novel, *Catherine*, began as a parody of Newgate novels but, as he admits in a letter to his mother, the novel failed because he developed a sly affection for the heroine.[67] Instead of enjoying the form and then revealing its hollowness, in *Catherine* Thackeray accidentally inverts this process: he asserts the emptiness of the form – and the moral claims that form makes for its heroes and heroines – only then to discover, shamefacedly, its pleasures. In both parodies, however, the literary experience is identical to the fetishistic experience of commodities: a process of attraction and of repulsion, of authenticity and of falsehood. And, just as she offers the most direct register of commodified social processes, the perfection of those habits the economy encourages, so Becky Sharp's discursive habits offer the best illustration of the consequences those processes have on discursive practices. Throughout *Vanity Fair* she gains approval for her abilities as a parodist and mimic: the Pinkertons, Lady Jane, Miss Briggs, Rawdon, Jos, and a variety of incidental figures suffer at her hands; and her social existence throughout the novel is, of course, in important ways a life of imitation.

Her parody expresses her scorn for the world around her. But, more significantly, it expresses the distance between that world

66  Thackeray, *Novels*, p. 470.

67  "It was not made disgusting enough that is the fact, and the triumph of it would have been to make readers so horribly horrified as to cause them to give or rather throw up the book and all its kind, whereas you see the author had a sneaking fondness for his heroine, and did not like to make her utterly worthless." Thackeray, *Letters*, vol. I, p. 433.

and her own. Becky mimics to ingratiate herself, but she ingratiates herself in this way rather than another because she is marginal, at the fringes of the social world. Poor, foreign, female, and (especially) motherless, she is removed from the powers that determine discursive norms, and parody, as many feminists have emphasized, can be an especially powerful habit of discourse available to those – especially women – who must speak from the margin and in a language they did not design themselves.[68] Becky as a mimic takes up forms of conversation which exist outside of her and uses them to her own ends, namely, to ridicule those who originally use the forms and to further her own career.

Thackeray was himself affiliated by some readers with this alienated position. His "mind was," Bagehot noted, "to some considerable extent, like a woman's mind" and his point of view was, as we've seen, that of a "footman," with an "instinctive sympathy with humble persons."[69] Thackeray generalizes from the specificity and intensity of the alienation which results from Becky's position as a woman in order to represent himself and to portray his male characters. This elision is indicative of a more widespread identification of female alienation as the sign or bearer of male estrangement; as Tania Modleski has argued, "male power frequently works to efface female subjectivity by occupying the site of femininity."[70]

Becky remains a threatening figure for Thackeray but, at the same time, he works to subdue this threat by identifying with her, by seeing her as the emblem for his own alienation. The identification and generalization of Becky's position into a human condition eradicates the specifically female characteristics of that threat. It sustains the generalized individual subject as a category of thought: everyone is failed by their language. "Only the word coined by commerce, and really alienated, touches them as familiar."[71] Language and literary forms are subject to the forces that

---

68 The literature here is extensive. For an early and influential formulation, see Luce Irigaray's "The Power of Discourse," in *This Sex Which is Not One*, trans. Catherine Porter (Ithaca, Cornell University Press, 1985), pp. 68–85; and, for a more recent essay which critically considers the complex political implications of the debate, see Tania Modleski, *Feminism Without Women: Culture and Criticism in a "Postfeminist" Age* (New York, Routledge, 1991), especially chapter 8.

69 Bagehot, "Thackeray and Sterne," p. 304; p. 307.

70 Modleski, *Feminism*, p. 7.   71 Adorno, *Minima Moralia*, p. 101.

commodify objects; they antedate the individual and resist his or her attempts to make them carry enduring significance. Thackerayan allegory suffers the same parodic evisceration as the goods those allegories describe. Benjamin's famous comment about Baudelaire – "Baudelaire knew how it stood with the poet: as a flaneur he went to the market; to look it over, as he thought, but in reality to find a buyer" – applies in a modified way to Thackeray's own *flanerie*.[72] He too went to the shops and shows, presenting himself merely as an observer, while looking, at the same time, for a buyer; in finding one, however, he found that he himself had been sold.

Thackeray's belief that literature implicates its authors fully in the market became more explicit in *Pendennis*: "That's the way with poets," says Warrington to Pen,

"They fall in love, jilt, or are jilted: they suffer and they cry out that they suffer more than any other mortals: and when they have experienced feelings enough they note them down in a book, and take the book to market. All poets are humbugs, all literary men are humbugs, directly a man begins to sell his feelings for money he's a humbug."[73]

Not surprisingly, this attitude provoked hostile commentary from fellow writers – among them Dickens, Forster, and Bulwer – who thought Thackeray's insistence on literature's necessary implication in the economy degrading to the profession. As Craig Howes has shown, Thackeray attempted to conciliate his critics by compromising: according to his revised understanding, writing is the result of valid, free, and dignified non-economic activities; its sale belongs to a distinct sphere. But, while creating this distinction helped to "resolve" the dignity-of-literature debate, Thackeray did not maintain it in his own work. Indeed, in the late novel *Philip*, the economic basis of literary work has become so explicit that it is a matter for self-reflexive commentary:

Ah! how wonderful ways and means are! When I think how this very line, this very word, which I am writing represents money, I am lost in a respectful astonishment…I am paid, we will say, for the sake of illustration, at the rate of sixpence per line. With the words "Ah, how wonder-

72 Walter Benjamin, *Charles Baudelaire: A Lyric Poet in the Era of High Capitalism* (London, New Left Books, 1979), p. 34.
73 Thackeray, *Pendennis*, p. 434.

ful," to the words "per line," I can buy a loaf, a piece of butter, a jug of milk, a modicum of tea.[74]

Words "represent" money: authorship and the process of writing are completely and unambiguously implicated in the exchange of commodities.

This recognition, assimilated in *Philip* by Thackeray's wit, is present in *Vanity Fair*, but not explicitly acknowledged. It exists there as a troubling pressure, external to the narrative but impinging upon it as an unexpected, unarticulated bitterness – a bitterness not arising out of events within the text, but arising *against* the text. It is most forcibly present at the novel's end:

> Which of us is happy in this world? Which of us has his desire? or, having it, is satisfied? – Come, children, let us shut up the box and the puppets, for our play is played out. (p. 878)

In the last image of *Vanity Fair* the characters retreat into materiality; and the last idea is the one that has governed the argument I have been making here: objects of desire are inaccessible in Thackeray's world, or, if acquired, unsatisfactory. But the anger behind these words cannot be integrated into the text thematically; it is instead a frustrated response to the novel's ending, to its form, if we understand form specifically as the form of the commodity. This object too has become self-enclosed and fungible, subject to a circulating economy of goods. As its puppets recede into the chest and its readers are reduced to children, *Vanity Fair* is seen to be like other objects of the reified world.

To return to Spec and the attorney's clerk gazing enraptured into Filch's pawnshop window, we can say that to read Thackeray is to experience the world as they do, able to see the objects we desire but unable to possess them. If Thackeray's work gives the "sentiment of reality," it does so not because it describes without exaggeration pokers and tunics but because it reproduces the fetishistic experience of living in a reified economy. We read Thackeray's writing as Spec sees the objects before him, through plate-glass windows.

---

74 William Thackeray, *Philip*, in Thackeray, *Works*, vols. xx–xxi, vol. xxi, p. 537.

# 2

# Spaces of exchange: interpreting the Great Exhibition of 1851

A man with a reflective turn of mind, walking through an exhibition of this sort will not be oppressed, I take it, by his own or other people's hilarity.                    William Thackeray[1]

The world exhibitions glorify the exchange value of commodities.
Walter Benjamin[2]

Thackeray exhibits the constantly circulating, incessantly dispiriting objects I considered in the last chapter in a curiously planar space; compared, for instance, to the involuted nooks and crannies, insides and outsides, of Dickens' novels, the space of Thackeray's failed allegories is remarkably depthless and two-dimensional. The contiguity of objects within the space of perspectival realism is rendered insignificant by the insistence with which those objects refer to an abstract level of meaning, represented most fully, as I argued, by death:

As you ascend the staircase of your house from the drawing- towards the bed-room floors, you may have remarked a little arch in the wall right before you, which at once gives light to the stair which leads from the second story to the third (where the nursery and servants' chambers commonly are), and serves for another purpose of utility, of which the undertaker's men can give you a notion. They rest the coffins upon that arch, or pass them through it so as not to disturb in any unseemly manner the cold tenant slumbering within the black ark. (*Vanity Fair*, p. 768)

The movement we saw Thackeray make in the last chapter, up from the gazing footmen to the "fine folks" in the drawing-room, is here negated by a contrary movement, made down the steps by the undertaker's men. However, although these steps and their arch are precisely located – on the second story, right before

---

1  *Vanity Fair*, p. 1.          2  *Reflections*, p. 152.

"you" – their existence is ostentatiously assumed by Thackeray rather than known: he is, after all, describing the reader's house which, in the singular, simply does not exist. As Thackeray's thought descends towards its stark, capitalized abstractions – "what a memento of Life, Death, and Vanity it is – that arch and stair" – precision of detail is of no greater moment than the slight hitch in the progress of the undertaker's men (p. 769).

In this way, the very variety of colorful objects Thackeray exhibits behind the windows of his novel – the cashmere from India, the bijoux from France – only sets off with greater clarity the monochromatic, unitary understanding to which he finally reduces them. And this insistent movement towards abstraction evacuates the area of the novel, flattens its domain until it becomes, in fact, like the circumscribed (if, in comparison to earlier displays, "lofty") space behind the brilliant windows spreading throughout London: "You must be prepared, when you come up to the gathering of the nations, to see some changes in the shop-fronts of the metropolis. Small panes and low-browed windows are fast disappearing from our leading thoroughfares, to make way for a brilliant and lofty expanse of plate-glass."[3] In a fashion similar to that of Thackeray's novel, the objects displayed at the Great Exhibition of 1851 – the "gathering of the nations" to which *Chambers's* readers were to travel – gained their significance not, primarily, by their contiguous relations to each other, but by gesturing towards a series of abstract codes constructed through them. Again, the display window provides a fitting emblem; indeed, as the *Illustrated London News* observed, "perhaps the earliest display of produce that can be called an 'Exposition,' in the French sense of the word, is that of the shelves of a retail-dealer's shop window."[4] Like the display space behind the shop-window at which Spec, Thackeray, and the reader gazed in *Sketches and Travels in London*, the Great Exhibition – "the Palace made o' windows," as Thackeray called it ("Mr. Molony's Account") – juxtaposed goods from all points in the globe, eliminating their original contexts and constructing new meanings in its austere space. Like the pawnshop or the auction, the Crystal Palace was not a space in which objects were either produced or

3  *Chambers's Journal* 15: 282 (26 April 1851), p. 269.
4  *Illustrated London News* 17 (16 November 1850), p. 390.

used; it was an intermediate space, another instance of what I call the space of exchange.[5] In this space, the upper-class goods one finds in Thackeray's novels were displayed near preserved larks and fruits from Prussia, sax-horns, sax-trumpets and saxophones from Adolphe Sax of Paris, gamboge from India, hog skins from Scotland, japan-ware from China, bowls, dishes and plates of felted, varnished rabbit fur from Russia, turnip cutters from England, artificial legs from the United States, and circular playing cards from India. "Just now we are an objective people," wrote *The Times*. "We want to place everything we can lay our hands on under glass cases, and to stare our fill."[6]

The extraordinary diversity of these things behind glass was arranged by and understood through a range of relational and contingent discursive structures. The organizers of the Exhibition officially classified the goods displayed according to two principles: objects were arranged by nation, with England occupying the western half of the Palace, the other nations occupying the east; and, secondly, objects were organized according to a four-fold Aristotelian arrangement of material, efficient, final, and formal causes: raw materials, machinery, manufactures, and fine arts. Commentators, however, collapsed these official categories and, in their writing, implicitly constructed a range of new relations between the manifold objects on display. Just as the most persuasive instance of Thackeray's fetishistic understanding of material culture is the formal pattern of his own novel, so, in the Exhibition, the discursive structures that define and redefine the goods on display are registered obliquely and indirectly, in implicit associations more than announced affiliations.

One of these tacit understandings of the Exhibition was distinctly Thackerayan. We saw that Thackeray articulated the material products of his culture into a form finally defined by the morbid impossibility of achieving utopian closure and satisfaction. Writing to her father, Charlotte Brontë similarly imagined the

---

5 Because the Exhibition claimed, in part, to be presenting a total representation of the world, a copy placed at a distance from the original, it is important to note that the representational technologies of the Exhibition were continuous with earlier types of display – like the display window, and, as Thomas Richards notes, the "space of [the] auction." *Commodity Culture*, p. 38.

6 *The Times* (13 October 1851), quoted in Timothy Mitchell, *Colonizing Egypt* (Cambridge University Press, 1988), pp. 19–20.

objects of the Exhibition as so many brilliant witnesses to the futility of material desire: "Yesterday we went to the Crystal Palace," she wrote. "The brightest colours blaze on all sides; and ware [sic] of all kinds, from diamonds to spinning jennies and printing presses, are there to be seen. It was very fine, gorgeous, animated, bewildering," like, in fact, "a mighty Vanity Fair."[7] The flaneurs walking through the Exhibition, like those walking through Thackeray's "exhibition," appear from this perspective to examine the shops and the shows, the flare, the noise and the gaiety, only to remain objective, impotent observers.

But this was not the only way participants in the Exhibition understood it, and, in what follows, I will describe various, more significant, discursive structures operating within the Exhibition, and the various, often contradictory, ideologies implicit in those structures. To do so, however, we must first analyze the means by which the spaces of production and consumption were evacuated and replaced in the Exhibition by one spectacular space of exchange. This depthless, abstract space encouraged its own patterns of behavior and thought, and allowed the production of the categories of meaning I will discuss.

# I

In an essay on the Exhibition, *Household Words* wrote that the extraordinary expansion of the railways in Britain had, by reducing the time required for travelling, "given new ideas of time and space to the civilised world."[8] These "new ideas" took a particular form, one which was concisely stated on the same day (two days after the opening of the Exhibition) by the *Illustrated London News* when it described "the practical annihilation of space and time which we owe to the railway system."[9] The "'annihilation of time and space'" as Wolfgang Schivelbusch notes, "was the *topos* which the early nineteenth century used to describe the new

---

7 Thomas James Wise, ed., *The Brontës: their Lives, Friendships, and Correspondence*, 4 vols. (Philadelphia, Porcupine Press, 1980), vol. III, p. 240.

8 *Household Words* 3: 58 (3 May 1851), p. 124. The argument developed through this section draws on material I have discussed at further length in "Epistemological Claustrophobia and Critical Transcendence," *Yale Journal of Criticism* 7: 2 (Fall 1994).

9 *Illustrated London News* 18 (3 May 1851), p. 343.

situation into which the railroad placed natural space."[10] More precisely, time itself "annihilated" space, reducing the significance of space in the collective sensorium of mid-Victorian culture and leaving an experience of time dominant.[11] "Our very language begins to be affected," wrote one commentator. "Men talk of 'getting up the steam,' of 'railway speed,' and reckon distances by hours and minutes.'"[12]

When we consider that goods and people circulated to and from the Great Exhibition by means of these newly built railways, it is not surprising that the cavernous space of the Palace, in spite of its extraordinary size ("the most extensive covered space ever seen or imagined by man" enthused *Sharpe's Magazine*), was understood through this *topos* as well.[13] "The railroad reorganized space. In architecture, a similar reorganization occurred with the introduction of glass and steel as new building materials."[14] In his lecture on the Exhibition, William Whewell wrote: "by annihilating the space which separates different nations, we produce a spectacle in which is also annihilated the time which separates one stage of a nation's progress from another."[15] As with the rail-

10 Wolfgang Schivelbusch, *The Railway Journey: The Industrialization of Time and Space in the Nineteenth Century* (Berkeley, University of California Press, 1986), p. 10.

11 *The Quarterly Review* (1839): "'distances were thus annihilated'" by trains; Constantin Pecqueur (1839): "'the railways' operation ... causes distances to diminish'"; Dionysius Lardner (1850): "'Distances practically diminish'"; Heinrich Heine (1843), "'Space is killed by the railways, and we are left with time alone.'" Quoted in Schivelbusch, *Railway Journey*, pp. 33–7. For a lengthy meditation of the effects of the railway on time – a meditation that suggests the penetration of anxiety about time into the bourgeois household – see *Chambers's Journal* 15: 390 (21 June 1851), pp. 392–5. More generally, see Schivelbusch, *Railway Journey*, pp. 42–4 and E. P. Thompson, "Time, Work-Discipline, and Industrial Capitalism," *Past and Present* 38 (December 1967), pp. 56–97.

12 J. Francis, *A History of the English Railways. Its Social Relations and Revelations*, 2 vols. (London, Longman, Brown, Green, and Longman's, 1851), vol. II, p. 139. Similarly, a writer for *Sharpe's Magazine* thought that "mile-reckoning will be eschewed, and minute-measure established ... and the infant mind will describe the mutual distances of nations by the time in which express trains perform the journey between them." 14 (1851), p. 265.

13 *Sharpe's London Magazine* 14 (1851), p. 250.

14 Schivelbusch, *Railway Journey*, p. 45.

15 William Whewell, "The General Bearing of the Great Exhibition on the Progress of Art and Science," in *Lectures on the Results of the Great Exhibition* (London, David Bogue, 1852), p. 11.

ways, however, commentators primarily understood the Exhibition as a reduction of space: "Here is the whole world concentrated in a mere point in space."[16] In fact, the Exhibition concentrated space so as to make time – understood as the relative historical progress of the various nations – more easily perceived. It was a process, as a writer for *Eliza Cook's Journal* wrote, of "laying out the industrial progress of the world, as it were, on a racecourse, and indicating the positions which the various countries occupy in respect to each other."[17] As travelling on the railway reduces space and emphasizes time, so the Exhibition brought objects and people from across the world to a single point, where their rates of development could be measured and compared.

This experiential relationship between the space of the Exhibition and the railway is, of course, grounded in a series of historical developments. It is fitting but not merely coincidental that the first sketch made by Joseph Paxton of his Crystal Palace was made on blotting paper of the Manchester, Buxton, Matlock, and Midlands Junction Railway: the entire development of the Exhibition and the Palace was both given its general shape and determined at crucial moments by railway companies. Paxton was not simply, as popular mythology has it, the Duke of Devonshire's gardener – "more accustomed to work with plants than with machinery" – but rather, by the late forties, a wealthy engineer who moved from the building of glasshouses to bridges and railways, and who, like other engineers, came to be a railway capitalist.[18] He was a partner of the Midlands Railway, and made this sketch while sitting at a board meeting.

The six million visitors who visited the Exhibition across the course of the summer and the (roughly) one million articles exhibited there were brought over Europe and to London by the network of railway lines built in the preceding decade. This was the first great moment of mass international tourism and railway contractors could see its potential benefits. When it appeared that funds would not be sufficient to support the project, contractors provided it with a financial guarantee. Their investment was amply repaid:

16  *Athenaeum* 1227 (3 May 1851), p. 478.
17  *Eliza Cook's Journal* 2: 40 (2 February 1850), p. 217.
18  Sigfried Giedion, *Space, Time, and Architecture* (Cambridge, MA, Harvard University Press, 1954), p. 255. Chadwick describes Paxton's career as a railway speculator and company board member (pp. 238–45).

receipts for the Great Western Railway, for instance, in the month of June 1851 were 31 percent larger than the same month of the previous year; for July they were 56 percent higher.[19] When the Crystal Palace was moved to Sydenham after the Exhibition, and was established as a public winter garden, the company that bought the building was chaired by the chairman of the Brighton Railway company; he provided a financial guarantee for the project on the condition that the building be moved to a point on the company's railway line. It is thus not wrong, though maybe reductive, to claim that railway contractors "made possible the Great Exhibition."[20]

As these financial negotiations suggest, it was not merely the technology of the railways that allowed the reduction of space and time exhibited by the Palace, but also, more starkly, the capital behind those railways. The veritable reorganization of space and time effected by the Exhibition was managed with the financial backing of railway contractors, and the technological expertise of engineers who were also capitalists. Commentators on the Exhibition inadvertently suggest this when they refer to the Palace as having arisen "like an exhalation": the allusion is to *Paradise Lost*, and Pandemonium, built by Mammon and Mulciber in Hell.[21] The productive forces of Mammon, whether infernal or not, provided the extraordinary resources required for the quick construction of the building, and the assemblage of goods. Marx describes the situation in *Grundrisse*: "While capital must on one side strive to tear down every spatial barrier to intercourse, i.e. to exchange, and conquer the whole earth for its market, it strives on the other side to annihilate this space with time."[22] Goods were

19 Henry Grote Lewin, *The Railway Mania and its Aftermath* (Newton Abbot, David and Charles, 1968), pp. 425–6.
20 Harold Pollins, "Railway Contractors and the Finance of Railway Development in Britain," in *Railways in the Victorian Economy: Studies in Finance and Economic Growth*, ed. M. C. Reed (Newton Abbot, David and Charles, 1969), p. 214.
21 The earliest allusion to Milton seems to have been in *Household Words* 3: 58 (3 May 1851), p. 121; for subsequent instances, see *Sharpe's London Magazine* 13 (1851), p. 311; Whewell, "General Bearing," p. 10.
22 Karl Marx, *Grundrisse*, trans. Martin Nicolaus (New York, Vintage, 1973), p. 539. "The Geography of Capitalist Accumulation," in David Harvey's *The Urbanization of Capital: Studies in the History and Theory of Capitalist Urbanization* (Baltimore, The Johns Hopkins Press, 1985), discusses the importance of this *topos* for Marx; Harvey's argument there has been useful more generally in its investigation of the relationship of capital expansion to geography.

not exchanged at "the shop of glass," or the "Crystal Store," but the space that was created there was defined by the demands of exchange, the circulation of commodities through time.[23]

The nature of this space of exchange can be seen with particular clarity if we compare the Palace with other commercial palaces that were developing in the middle of the century: the palatial department stores like Bon Marché in Paris and Whiteley's in London.[24] The characteristics of these institutions – their physical arrangement and the behavior encouraged by that arrangement – underscore the relationship of space to exchange. Both department stores and exhibition halls created spectacles before which people adopted an attitude of solitary and passive observation. Glass walls allowed sunlight to enter, iron reduced the number of obstacles in the line of vision, and the objects on display were allowed to stand out for view. In department stores, passivity was further encouraged by the establishment of fixed pricing: consumers no longer bargained with salespeople; this social and active element of selling and buying was replaced with a more disengaged, solitary and reflective practice. Walking through the shops and shows was a private affair. Furthermore, the general emphasis on exhibition and spectating reminded viewers that they too were on show both to the police-force, "our

23 *Punch* 20: 188 (1851), p. 195. Subsequently, in 1858, a "Crystal Palace Bazaar" was built according to the architectural principles of the original Palace; while it was considerably smaller than its namesake, it was intended for the display and sale of goods. See the *Illustrated London News* (16 November 1858), pp. 440–2. David Van Zanten mentions the Bazaar in two discussions of Owen Jones' polychromy: *The Architectural Polychromy of the 1830's* (New York: Garland Press, 1977) and "Architectural Polychromy: Life in Architecture," in Robin Middleton, ed., *The Beaux-Arts and Nineteenth Century Architecture* (Cambridge, MIT Press, 1982).

24 C. R. Fay reports that William Whiteley was inspired by the Exhibition to develop a great shop in which customers could see a variety of goods without being expected to buy any of them. See *The Palace of Industry 1851* (Cambridge University Press, 1951), pp. 90–1. Of the many analyses of Victorian department stores, I have found Richard Sennett, *The Fall of Public Man: On the Social Psychology of Capitalism* (New York, Vintage, 1978); Michael Miller, *The Bon Marché: Bourgeois Culture and the Department Store, 1869–1920* (Princeton University Press, 1981); Susan Benson, *Counter Cultures: Saleswomen, Managers, and Customers in American Department Stores* (Urbana, University of Illinois Press, 1986); and Rosalind Williams, *Dream Worlds: Mass Consumption in Late Nineteenth-Century France* (Berkeley, University of California Press, 1982) especially useful.

Metropolitan Argus,"[25] and to fellow-spectators. Passivity and orderliness – what was called "Good Behavior before Strangers" in, appropriately enough, the *Spectator* – was encouraged.[26]

This passivity and its primarily visual origins took its strongest form in the "mental helplessness" – a version of the "shock experience" Benjamin later saw typifying modern metropolitan life – that visitors recurrently noted as they entered the Palace. The insubstantial, fairy qualities of the building produced a "moment of amazement" during which "the Soul was approached through its highest senses, flooded with excitement; all its faculties were appealed to at once, and it sank, for a while, exhausted, overwhelmed."[27]

Through the course of commentary on the Exhibition, this sublime effect repeatedly has been associated with the roughly contemporary aesthetics of Turner's paintings:

J. M. W. Turner's study of the Simplon Pass ... uses a humid atmosphere to dematerialize landscape and dissolve it into infinity. The Crystal Palace realizes the same intention through the agency of transparent glass surfaces and iron structural members ... an equivalent insubstantial and hovering effect is produced.[28]

This critical observation, like the more casual comparisons made, for instance, with Aladdin's cave, suffers from being, precisely, impressionistic; critical commentary has seemingly been infected by its subject. If these articulations of the experience of the Exhibition and the paintings of Turner and impressionists seem tenuous, however, the connections satisfying but theoretically dubious, the following quotation from *Punch* is to the point: "The

25  *Illustrated London News* 18 (1 February 1851), p. 72.
26  *Spectator* 24 (26 April 1851), p. 394.
27  Benjamin, *Reflections*, p. 160; James Ward, *The World in its Workshops* (London, Wm. S. Orr & Co, 1851), p. 3; Samuel Warren, *The Lily and the Bee* (Leipzig, Tauchnitz, 1851), p. 12. Schivelbusch also notes the "perceptual shocks," experienced by both the travellers on the railways and the visitors to the Exhibition. *Railway Journey*, p. 46.
28  Giedion, *Space*, p. 254. More recently, Schivelbusch has argued that Turner's paintings and later impressionist work implied "a codification of a certain nineteenth-century perception of an evanescence whose most powerful material manifestations are the railroad and ferro-vitreous architecture." *Railway Journey*, p. 49. In *All That's Solid Melts into Air*, Marshall Berman similarly joins the Palace with Turner and, in particular, with *Rain, Steam and Speed. All That is Solid Melts into Air: The Experience of Modernity* (New York, Simon and Schuster, 1982), p. 237.

THE HAPPY FAMILY IN HYDE PARK.

Plate 4. Prince Albert displaying his domestic nation

dazzling effect we can only compare to a series of Turner's pictures being viewed, on a summer's day, through the windows of an express train going at the rate of sixty miles an hour."[29] The impressionism of the scene – the visual phenomenon which has dissolved material nature, and especially the ponderous

29 *Punch* 19 (1850), p. 10.

industrial materials of the Palace, into an insubstantial unity – is replicated by an impressionistic analytical response that renders apparently discordant experiences identical to the hasty glance. The elision of boundaries effected by the Palace has its corollary in the dazzling effect achieved critically by blurring the boundaries between the Palace, train travel and Turner's paintings – paintings viewed in an exhibition. Indeed, perhaps it is not taking the point too far to say that Benjamin's critical work on the arcades was similarly infected by the object of his study. Sections of his work on the arcades were written in the Bibliothèque Nationale – the ferro-vitreous construction of which, like that of the Department store and the Exhibition, encouraged clear vision and the quiet passivity of a resting *flaneur*.

## II

The logical principle behind the construction of this fairy palace, like that behind the railways, was the rationalization of parts; along with the large work force assembled for the job, standardized construction units allowed the building to be rapidly assembled. All the panes of glass used in the Palace were 49 by 10 inches, each girder either 24, 48, or 72 feet long, all the planks of wood "cut and fashioned by machinery, so as to be precisely similar, even to a hairbreadth of length, or to the bored hole of a nail." This stark regularity provided a dialectical complement to the extraordinary miscellaneity and ornamentation of its contents.[30] Whereas ornamentation inside the Exhibition was lavish, the Palace itself offered no ornamentation but that which resulted from the strictest functionality.

As Manfredo Tafuri claims, the 1840s initiated the development of a "utopia of form" that strives to order and comprehend the burgeoning productivity of commercial production:

---

30 *Chambers's Journal* 15: 374 (1 March 1851), p. 130. Noting, after Richards, that the exotic or foreign displays in world fairs were less coherently presented than the Western displays, Meg Armstrong similarly argues that "the dialectic between the sublimely monumental or gigantic and the disarticulated fragment or ruin of the exotic is integral to the politics of world fairs and their display of power in the nineteenth and early twentieth centuries." "'A Jumble of Foreignness': The Sublime Musayums of Nineteenth-Century Fairs and Exhibitions," *Cultural Critique* 23 (Winter 1992–3), pp. 199–250, p. 234.

"Architectural, artistic, and urban ideology was left with the *utopia of form* as a way of recovering the human totality through an ideal synthesis, as a way of embracing disorder through order."[31] But discovering the conceptual equivalent of the orderly building in which the goods were housed was a difficult project. The objects displayed, like those behind plate-glass display windows, were accessible only to the loosest of tropes: statistical charts and anaphoric catalogues. The *Annual Review* calculated the articles displayed, the countries from which they came, the materials from which they were made, and their value: the furniture fabricated in papier mâché and japan-ware, for instance, was worth £45,925. But the goods actually on display only begin the catalogue of things calculated: the volume of refreshments bought at the Palace was estimated (260,000 pounds of beef and tongue, 930,000 bath buns); the plans and guides sold in each of the Penny, Twopenny (English, French, and German translations), and Sixpenny versions were counted; the number of carriages arriving on open-ing day was described (stretched in a line, they would extend 20 miles), and their various types specified (800 Broughams and 300 Clarences); the money brought in was noted and its weight assessed (35 tons of coins). Most significantly, the number of visitors was calculated for each day and week, even for some hours – *The North British Review* reported that on 7 October, 93,224 people were in the Palace.[32] As Thomas Richards suggests, in discussions of the Exhibition people appear most strikingly as numbers, what he calls "statistical subjects." The 1851 census in this light appears as a fitting corollary for the Exhibition.

Other writers organized the Exhibition in catalogues or cyclo-pedias such as *Knight's Cyclopedia of the Industry of all Nations* which, across 1,800 pages, provides *"a full explanation of every sub-ject that can suggest itself to the enquiring visitor"*: Abacus, abandon-ment, abattoir, Aberbrothwick, Aberdeen, Aberdeenshire, Abies

31 Manfredo Tafuri, *Architecture and Utopia: Design and Capitalist Development*, trans. Barbara Luigia La Penta (Cambridge, The MIT Press, 1976), p. 48; see also Georg Simmel, "The Berlin Trade Exhibition," Sam Whimster, trans., *Theory, Culture & Society* 8 (1991), p. 120.
32 *North British Review* 17: 34 (1851), p. 535.

... [33] "As the subject is quite inexhaustible, there is no hope of ever coming to a regular finish," wrote Lewis Carroll,[34] and many of the poems written for the Exhibition demonstrate this:

> There's Fountains there
> And Crosses fair;
> There's water-gods with urrns [sic]
> There's organs three
> To play, d'ye see,
> "God Save the Queen" by turns.

> There's Statues bright
> Of marble white
> Of silver, and of copper;
> And some in Zinc
> And some, I think
> That isn't over proper ... (Thackeray)[35]

> Harvest-tool and husbandry,
> Loom and wheel and enginery,
> Secrets of the sullen mine,
> Steel and gold, and corn and wine ... (Tennyson)[36]

> These are the goods – a most infinite store
> Of ebony, jewels, gold, silver, and ore;
> Statues of marble ... (Anon.)[37]

33 *Knight's Cyclopedia of the Industry of all Nations* (London, Charles Knight, 1851); emphasis in original. Over the course of the summer, the *Illustrated London News*, the *Athenaeum* and the *Morning Chronicle*, among other publications, provided detailed descriptions of the contents of each division of the Exhibition.

34 Lewis Carroll, *The Letters of Lewis Carroll*, ed. Morton Cohen, 2 vols. (New York, Oxford University Press, 1979), vol. I, p. 18.

35 William Thackeray, "Mr. Moloney's Account of the Crystal Palace" (lines 79–90), *Punch* 20 (1851), p. 1.

36 Alfred Tennyson, "Ode Sung at the Opening of the International Exhibition" (lines 14–17), in *Tennyson: Poems and Plays* (Oxford University Press, 1965), p. 207.

37 Anon., *The Crystal Palace that Fox Built*, illus. John Gilbert (London, David Bogue, 1851), p. 13 (lines 13–15). See Karen Newman on the catalogue as a mode of representing commodities: "seemingly excessive and extravagant, [it] paradoxically produces lack or scarcity and the desire for more," "City Talk: Women and Commodification in Jonson's *Epicoene*," *ELH* 56: 3 (Fall 1987), p. 511. And compare Robert Browning's description of plate-glass display windows in "Shop": "Its front, astonishing the street, / Invited view from man and mouse / To what diversity of treat / Behind its glass – the single sheet! ... What gimcracks, genuine Japanese: Gape-jaw and goggle-eye, the frog / Dragons, owls, monkeys, beetles, geese; / Some crush-nosed human-hearted

In giving the objects in the Palace a greater order than that of these lists, the most common principle of classification was commercial. If the Exhibition was perceived as "the crystal store," a huge market gathered together by the forces of capital, it would be logical to see the objects as "merchandise."[38] For these observers, the Exhibition did come to resemble the Vanity Fair Brontë saw:

The spirit of industrial activity and commercial competition creates all these scenes [similar to the Exhibition], and as we trace them to their source we cannot help noticing the desire of acquisition, one of the original principles of human nature, which often and most generally kindles and keeps that spirit alive.[39]

Initially, the Exhibition had been envisaged as harboring the wares of a gigantic store, in which priced objects would be available for sale. Sir William Reid, the chair of the Executive Committee, announced that "a price may be attached to the objects exhibited, and the objects, if sold, may be marked." Reid's decision was soon reversed, however, and displaying prices explicitly forbidden: "The Exhibition being intended for purposes of display only, and not for those of sale ... the Commissioners have decided that the prices are not to be affixed to the articles exhibited."[40] All signs of commerce were banished and the objects displayed were thus not to be considered in relation to their monetary value.

Charles Babbage was among those who argued vainly against the implementation of this policy:

The exchange of commodities between those to whom such exchanges may be desirable, being the great and ultimate object of the Exposition, every circumstance that can give publicity to the things exhibited, should be most carefully attended to. The price in money is the *most important ele-*

dog: / Queer names, too, such a catalogue!" (lines 2–10). *Robert Browning, The Poems*, 2 vols. (New Haven, Yale University Press, 1981), vol. II, p. 439.

38 Martin Tupper, "The Great Exhibition" (line 10), *Three Hundred Sonnets* (London, Arthur Hall, Virtue & Co., 1860), p. 228.

39 *The Palace of Glass and the Gathering of People* (London, The Religious Tract Society, 1851), p. 86.

40 Quoted in Charles Babbage, *The Exposition of 1851*, in *The Works of Charles Babbage*, 11 vols., ed. Martin Campbell-Kelly (London, William Pickering, 1989), vol. X, p. 49.

*ment* in every bargain; to omit it, is not less absurd than to represent a tragedy without its hero, or to paint a portrait without a nose.[41]

Babbage sees economics as the principal end of the Exhibition, not the gathering of nations or the celebration of labor; and the suppression of the prices thus undermines the central purpose of the event. Nonetheless, in spite of complaints from several of the exhibiting countries and cities, no prices were marked on goods; the Exhibition appeared to have banished commerce from its halls. In its place, relational categories of gender, nationality, labor, and taste implicitly articulated objects into new practical and conceptual orders.

## III

At the close of *Vanity Fair* we saw all its characters, male and female alike, turn into objects; but it was the women of the novel, and Becky Sharp in particular, who were most obviously com-modified and most skillful at manipulating that commodifica-tion. In the Great Exhibition, women similarly oscillate from one side of the display glass to the other, from being objects viewed to being ideal viewers.

To an extent, the various representations of women at the Exhibition merely extended (and momentarily supplanted) the images of them as patrons of metropolitan shops: "The Exhibition has, in a great measure, put an end to the visits of ladies in their carriages to the shops of Piccadilly and Regent Street, and of this, as may well be imagined, the tradesmen complain bitterly."[42] After the Exhibition, as large stores continued to develop, the implication of women into the discourses of consumerism became more complete. In the "'Adamless Eden'" of the department store, women abound: "'Buying and selling, serving and being served – women. On every floor, in every aisle, at every counter, women ... Behind most of the counters on all the floors, ... women. At every cashier's desk, at the wrapper's desk, running back and forth with parcels and change, short-skirted women ... Simply a mov-ing, seeking hurrying, mass of femininity.'"[43]

41 Babbage, *Exposition*, p. 49.     42 *Sharpe's London Magazine* 14 (1851), p. 251.
43 Quoted in Benson, *Counter Cultures*, p. 76.

In the Exhibition, as in these department stores, women were discovering the attractions of "just looking"; one entered casually, for entertainment, rather than with a particular purpose in mind.[44] Because women often did not have control over purses, *entrée libre*, the ability to enter stores without purchasing anything, freed them up to shop with greater liberty. The Exhibition made this principle a rule: there, one could not buy anything. In *Punch*, under the heading, "A Lady's Reason for Liking the Great Exhibition," we read:

"My Dear, it is so very agreeable. You cannot tell how amusing it is! It is much better far than going a-shopping. The whole place is full of some of the prettiest things in the world – laces – silks – brocades – and such lovely jewels – and the beauty is, you may look at them ever so long, without being expected to buy a single thing!"[45]

*Entrée libre* expanded the experience of shopping, made it spectacular and fantastic, a colossal entertainment – indeed, "entertainment" in its contemporary form can be said to begin with spectacular events such as the Exhibition. "In the face of the richness and diversity of what is offered," wrote Simmel about the Berlin Trade Exhibition in 1896, "the only unifying and colorful factor is that of amusement. The way in which the most heterogeneous industrial products are crowded together in close proximity paralyses the senses – a veritable hypnosis where only one message gets through to one's consciousness: the idea that one is here to amuse oneself."[46] In 1851, fantasy combined with the architectural characteristics of the Palace to create a "fairyland," an "Aladdin's Hall," a "paradise." In this realm, objects were set apart from the everyday world of routine, work, and more incidental pleasures, and became so many instances of Lacan's *objet petit a*, available for desire but accessible only in fantasy:

Ever since the 1st of May, I've driven directly after early breakfast to the Palace of that great Jin, PAXTON, in Hyde Park, where for hours I've done nothing but think myself a great Princess of the Arabian Nights, with the Koh-i-noor my own property, whenever I liked to wear it.[47]

---

44 The relations between vision, gender, and commercial display have been most widely developed in the work of feminist film theorists; on "just looking" in the field of Victorian commerce, see Rachel Bowlby, *Just Looking: Consumer Culture in Dreiser, Gissing, and Zola* (New York, Methuen, 1985).

45 *Punch* 20 (1851), p. 212.

46 Simmel, "Berlin Trade Exhibition," p. 119.

47 *Punch* 20 (1851), p. 222.

The space of the Exhibition, like that fabricated by Spec and Isidor in *Sketches and Travels in London* and *Vanity Fair*, became a fantasy utopia. The attitude of the *Punch* writer, like Thackeray's, is significant: both are satirizing the wishful desires created within, in one instance, servants, in the other, women. But the existence of such fantasy is attested to while it is satirized.

These fantasies menaced the very display which produced them. "The artist of the [display] window," as Stuart Culver writes, "never quite manages to domesticate the desire he provokes" – whether the desiring subject is a woman or a man.[48] Identifying too fully with their fantasies, refusing to leave the space of their desires, women can accost the social order. Like Becky Sharp, whose insistent appetites threatened the window-dresser who created her, women at the Exhibition were daunting and required restraint. Satire, like that of *Punch*'s cartoon, was one attempt to restrain women's fantasies, to undermine them by making them ridiculous. More effectively, however, the desire for goods was contained by representing women as objects themselves: "Why – but that the women of England are the loveliest in the world – should we not rear young ladies under glass, and see if we cannot grow Circassian beauties," wondered *Punch*.[49] Placing women on the other side of the window turned them into mannikins, puppets, and statues bright at which both men and other women gazed. For women, observing their own objectification could shape the desire it attempts to contain, inculcating self-regulation and making them fantasize now about becoming the object of the gaze; later, we will see a version of this desire in Rosamond Vincy, and will see the dangers George Eliot believed it poses for culture. For men, this objectification produces – indeed, it has been argued, is identical to – conventional heterosexual desire: "objectification," as Teresa de Lauretis writes, "or the act of control, defines woman's difference (woman as object/other), and the eroticization of the act of control defines woman's difference as sexual (erotic)."[50] The desire which is this

48 Stuart Culver, "What Manikins Want: *The Wonderful Wizard of Oz* and *The Art of Decorating Dry Goods Windows*," *Representations* 21 (Winter 1988), p. 113.
49 *Punch* 19 (1850), p. 229.
50 Teresa de Lauretis, "Eccentric Subjects: Feminist Theory and Historical Consciousness," *Feminist Studies*, 16: 1 (Spring 1990), p. 118.

Plate 5. The threat of women's desire for goods

objectification can be disturbingly unmanageable even for the desiring subjects themselves. Thackeray's volatile relation to his "famous little Becky puppet,"[51] the fascination, identification and repugnance which he simultaneously felt toward her, again provides a demonstration. Her appetites cannot be clearly domesticated within the text, and remain within no single home; when Thackeray attempts to manage those desires by creating a display of them, however, his own desire escapes his control. Thus, at the novel's end, Becky becomes an object and the writer is left only with the sense of a longing which cannot be satisfied or managed.

For men, the "ladies under glass" at the Crystal Palace and at more conventional bazaars embodied fear as well as this ambivalent desire; the fairy-tale princess in the crystal casket could come to life – but she could also remain dead for eternity. The fear which women behind glass provoke similarly calls for a reassertion of their objectification. As Deborah Nord has written, "in the male discourse of urban description ... public woman is fallen woman: she may function as a projection of the male stroller's alienation or as an emblem of social contamination that must be purged, but in either case she is an object."[52] In *Vanity Fair*, again, we saw Becky Sharp serve both these functions: she is placed at or beyond the margin of the novel, partially submerged in its waves; and in that liminal position, she acts as a vehicle bearing the alienation of her author.[53]

Freud provides a more striking instance of this troubled fascination with women behind glass, and one more immediately relevant for the public display at the Palace. In another city at another time, Freud "found [him]self" uncannily, insistently drawn to these images:

I found myself in a quarter the character of which could not long remain in doubt. Nothing but painted women were to be seen at the windows of the small houses, and I hastened to leave the narrow street at the next

---

51 Thackeray, *Vanity Fair*, p. 2.
52 Deborah Nord, "The Urban Peripatetic: Spectator, Streetwalker, Woman Writer," *Nineteenth-Century Fiction* 46: 3 (December 1991), p. 374.
53 Gary Dyer has traced out the historical connections between images of prostitution and the East as they are present in *Vanity Fair* and Victorian attitudes towards "bazaars." See "The 'Vanity Fair' of Nineteenth-Century England: Commerce, Women, and the East in the Ladies Bazaar," *Nineteenth-Century Fiction* 46: 2 (September 1991).

turning. But after having wandered about for a while without being directed, I suddenly found myself back in the same street, where my presence was now beginning to excite attention. I hurried away once more, but only to arrive yet a third time by devious paths in the same place.[54]

Freud's text merely presents this as an instance of the uncanny "recurrence of the same situations"; but the circumstances of the repetition are crucially significant.[55] Behind the glass window, the male viewer perceives a partial representation of the female body, and is encouraged to complete that partial view, to create a complete sense of the woman's body, to fill in what they lack.[56] In "The Uncanny," the confrontation with female lack assumes traumatic proportions; repetition attempts to master that trauma while it forces upon the viewer the sense of uncanny fate or obsession. Elsewhere, this confrontation was blithely represented as a mundane fact of normative masculine desire: "There is no doubt but that love caught from a window is infinitely more overpowering than that inspired from any other source. We see but the beautiful face – perhaps the lovely bust or entrancing three-quarter length – imagination supplies the rest."[57] Fetishistic fantasy, supplying what women lack, is here fully normalized.

54 Sigmund Freud, "The Uncanny," in *Collected Papers*, vol. IV, p. 389.
55 Freud, "Uncanny," p. 389.
56 In "What Manikins Want" Culver argues that manikins are not images promising a totality (fragmented bodies gesturing towards a whole body) but that viewers are attracted to their very fragmentariness, enjoy a "break in the self's integrity," and experience "desire in its purest form" (p. 116). But the experience of desire before such images must vary in relation to gender, erotic habits, and the particular object of desire. Thackeray certainly desires a false totality, a utopian whole – while at the same time finding compensations in his failure to find it.
57 *Hoggs' Instructor* 7 (1851), p. 320. A writer for *Chambers's Journal* 171 (11 April 1857) similarly describes his fascination with "one fair item" on display behind the window of a bonnet shop, a woman working there whose parts he itemizes (eyes like gems, lips like a bright flower, and glossy locks of hair) as he stands each morning admiring her. "I was known to her by sight, for a smile of half recognition would sometimes wander over her face, as she wondered perhaps what I could possibly see to interest me so much in the shop and its doings. She never, I am sure, resented my incessant supervision as an impertinence" (p. 227). Like Spec at the windows of the pawnbroker, this enraptured observer has his hopes frustrated: his little romance comes to an end when he sees a man enter the shop and be greeted as a lover.

On sale for women during the Exhibition were gloves "with a map of London showing the Crystal Palace on its palm, enabling the wearer to find her way around the metropolis with discretion."[58] Men coming to London for the Exhibition could avert uncanny experience – could receive the guidance Freud lacked – by purchasing a guide to the display of commodified fetishes. *The Bachelor's Pocket Book for 1851*, a handbook to the bordellos and prostitutes of the city, has on its busy cover railway trains carrying Mr. Punch himself, figures from China and America, and "a young lady in a see-through skirt holding a sign which identifies her as the representative of 'Fine Arts'"; above the trains, meanwhile, supported by two female angels, is a model of the Crystal Palace.[59] The women in the pages of the *Pocket Book* were catalogued, pictured, and placed on display.

## IV

A month before the Exhibition opened, the Home Secretary, Sir George Grey, was asked in the House of Commons whether the Government knew of the meetings in London of a certain "Committee of Central European Democracy," a group committed to "insurrection against and the extermination of the existing sovereigns" of Europe.[60] Although Grey turned the question aside, inquiries like it were being asked throughout the metropolis. Lord Brougham, in the House of Lords, had earlier predicted that the Exhibition would bring to the city "some good specimens of Socialists and men of the Red colour, whose object it would be to ferment the mass."[61] And *Fraser's Magazine* saw, in the crush of foreigners "careering in full swing of strangeness and bewilderment through the streets of London," the penetration of foreign lawlessness into the daily motion of British public life:

58  Sarah Levitt, *Victorians Unbuttoned: Registered Designs for Clothing, their Makers and Wearers, 1839–1900* (London, George Allen & Unwin, 1986), p. 20.
59  Michael Slater, "The Bachelor's Pocket Book for 1851," in Don Richard Cox, ed., *Sexuality and Victorian Literature* (Knoxville, University of Tennessee Press, 1984), p. 129.
60  *Hansard's* 115 (17 March–10 April 1851), p. 883.
61  *Hansard's* 112 (18 June–18 July 1850), p. 871. This anxiety encouraged (and was encouraged by) false estimates of the number of visitors. 42,000 more foreigners came to London in 1851 than in the previous year, many fewer than the 3,500,000 *Fraser's* anticipated.

By what means are we to preserve English decorum in the streets? ... These foreigners have no notion of being restrained within the boundaries of the kerb-stones. At home they straggle out all over the open streets of their uncomfortable, stony, picturesque, old towns: here they will try to do the same thing ... Who is to pay for the broken [shop-] windows? ... Who shall preserve order amongst a heterogeneous mob gathered indiscriminately from all parts of the world, and bringing into the multitudinous collision an infinite medley of customs, costumes, and conflicting temperaments? ... Where will the millions retreat to in moments of emergency – when there happens to be a broiling sun, for instance? Where are the porches and awnings to shelter them? They will rush, perhaps, *en masse*, to the shady side of the street ... [a] jammed and panting multitude.[62]

Decorum and restraint are seen – in this unrestrained, indecorous essay – as particularly English, while straggling lawlessness is peculiarly foreign, at its best quaint, at its worst dangerous. Display windows will break, the boundary between desire and its objects will shatter, and the nation of shopkeepers will be looted. *Fraser's* went on to describe one danger of foreign visitors more fully, wondering whether the advertising columns of *The Times* were being used as a channel of clandestine communication between French Socialists and English Chartists.[63]

When not figuring visitors from other countries as lawless and uncontrollable threats, writers on the Exhibition regularly attempted to control them by representing them as objects; the visual technology of exhibitions encouraged this mode of social control for foreigners as it did for women. As Timothy Mitchell has shown, the writing of Egyptian visitors to European exhibitions vividly evokes the experience of being transformed into exhibitions and displays: believing that, as one early traveller to Europe had it, "'the gaze has no effect,'" Europeans framed Egyptians as objects on display in theatres and museums.[64] But, Mitchell shows, the Egyptians saw more clearly than contemporary Westerners that Europe was in the process of constructing itself as an exhibit, a strictly ordered world organized for the spectator's view. As we will see below, the world of the display window comes to extend beyond Hyde Park as stores, museums,

62  *Fraser's Magazine* 43 (February 1851), pp. 131–2.
63  *Fraser's Magazine* 43 (February 1851), p. 136.
64  Mitchell, *Colonizing Egypt*, p. 2.

cafés, and "even the Alps once the funicular was built" were seen as displays.[65] If the Great Exhibition was "the World Daguerrotyped," as one American visitor had it, the world itself, outside the crystal walls, was little different: "everything seemed to be set up before one as though it were the model or picture of something."[66]

When considering the objects produced by foreign exhibitors, commentators' observations were informed by national stereo-types. England's ability to order and restrain the influx of goods and people from across the world – to accommodate, in its stable, homogenous capital, the wild profusion of nations – resulted from its sober regularity. "The concentrated energies of a nation beating with a common heart could alone have achieved a result which, powerful in its own unity, has had power to assimilate to itself even the discordant elements abroad and build them into a unity of nations."[67] English regularity – the equivalent in national char-acteristics of the regular structure of the Palace, the rationalized classification of the Exhibition's contents, and the extensive British network of railways – keeps the unruly foreign visitors within the kerb-stones. The arrangement of the goods in the Palace also contributed to the impression of British order. Although overflowing with material, the English section of the Exhibition, covering half the entire area, was at least arranged as a whole; the eastern half of the building, into which all other coun-tries were placed, was, as Richards says, balkanized and chaotic.[68]

This definition of national regularity was shaped in particular by rhetorically positioning England amidst the opposed exam-ples furnished by rival countries; simply by describing the pro-ductions of these countries writers could implicitly or explicitly present British productions as normal and standard. In particular, commentators repeatedly returned to France, America and China as they attempted to define England's national profile and answer the frequently asked questions, "Wherein is our superior-ity? In what do we see the effect, the realization, of that more

65  Mitchell, *Colonizing Egypt*, p. 12.
66  William A. Drew, *Glimpses and Gatherings During a Voyage and Visit to London and the Great Exhibition in the Summer of 1851* (Augusta, ME, Homan & Manley, 1852), p. 336; Mitchell, *Colonizing Egypt*, p. 12.
67  *Athenaeum* 1228 (10 May 1851), p. 500.
68  Richards, *Commodity Culture*, p. 25.

advanced stage of art which we conceive ourselves to have attained?."[69]

"France has chosen the flowered path," wrote *Sharpe's*, and to the Exhibition she sent the objects of flowery luxury she excelled in creating. "She can produce only beautiful objects; she can work only for the wealthy."[70] Even the French superintendents sent to guard the exhibits were thought to be too opulently dressed. By defining the French as the producers of luxury – "this light and pleasure-loving nation" – the British could uphold their own superiority in attending to the needs of the multitude: "England, the land of aristocracy, produces good things for the people only, while France, the country of democrats, works only for the aristocracy."[71]

This insistence on standards of democratic utilitarianism broke down, however, as soon as observers moved through the Palace to evaluate the American section. America was depicted as the land of austere functionality, constitutionally incapable of attractive ornament: "The inhabitants of the Old World do not seek the shores of the New to indulge their taste in the fine arts, or provide themselves with luxuries to deck their tables and adorn their palaces."[72] This characterization owed much to a barely concealed anxiety that the United States had surpassed Britain in producing "good things for the people." Indeed, as the Exhibition was drawing to a close, *The Times* wrote that "it is beyond all denial that every practical success of the season belongs to the Americans."[73] To distinguish themselves from such success, the British were forced to associate themselves with the luxury and refinement they had derogated in the French. The rational and measured order of England thus could act as a mean between French and American extremes. "In its general aspect," wrote *Sharpe's*, the English exhibition "appears, thus to speak, to take its stand midway between America, the country of the useful, and France, the land of the agreeable."[74]

69 Whewell, "General Bearing," p. 13.
70 *Sharpe's London Magazine* 14 (1851), pp. 319–20.
71 *Sharpe's London Magazine* 14 (1851), p. 319.
72 *Athenaeum* 1229 (17 May 1851), p. 526.
73 Quoted in Robert Dalzell Jr., *American Participation in the Great Exhibition of 1851* (Amherst College Press, 1960), pp. 50–1.
74 *Sharpe's London Magazine* 14 (1851), p. 318.

The sobriety that prevented England from the excesses of either frivolous luxury or graceless efficiency carried an extra reassurance. For English order could also demonstrate its imperviousness to the political sedition that both these nations, France and America, represented. That French superintendents, for instance, were needed at all was a demonstration of the insubordinate volatility of the French character: "Our neighbors have yet to learn from us, how to esteem and respect the constituted authorities."[75] The Americans, in turn, were seen as bringing their own brand of rebellion:

> YANKEE DOODLE's come to town,
> To see the Exhibition,
> And strike a blow at England's Crown,
> By stirring up sedition.[76]

Britannia, her "calm, imperturbable lion crouched at her feet," could by her disciplined efforts easily repress any attempt at disruption: "that quiet lion that looks so slumberous in the sun, opening and shutting his placid eyes so lazily, and sprawling out his great paws in a sort of dream, is by no means so sleepy as he looks."[77]

Like France, China was seen to be a country in which the needs of the few were gratified before those of the many; however, in China, luxury was seen to be "soporific," a mark of the nation's stagnation rather than of its advanced refinement. Progress became one of the crucial valuative terms of the event, transcoding the rhetorics of nationalism and imperialism into quantifiable terms in order more effectively to define and affirm what is British. The Chinese suffer under the malediction of being unoccidental, and their products only enter into consideration when they illustrate the superiority of future-minded Westerners. Charles Dickens and R. H. Horne, writing in *Household Words*, assimilated the East fully to an abject position within a Western notion of progress.[78] They compared this "progress" with the

---

75  *Sharpe's London Magazine* 14 (1851), p. 320.
76  *Punch* 20 (1851), p. 161.
77  *Fraser's Magazine* (February 1851), p. 137.
78  For an analysis of the range of Victorian attitudes towards progress, see Patrick Brantlinger, *Spirit of Reform: British Literature and Politics, 1832–1867* (Cambridge, Harvard University Press, 1977), especially pp. 196–203; for

"stoppage" of the East by juxtaposing the Great Exhibition in Hyde Park with the "Little Exhibition," a display of Chinese goods nearby:

Well may the three Chinese divinities of the Past, the Present, and the Future be represented with the same heavy face. Well may the dull, immovable, respectable triad sit so amicably, side by side, in a glory of yellow jaundice, with a strong family likeness among them! As the Past was, so the Present is, and so the Future shall be, saith the Emperor. And all the Mandarins prostrate themselves, and cry Amen.[79]

China is seen as diseased, its intellect subservient to a foolish political authority, the undifferentiated bodies of its inhabitants registering not only their alien qualities but also the nation's stagnation. It is appropriate that the Chinese Mandarins only break their silence to speak "Amen" in English, for the representation of the East here is more English than Chinese.

*Hoggs' Instructor* made graphic the idea that emerged from this understanding of the world's goods:

Britain stood out in bold relief the principal figure in the picture of the world, occupying and engrossing mainly the foreground, a rich and troubled sky above her, the principal light issuing from one cloudless spot, and of which she was the recipient, her surrounding grouped neighbors being but partially within its blaze, dimness and darkness increasing with the distance, till the horizon and sky blended, completing the picture.[80]

While this quasi-religious image was presented as a deduction from the Exhibition, as something that the Exhibition had revealed to its observers, other commentators understood the fact of the Exhibition itself to be sign of England's superiority. Rather than being an occasion for the evaluation of progress, the

perhaps the most famous Victorian description of Chinese "stoppage," see J. S. Mill, *On Liberty* (Harmondsworth, Penguin, 1982), pp. 136–40; and for an analysis of such stereotypes as fetishes which structure the apprehension of racial differences, see Homi Bhabha, "The Other Question: Difference, Discrimination, and the Discourse of Colonialism," in *Out There: Marginalization and Contemporary Cultures*, ed. Russell Ferguson et al. (Cambridge, MIT Press, 1990), pp. 71–87.

79  Charles Dickens and R. H. Horne, "The Great Exhibition and the Little One," in Harry Stone, ed., *Charles Dickens Uncollected Writings from Household Words* (Bloomington, Indiana University Press, 1968), pp. 322–3.

80  *Hoggs' Instructor* 6 (1851), p. 285.

Exhibition was final evidence of England's preeminence:

The invitation we have given the world, to send its treasures to enrich and bedeck our Crystal Palace, and its tribes to visit us, for the sake not only of inspecting that great emporium but of witnessing our national conditions under its various aspects, implies a conscious greatness, on the part of our country sufficient to warrant such a bold and unprecedented step. It would be presumptuous and idle for an inferior state to ask her potent neighbors thus to honor her, and no such state would venture the experiment.[81]

Presented as an "experiment" or contest, a race of nations along a historical racetrack, the Exhibition was at the same time the trophy exhibited by the victor.

## V

The classification of the actual objects of the Exhibition into divisions tended to gather into two patterns. Discussion turned around questions of labor and laboring people – the efficient cause that led raw materials to become manufactures – and taste, illustrated in the sculpture displayed and the designs of the various manufactures. Those who thought the Exhibition was a display of labor's products saw it in one of two ways: as a historical demonstration of labor's proper dignity, or, conversely, as a major diversion from the unjust social position of laborers. Blanchard Jerrold wrote that the Exhibition marks "a great and decisive epoch in the history of the working classes of the world," for it proved that "industry, whether exercised to fell an oak or to create an Act of Parliament, is equally meritorious."[82] Early in the Exhibition, however, *Punch* took the more cynical position that the Exhibition marked a triumphant occlusion of the laborers' condition:

A real exposition of Industry would require that the INDUSTRIOUS themselves should be exhibited as well as their productions. In a glass hive we ought to show the bees at work. However, as needlewomen cannot be starved, nor tailors "sweated," nor miners blown up, amongst a multitude of people, with any degree of safety, it is suggested that paintings of

81  *Palace of Glass*, p. 53.
82  *Illustrated London News* 18 (3 May 1851), p. 372.

our various artizans, labouring in their usual vocations, should accompany the display of the substances and fabrics which we owe to the labour or ingenuity of the respective classes ... Shall we ostentatiously show off all manner of articles of comfort and luxury, and be ashamed to disclose the condition of those whom we have to thank for them?[83]

These divided attitudes towards the role of labor reappear in the various images produced of the Exhibition. The *Illustrated News*, for instance, published an extraordinary series of engravings of the Palace, its parts, their construction, the machinery required for that construction, the arrival of goods to London, and the situation of the Palace in Hyde Park, beginning in mid-November 1850 and appearing virtually every week until the Exhibition opened the following summer. In each of these illustrations, the workers constructing the Palace are prominent. In contrast, the *Art Journal Illustrated Catalogue*, published when the Exhibition closed, presents the objects standing out in solitary glory, framed by the fine print of the text, with little sign of the labor of those who made them. Tony Bennett generalizes from such images to describe one dominant effect of the Exhibition as a whole. In the Palace, he writes,

the stress was shifted from the *processes* to the *products* of production, divested of the marks of their making and ushered forth as signs of the productive and co-ordinating power of capital and the state. After 1851, world fairs were to function less as vehicles for the technical education of the working classes than as instruments for their stupefaction before the reified products of their own labour, "places of pilgrimage," as Benjamin put it, "to the fetish Commodity."[84]

But the most telling indicator of the attitude towards workers expressed at the Exhibition lies in the designs copyright law developed for the event. As the Exhibition approached, there was great fear that the designs for newly created objects would be copied by visitors and reproduced. A designs copyright existed

83   *Punch* 20 (1851), p. 42.
84   Tony Bennett, "The Exhibitionary Complex," *New Formations* 4 (Spring 1988), p. 94. Similarly, James Clifford argues that in such collections, "the objective world is given, not produced, and thus historical relations of power in the work of acquisition are occulted. The *making* of meaning in museum classification and display is mystified as adequate *representation*. The time and order of the collection erase the concrete social labor of its making." "On Collecting Art and Culture," in Ferguson, ed., *Out There*, p. 144.

prior to 1851, but the cost of obtaining a copyright under it was prohibitive for many of the workmen whom, it was expected, were going to display objects. A new law was enacted, providing temporary, inexpensive protection against such reproductions. However, the law was rendered void if the designs were used for objects offered for sale: "This provisional copyright is given strictly on condition that there be no sale or exposure for sale. If the proprietor of such copyright sell, expose, or offer for sale any article, substance, or thing to which his design is applied, he forfeits the provisional copyright."[85] Thus design was cordoned off from the economic in two ways. By lowering the price of the copyright, Parliament supported arguments that inventive ability is independent of wealth and class; and by prohibiting the sale of designed objects, it made designs themselves a peculiar kind of property, from which no profit could be made. A worker was permitted to own his or her design and "sell or transfer his right and property in the design itself, without injuring the copyright,"[86] but he or she was not allowed to treat the design as capital from which profits could be made. Workers were allowed, that is, to be property-holders but not capitalists.

This wary, firmly controlling attitude towards workers reemerges in the writing of even those commentators who claimed to celebrate them. These writers tended to think of the worker in abstract terms and to impose on him a stereotyped character: "For the first time since the world began an ovation had been accorded to Labour! Here thought, and skill, and the rude might of the horny hand, shewed themselves in their majesty; and industry, wondrous in form and exhaustless in energy, triumphed over the idle, the incapable, and the inane."[87] While repeatedly seen as a celebration of Victorian industrial strength, the Exhibition also revealed middle-class fears about that strength. The "rude might of the horny hand" suggests one source of the anxieties that such restrictive and stereotyping celebrations were attempting to allay. Condescending praise covers fear: "The poorest labourer and the humblest artisan have been among the visitors, and yet no vulgar word has been heard, and

---

85  Quoted in *Illustrated London News* 17 (11 January 1851), p. 526.
86  *Illustrated London News* 17 (11 January 1851), p. 526.
87  *Chambers's Journal* 15: 387 (31 May 1851), p. 350.

no vulgar deed perpetrated within its crystal walls."[88] As we have seen, the simultaneous entry of foreigners into the metropolis from abroad and of workers from across the country had elicited from writers fears about sedition and rebellion:

> I DREAMT that I stood in the Crystal Halls,
> With Chartists and Reds at my side,
> And that all who assembled in those glass walls,
> Came there the contents to divide[89]

Fears such as those parodied here by *Punch* raised questions as to whether the laborers themselves should be allowed to visit the Exhibition, and at what cost. Early in the planning of the Exhibition, a Working Classes Committee, including among its members Thackeray, Dickens, Lord Ashley, William Lovett, Francis Place, and Henry Vincent, met with the Royal Commission to obtain approval for efforts to encourage visits by workers; the Commission refused to sanction these ventures.[90] As it happened, local committees were formed, and a good number of employers, both in London and elsewhere, gave workers time off to see the event.[91] Workers, like women and servants in Thackeray, came to gaze through the windows in huge numbers.

The anxieties over the simultaneous presence of street-sellers, workers and foreigners activated fears of the mob. Mayhew notes rumors that "a great many persons" were coming to London to sell penny medals commemorating the event: "'The great eggs and bacon,'" one called it, "'for I hope it will bring us that sort of grub. But I don't know; I am afraid there'll be too many of us. Besides they say we shan't be let sell in the park.'"[92] Often the anxieties over the mob joined with fear of plague and disease, because it was considered not only that the sheer number of people would cause illness, but that these types of people, laborers and the non-English, were more apt to spread disease. To allay

---

88 David Brewster, review of *Exposition of 1851*, by Charles Babbage, in *North British Review* 15: 30 (August 1851), p. 536.

89 *Punch*, 20 (1851), p. 245.

90 Audrey Short, "Workers Under Glass," *Victorian Studies* 10: 2 (December 1966), pp. 194–5.

91 R. J. Morris, "Leeds and the Crystal Palace," *Victorian Studies* 13: 3 (March 1970), pp. 293–4.

92 Henry Mayhew, *London Labour and the London Poor*, 4 vols., (New York, Dover Publications, 1968), vol. I, p. 350.

these fears, a number of writers, including Dickens, advertised the strength of the metropolitan police. Indeed, the Exhibition in the Crystal Palace became both a great demonstration of and emblem for the panoptical powers of the recently established force: "The Police of England," wrote *Punch*, "have eyes, that, like the eyes of LYCENAUS, could, upon occasion, see into the bowels of the earth, as if the earth were no other than the inverted Crystal Palace itself."[93] The rationalized powers of the police extended over the entire metropolis, and were to restrain possible outbreaks. From the vantage of those street-sellers who wanted to capitalize on the Exhibition, this surveillance appeared unjust. Mayhew records the anger of street-sellers who were prevented by the police from selling "Exhibition cards" – envelopes containing gelatine postcards decorated with sketches of the Palace: "Why," said one man,

when I couldn't be let sell my cards, I thrust my hands into my empty pockets, and went among the crowd near the Great Exhibition place to look about me. There was plenty of ladies and gentlemen … Some had newspapers they was reading – about the Exhibition, I dare say – papers which was bought, and, perhaps, was printed that very blessed morning; but for us to offer to earn a crust then – oh, its agen the law. In course it is.[94]

More appealing to readers than imposed surveillance were various schemes of self-regulation that would render the police unnecessary. Charles Babbage argued that a limited number of workers, recommended by their employers, should be admitted free of charge and then required to report thieves or "improper persons" to the police; additionally, because of their expertise, these workers/observers might also be enlisted to report on any defects in the machinery exhibited.[95] While this plan draws up a segment of the working class into the surveilling body, it calls attention to conflicting assumptions about workers; even though they may best know the machines and how they operate, workers must themselves be regulated and recommended for approval before their "trustworthiness" can be believed.

93 *Punch* 20 (1851), p. 210; see also Charles Dickens and W. H. Wills, "The Metropolitan Protectives," in Stone, ed., *Charles Dickens Uncollected Writings*, pp. 253–74.
94 Mayhew, *London Labour*, vol. I, p. 266; see also vol. I, p. 353.
95 Babbage, *Exposition*, p. 74.

But the workers who visited the Exhibition proved to be self-regulating without requiring a plan such as Babbage's or necessitating the overt use of force by the metropolitan Argus or Lycenaus. There are a range of possible reasons for the quiescence of the workers at the Exhibition. The most obvious is simply that the anxiety was, if not entirely unfounded, certainly exacerbated by the popular image of the rude and horny-handed workers. The conditions for an insurrection were not present at the Exhibition, and it was mainly middle- and upper-class fear that lead them to exaggerate its likelihood. In the years following 1848, the labor movement did not have the coherence and power to organize at a mass level. The apparent financial stability of the "Victorian noon" (fuelled by the imperialism on display at the Exhibition) and a domestic tradition of civil freedom encouraged significant sections of the working class to believe that their interests lay in peaceable cooperation with authorities.[96] Had the Exhibition taken place a few years earlier, the system of relationships then active among laborers would have provided a stronger basis for working-class action. The gathering in Hyde Park was regularly imagined in relation to the Chartist meeting at Kensington Gardens:

On the 10th of April, 1848, affrighted London beheld a muster of a hundred thousand disaffected men on Kensington Common; and three weeks later in this year is joyfully witnessed an assembly more numerous still by far, covering Hyde Park and all its avenues; while through that sea of people slowly rode the Queen, amidst shouted blessings in every language of earth.[97]

As it was, *Chambers's* smug analysis proved correct: "There will be no 10th of April Chartism here – our Exhibition of '51 is better than a revolution."[98]

Furthermore, had an uprising been possible, three forces were present which would have acted as restraints on an insurrection. The first is simply the passivity we have seen the Exhibition

96 "The combination of higher wages associated with imperial power, and civic freedoms associated with a national heritage prior to landlord or capitalist rule, had already quieted impulses of popular rebellion by the time of the Great Exhibition." Perry Anderson, "The Figures of Descent," *New Left Review* 161 (January/February 1987), p. 50.

97 *Hoggs' Instructor* 8 (1852), p. 305.

98 *Chambers's Journal* 15: 374 (1 March 1851), pp. 129–30.

encourage; the space of exchange prompts viewing rather than action. While the objects in the Palace seemed to invite the anger of workers, they invited their gazes more effectively. Secondly, the presence of visitors, rather than inciting rebellion, actually worked to restrain it: while in *Punch's* illustration (plate 4, above), foreigners were held up for display by the State (in the form of the Prince Consort), the English of all classes were equally aware of an opportunity to impress their visitors. The glass and girders of the Palace contained and controlled all members of the "Happy Family." A poem for children provided rules that adults also were instructed to follow:

> Be gentle and kind, little Children, and show
> That the rules of behavior you practice and know
> That the foreigners when they go home may all tell
> What good boys and girls in this free country do dwell.[99]

Finally, the orderliness of the objects exhibited was infectious and overwhelming. One stated task of the Exhibition was the inculcation of respect for constituted authorities. Thus, in an early stage of planning, the Art Union maintained that "the loyalizing effect of such an exhibition is not the least of its moral recommendations. Every man who visited it would see in its treasures the result of social order and reverence for the majesty of the law."[100] I suggested above that this internalized culture of self-regulation was felt in a particularly acute fashion by women gazing at the objects they desire; Tony Bennett argues that the Exhibition produced this disciplinary effect more generally, perfecting, particularly among the working classes, "a self-monitoring system of looks in which the subject and object positions can be exchanged, in which the crowd comes to commune with and regulate itself through interiorizing the ideal and ordered view of itself as seen from the controlling view of power – a site of sight accessible to all."[101] The fear of revolution was a middle-class anxiety; the Exhibition acted as an antidote.

---

99  "The House that Paxton Built" (London, Darton & Co., 1851).
100  Quoted in Paul Greenhalgh, *Ephemeral Vistas: Expositions Universelles, Great Exhibitions and World Fairs, 1851–1939* (Manchester University Press, 1988), p. 30.
101  Bennett, "Exhibitionary Complex," p. 82.

The ordering of objects, the rationalized classification of the extraordinary material wealth of the nation, its colonies, and the world's countries, simultaneously ordered the viewers who perceived them. The classes were seen to be united by the "genius of the spot":[102]

> HEAVEN's duteous sunshine waits upon her going,
> And with it blends a sunshine brighter still –
>    The loyal love of a great people, knowing
> That building up is better than o'erthrowing;
>    That Freedom lies in taming of self-will.[103]

If Thackeray imagined revolution as a valet longing for the conspicuous goods of his master, the Exhibition suggests that the display of objects can be used to regulate class desire as well.

Criticism of the Exhibition by members of the working class remained, but emerged only at the edges of popular discussion. Julian Harnay, in *The Friend of the People*, saw the Exhibition as "so much plunder wrung from the people of all lands by the men of blood, privilege and capital met to exult over the prostration of labour."[104] The unwillingness of some members of the working class to exhibit their inventions even after the passage of the new designs act also indicates a suspicion that the event was to their disadvantage.[105] Less confrontational artisans who remained dissatisfied with the Exhibition simply resisted offering their inventions for the display; and, in the years after 1851, others formed their own exhibits of industrial products:

In those undertakings [the Exhibitions of 1851 and 1862] the Working Classes were chiefly represented by their employers, who devoted their capital to the production of the best specimens of skilled workmanship, and received the honors awarded without any material prejudice to the interests of the actual producers ... It may be inferred, therefore, that although Working Men were not excluded from these displays as exhibitors, the expenses attendant upon producing objects worthy to be placed in competition with those of the capitalist prevented their avail-

---

102 *Athenaeum* 1235 (28 June 1851), p. 685.
103 *Punch* 20 (1851), p. 195.
104 Quoted in Short, "Workers Under Glass," p. 199.
105 Morris, "Leeds and the Crystal Palace," p. 293.

ing themselves of the privilege; and that, consequently, a fair representation of the Working Classes did not take place til the inauguration of the NORTH LONDON INDUSTRIAL EXHIBITION.[106]

Working men were not excluded from the 1851 event – and the Exhibition thus had the appearance of being an open affair – but were only included on grounds that made difficult their "fair representation."

## VI

These questions about the working class could be elided if commentators focused on the aesthetic merits of products, on what Simmel called "the shop-window quality" of the things at the Exhibition.[107] From this vantage, issues of wages and the control of the means of production fade behind issues of form and beauty:

The *Poet*, as the Greeks called him, was the *Maker*, as our English fathers, also, were wont to call him. And man's power of making may show itself not only in the beautiful *texture* of language, the grand *machinery* of the epic, the sublime display of poetical *imagery*; but in those material works which supply the originals from which are taken the derivative terms which I have just been compelled to use: in the Textures of soft wool, or fine linen, or glossy silk, where the fancy disports itself in wreaths of visible flowers; in the Machinery mighty as the thunderbolt to rend the oak, or light as the breath of air which carries the flower-dust to its appointed place; in the Images which express to the eye beauty and dignity, as the poet's verse does to the mind; so that it is difficult to say whether Homer or Phidias be more truly a poet.[108]

For many like Whewell, the Exhibition was a colossal work of art; accordingly, to them the best measure by which it could be judged was aesthetic. In his prize-winning essay, representative of this way of thinking, Ralph Wornum argued that "taste" – rather than commercial progress, international solidarity, or the improvement of working people – was "the great object of attainment" in the Exhibition.[109]

---

106 J. F Wilson, ed., *A Memorial to the North of London Working Classes' Industrial Exhibition* (London, Petter and Galpin, n.d.), p. 1.

107 Simmel, "Berlin," p. 122.

108 Whewell, "General Bearing," p. 4.

109 Ralph Wornum, "Prize Essay: The Exhibition as a Lesson in Taste," *The Crystal Palace Exhibition Illustrated Catalogue* (New York, Dover Publications, 1970), p. i***.

Despite Wornum's claims for exclusivity, an aesthetic outlook was firmly implanted in the other discursive perspectives: if the rude hand of labor provided the might of the Exhibition, for instance, it was generally seen to be the place of the other classes to provide its aesthetic form. Wornum justifies the "demand" for costly works of art by arguing that they provide a standard of taste and foster a "legitimate rivalry" that extends to a "humbler class of production."[110] Capital thus indirectly provides the criteria by which aesthetic objects are judged; the desire for profit encourages legitimate competition, both of an economic and an aesthetic variety.

However, while describing the practical integration of the aesthetic with the economic, Wornum at the same time wants to distinguish taste at a more abstract level. Thus he writes,

When a costly work is distinguished by exquisite taste, it is something more than a specimen of costliness, which is sufficiently distinct from taste or beauty, and a skillful work will be beautiful, not by virtue, but in spite, of its materials. Good taste is a positive quality, however acquired, and can impart such quality in perfection to even the rudest materials; it is taste, therefore, that must ever be the producer's most valuable capital.[111]

What Wornum is describing here is the formation of an aesthetic capital distinct from that of the economic; and he clearly states that the production of aesthetically pleasing objects available to "the world of taste in general"[112] is more meritorious than the production of a few singular pieces of great luxury. His argument, however, working from the practical economic conditions of the moment, acknowledges that this distinction exists primarily on a theoretical level. In practice, the standard and key of aesthetics is provided by costly and magnificent means.

Wornum makes the same argument from the opposite direction when he claims that "ornament is not a luxury, but, in a certain stage of the mind, an absolute necessity."[113] The aesthetic is subsumed in the economic not as a refined indulgence – a position difficult to maintain, given the rest of Wornum's argument –

110  Wornum, "Prize Essay," p. vii***.
111  Wornum, "Prize Essay," p. vii***.
112  Wornum, "Prize Essay," p. vii***.
113  Wornum, "Prize Essay," p. xxi***.

but as a necessity. This is clearly an instance of what Baudrillard calls "the ideological genesis of needs," the discursive production of requirements which serve not biological but political and economic functions. Wornum continues:

> Where manufactures have attained a high mechanical perfection, or have completely met the necessities of the body, the energy that brought them to that perfection must either stagnate or be continued in a higher province – that of Taste; for there is a stage of cultivation when the mind must revolt at a mere crude utility.[114]

The aesthetic faculty, while distinguished from the body (being beyond and above it) is nonetheless put on a continuum with it, and is seen as governed by similar demands. The evolutionary development of "manufactures" brings manufacturing when it has satisfied biological needs to the higher, aesthetic realm of necessity, and the economic there merges with the aesthetic; the objects displayed at the Exhibition were called "Art-Manufactures."[115]

## VII

The return to economic considerations in Wornum's discussion of taste suggests that the various discursive formations constituting the Exhibition define themselves in relation to each other. The independence of the cultivation of taste from the cultivation of economic desire, for instance, should not be exaggerated; both processes are linked by what Wolfgang Haug has called the "technocracy of sensuality,"[116] the inculcation of economic desire through aesthetic discrimination. Or, again, the discourse of progress, as exemplified by the article by Dickens and Horne, is fully implicated into economic arguments. Against protectionists who, like Lord Brougham, warned that the Exhibition would "lower the price of all goods and wares" made and consumed in England, proponents of free-trade saw the event as a triumph, demonstrating that progress was a function of unrestrained inter-

---

114 Wornum, "Prize Essay," p. xxi***.
115 Wornum, "Prize Essay," p. i***.
116 Wolfgang Haug, *Commodity Aesthetics: Appearance, Sexuality, and Advertising in Capitalist Society*, trans. Robert Bock (Cambridge, Polity Press, 1986), p. 45.

course between countries. Thus China is a land of "stoppage" because it has remained isolated and without commercial contact with the West: "In the comparison between the Great and Little Exhibition, you have the comparison between Stoppage and Progress, between the exclusive principle and all other principles, between the good old times and the bad new times, between perfect Toryism and imperfect advancement."[117] The passion of the caricatures used by Horne and Dickens is fuelled by anger over the free-trade argument; China is no longer even a country to be caricatured on its own right, but the occasion for an argument much nearer to home.

In ways like this, commercial discourse, supposedly banished from the Exhibition, surreptitiously returns to what it in any case provided the occasion and means for; the tautological assertion of the *Illustrated London News* – "the object of the Exhibition is the display of articles intended to be exhibited, and not the transaction of commercial business"[118] – encircles a vacuum which the economic quickly filled. The Commission reconsidered their decision not to mark the prices of goods when a number of exhibitors and countries – from Leeds, Denmark, Prussia, Hamburg – complained. It was decided to permit exhibitors to send their prices to the committee which would then note their "cheapness" and allow the various juries to evaluate them with this in mind. More significantly, however, arguments raged over whether the Exhibition would stimulate or inhibit English manufactures: "Always practical and looking to the main chance, Englishmen have asked what is to be the use of it all – is it to do any good to trade?"[119]

Observers of the Exhibition worried that the Exhibition would drain money from trade by simply distracting potential buyers. To concerned merchants, the Exhibition seemed to have replaced the practice of buying with the spectacle of exhibiting. *Chambers's* reported their disenchantment:

The Exhibition continues to be an absorbing subject in more ways than one, as most of our west-end shopkeepers have found out by the exiguity of their exchequer. In the supereminent attractions of the Crystal

---

117 Dickens and Horne, "The Great Exhibition," p. 329.
118 *Illustrated London News* 16 (23 March 1850), p. 186.
119 *Chambers's Journal* 15: 387 (31 May 1851), p. 339.

Palace minor considerations appear to be lost sight of: mercers complain that silks and satins remain unsold on their shelves in consequence of the grander display in Hyde Park; cabinetmakers mourn over undiminishing stocks of chairs and tables; chemists aver that pharmacy was never less in request; and empty benches are seen at theatres to a much greater extent than is agreeable to managers. How can it be otherwise? After spending their money and their time in the Great Exhibition people are too economical and too tired for any other pursuit of business or pleasure; and while the commissioners are taking their thousands daily, there is so much diverted from the pockets of retailers.[120]

Clothing shops, furniture stores, pharmacies, and theatres: *Chambers's* casually classifies sites of commerce with those of theatrical exhibition. If the Palace replaced shops in the recreational life of London crowds, this suggests that the original appeal of the shops, the basis of their commercial success, was not entirely need but those pleasures which the Exhibition (where no necessities could be purchased) would also satisfy: the pleasure of consuming displays.

Shopkeepers quickly began to invert this dismal situation by enlisting the Exhibition as an incentive for selling novel goods; the *Illustrated London News* carried advertisements for "the exhibition Mantelet," "the Paxton Quadrilles," "Rimmel's Perfumery [which] will be found in Section 29" of the Exhibition, a "bonnet intended for the exhibition, but [which] from informality was too late," "Great Exhibition Pomade," a Great Exhibition handkerchief, "exhibition carpets." Songwriters marketed the "Quadrille of all Nations," "Crystal Palace Polkas," and lyrics such as "I met her in the Crystal Halls." The Pantechnicon, a prototype of the department stores discussed above, located "within five minutes' walk of Hyde Park," set apart "a large portion of [its] South Building for the Exhibition and Sale of Works of Art, &c., which the owners may fail to secure space for in the Grand Exhibition."[121]

In this way, the space of the Exhibition, rather than being a transparent or value-free arrangement of physical objects, a space for the display of objects already considered valuable, comes to be an institution that conferred value on objects. Its power extends beyond its spatial limits, so that even objects

120 *Chambers's Journal* 15: 391 (25 June 1851), p. 411.
121 *Exhibition Catalogue Advertiser* (London, Spicer and Clowes, 1851), p. 48.

not admitted to the Exhibition but merely associated by advertisers with it can acquire new value; but the existence of the spatial arrangement I have described is a prerequisite for the value conferred. The technologies of display and exchange, the shop windows and crystal walls, as they themselves circulate out of the Exhibit, help to define what is valuable and worth representing; from being a mimetic copy of the external world, realistically presenting the objects of that world for view, the technologies of display shape what is worth considering as part of the world itself. Like the scenic vistas perceived by present-day tourists – travelling with an eye out for good photo opportunities, the visual field perceived before all else as a potential picture – the world comes to appear as a series of display windows.[122]

Most of the aspirations embodied in the Exhibition – the promotion of international peace, the reconciliation of the classes, the development of a new industrial aesthetic – faded soon after the Exhibition closed. But the development of the space of exchange and its display-window appreciation of the world did not. The Exhibition, wrote *Eliza Cook's Journal*, was "to industry what galleries of painting and sculpture are to art – what a library is to literature – what a museum is to science – what a zoological and botanical garden is to natural history – a chart of the progress of mankind."[123] In each of these institutions, whether because of the association with ideas of "progress" or with the other discursive categories I have discussed, the arrangement of material culture in the abstract, chart-like space of exchange became an active agent in the production of value. The fragmentary, evanescent emblem of totality produced by these relational, articulatory

---

122 This is one of the central points of Mitchell's *Colonizing Egypt*: "'Reality', it turns out, means that which can be represented, that which presents itself as an exhibit before an observer. The so-called real world 'outside' is something experienced and grasped only as a series of further representations, an extended exhibition" (p. 29). Thus as the American William Drew commented in his *Glimpses and Gatherings* (Augusta, ME, Homan and Manley, 1852), London itself "is at the present season, almost itself one grand fair … so that the Crystal Palace loses in a measure its pre-eminence of attraction" (pp. 194–5). See also Richards' argument that the Exhibition created a spectacular and "consolidated rhetoric of public representation." *Commodity Culture*, p. 70.
123 *Eliza Cook's Journal* 2: 40 (2 February 1850), p. 217.

practices – "The Great Exhibition of the Industry of All Nations" – modifies each of the elements, the objects and viewers, which constitute it.

Finally, and inevitably, the Exhibition and the Palace which housed it became commodities themselves. If, as Charles Smith enthused, "whatever art has to glory in, or science to boast of, the shopwindow exhibits to the admiration of mankind," then the Crystal Palace itself, with its technology of display developed by art, science, and commerce together, was fated to find its place behind glass.[124] In describing swag-shops across the city from Hyde Park, in the East End, Mayhew first describes their windows: behind the crystal wall "there is little attempt at display; the design aimed at seems to be rather to crowd the window – as if to show the amplitude of the stores within, 'the wonderful resources of this most extensive and universal establishment' – than to tempt purchasers by exhibiting tastefully what may have been tastefully executed by the artificer."[125] One such window is awash with "ear-drops ... shawl-pins, shirt-studs, necklaces, bead purses, small paintings of the Crystal-palace [sic] in 'burnished "gold" frames,' watch-guards, watch-seals ... silver' tooth-picks, medals, and snuff-boxes."[126] Behind another window, amidst a similar array of goods, Crystal Palace mugs are displayed; and, elsewhere, "Exhibition medals."[127] The Crystal Palace itself, reduced and made accessible to circulation and exchange, has taken its place amid the multifarious commodities for sale behind the display windows of the city – from which, as *The Illustrated London News* remarked, it may be said to have originally emerged. The technologies of display exercised at the Palace, however, and the space of display supported by those technologies have since migrated out of Hyde Park to shape the visual aesthetics of commerce in modern culture.

124  Charles Smith, *Little World*, p. 330.
125  Mayhew, *London Labour*, vol. I, p. 333.
126  Mayhew, *London Labour*, vol. I, p. 334.
127  Mayhew, *London Labour*, vol. I, p. 334.

# 3

# The fragments and small opportunities of *Cranford*

The return of the Crystal Palace to the display window suggests the dexterity with which commodity culture turns objects into marketable goods. The Palace, with its origins in the technology of the window, may seem an object particularly susceptible to exchange; more difficult to imagine is the reduction and exchange of the home, conventionally considered a haven from exchange, the one realm not defined by the cash-nexus. Although the Exhibition did display objects intended for the home within its walls, viewers regularly distinguished the perception of objects on display in Hyde Park from that of domestic goods. Responding in Thackerayan fashion to the Exhibition of 1862, George Eliot invoked Ecclesiastes to contrast public display with domestic privacy: "'this also is vanity,' compared with a quiet life of home love."[1] Even today, when technologies of display have been extended from the shop-window to enclosed shopping malls and mail-order catalogues, display windows reduced and posted through the mail, and when the commodification of domestic material culture has become a banal fact of daily life, the common sight of an uninhabited domestic interior beyond the window of a furniture store remains odd and unsettling. In these still interiors, painterly images of *nature morte*, the absence of human life exaggerates the funereal weightiness of the furniture itself. Benjamin's comment on the "soulless luxuriance of the furnishings" in late-nineteenth-century interiors remains poignant: "The bourgeois interior of the 1860's to the 1890's, with its gigantic sideboards distended with carvings, the sunless corners where palms stand, the balcony embattled behind its balustrade, and the long corridors with their singing gas flames, fittingly houses only the corpse. 'On this sofa, the aunt cannot but

1 Eliot, *Letters*, vol. IV, p. 46.

be murdered.'"[2] The demand for domestic comfort reaches its mannerist extreme in these ponderous, overstuffed Victorian interiors, and is transformed into its dialectical opposite, dread. Private rooms can no longer be imagined without a public audience for their conspicuous and expensive display; and, opening their doors to the public world of society, this imagination also opens those doors to the mortifying expectation of exchange. The association of women with commodities and commodities with death has migrated, in Benjamin's critical vision, into a domestic mausoleum, where allegory is flattened into the linear plot of the detective novel, and where the death of objects has been displaced onto the violent death of women.

Elizabeth Gaskell's *Cranford* furnishes a critique of such inert and brutal private spaces. The frenetic animation of that novel presents the everyday life of the interior as anything but moribund. Gaskell's attention to domestic material culture has often been misread as a sentimental and nostalgic affection for the trivial details of the past. More severely, formalist critics have argued that fascination with domestic minutiae prevents the novel from achieving a proper structural coherence: "The author of 'Mary Barton' and 'Ruth' cannot write badly, even when, as now, she has almost nothing to write about. 'Cranford' is a picture of life in a secluded country town; the sketch is graphic; and as interesting as an almost total want of plot can make it."[3] The remarkable poise and assurance of Gaskell's writing appears to hover over an insubstantial narrative of insignificant events; indeed, according to this early reviewer, Gaskell's prose rests on "almost nothing." The book's "want of [a] plot" implicitly is connected to its subject matter: because nothing happens in this secluded town, a "picture" or "sketch" of the life there can have no narrative propulsion. "The incidents are few, there is hardly any thing that can be called a plot."[4] Through the course of its critical reception, this understanding of *Cranford* became conventional. Martin Dodsworth has summarized and developed the "familiar view"

---

2  Walter Benjamin, *Reflections*, p. 65. He writes elsewhere that "petit-bourgeois rooms are battlefields over which the attack of commodity capital has advanced victoriously; nothing human can flourish there again." *Reflections*, pp. 108–9.
3  *Peterson's Magazine* 24: 4 (October 1853), p. 215.
4  *Graham's Magazine* 43: 4 (October 1853), p. 448.

of the book: *Cranford* is "ever held by a room's arrangement or a bonnet's trimming. This ... view is usually accompanied by a subsidiary judgement: that the book has no structure."[5] Attention to domestic life determines the text's incondite organization: "held" by the material culture of every-day life, the narrative cannot progress.[6]

But *Cranford* does, in fact, develop a conventional teleological structure; Gaskell carefully interweaves stories of detection and financial failure in a propulsive, linear plot. These narratives, however, coexist with a cyclical movement, an alternative narrative form which emerges out of and represents the routines and material culture of everyday life. This second narrative form has eluded the appreciation of critics accustomed to considering linear stories; as a result, the complex play between its recursive movement and the linearity of the novel's more familiar plots has gone unconsidered. Furthermore, the unstable narrative congeries which emerges from the juxtaposition of these linear and recursive forms also inflects other elements of *Cranford*, most centrally, its representation of female subjectivity. In *Vanity Fair* and the Great Exhibition, we have seen women fluctuate between being objects under the gaze of men and being agents desiring goods on their own; these women have been central, troubling elements in discursive structures which present volatile commodities to the fetishistic desires of daunted consumers. In *Cranford*, Gaskell resists understanding material culture as the instigator of unsettling appetites and, simultaneously, works to represent female subjectivity as open and flexible rather than insular, fungible, and threatened.

# I

The particular vexations of representing the everyday life of the historical past derive from the contradictory temporal structures

5  Martin Dodsworth, "Women Without Men at Cranford," *Essays in Criticism* 13: 2 (April 1963), p. 132.
6  Dodsworth argues against this proposition by claiming that the text moves from an adolescent belief that feminine society is good in itself to a mature understanding that women must accommodate the "reality-principle" – which, in turn, Dodsworth briskly conflates with "the masculine predominance" of the day. "Women Without Men," p. 145.

which such a project must entertain. On the one hand, there is the representational mode of history, of "time as project, teleology, linear and prospective unfolding: time as departure, progression, and arrival," as Julia Kristeva has it.[7] Linguistic representation accommodates this temporal mode with relative ease because the structural properties of this medium and mode are congruent; but, at the same time, that congruence is not without its cost. "Linear time," as Kristeva continues, "is that of language considered as the enunciation of sentences (noun + verb; topic-comment; beginning-ending), and ... this time rests on its own stumbling block, which is also the stumbling block of that enunciation – death."[8] The mystery story thus emerges as the exemplar of this form of history when carried out in the domestic realm; the linear plotting of the murder is typically recounted in a linear process of reconstruction. The aunt's corpse rises almost inevitably as the image of history's end.

But the domestic simultaneously frustrates this "obsessional" temporality, encouraging instead the time of "the hysteric" and a syntactical structure that is repetitive rather than linear: "The hysteric (either male or female) who suffers from reminiscences would ... recognize his or her self" in temporalities either "cyclical or monumental."[9] Rather than leading to the discovery of a woman's corpse, reminiscence attempts to recuperate and repeat. The philosophy of history operative here is thus akin to that offered in Benjamin's ninth thesis: reminiscence resists notions of progress which propel narrators onwards, and attempts instead "to stay, and awaken the dead, and make whole what has been smashed."[10]

For Gaskell, this is to say, historical memory does not solely exist under a malediction of death and loss. Her prose is so unruffled that one would not readily call it either obsessional or hysterical; but placing her narrative *Cranford* against Kristeva's distinctions should underscore its participation in a cyclical form

---

7 Julia Kristeva, "Women's Time," in Toril Moi, ed., *The Kristeva Reader* (New York, Columbia University Press, 1986), p. 192.

8 Kristeva, "Women's Time," p. 192. Compare with Foucault's description of the order that regulates wealth and tends towards death in *The Order of Things*, quoted above in Chapter 1.

9 Kristeva, "Women's Time," p. 192.

10 Benjamin, *Illuminations*, p. 257.

like that of the hysteric; and it should also throw into relief the tensions implicit in any attempt to write domestic history. The opening of "The Last Generation in England," the early essay in which she included material later used in *Cranford*, lays out Gaskell's historical project:

I have just taken up by chance an old number of the Edinburgh Review (April 1848), in which it is said that Southey had proposed to himself to write a "history of English domestic life" ... This quarter of an hour's chance reading has created a wish in me to put upon record some of the details of country town life, either observed by myself, or handed down to me by older relations; for even in small towns, scarcely removed from villages, the phases of society are rapidly changing; and much will appear strange, which yet occurred only in the generation immediately preceding ours.[11]

These "details of country town life" retrieved from the past will be told with empirical specificity: "every circumstance and occurrence which I shall relate is strictly and truthfully told without exaggeration."[12] The recuperative impulse acting within this attention to detail is neatly brought out by Hilary Schor, who associates the tales from Knutsford with Geertzian "thick description": "One might also read Gaskell's description of lost village life in terms of what Clifford Geertz calls a 'thick description,' one in which she read behavior as 'trying to rescue the "said" of [social] discourse from its perishing occasions and fix it in perusable terms.'"[13] The "'said' of discourse," the instances of enunciation rather than of the syntactical linearity, are the object of Gaskell's recuperative history.

The circumstances and occurrences thus rescued resist system: Geertz describes the ethnographic difficulties in moving from particular observations in the field to theoretical or general statements, and the tales Gaskell tells have all the heterogeneity, the unsystematic specificity, of the "said." What a reviewer for *Gentleman's Magazine* called the "microscopic contemplation" of *Cranford* admirably meets Geertz's demand that ethnological

11 Elizabeth Gaskell, "Last Generation," in *Cranford* (London, Oxford University Press, 1972), p. 161.
12 Gaskell, "Last Generation," p. 161.
13 Hilary Schor, "Affairs of the Alphabet: Reading, Writing, and Narrating in Cranford," *Novel* 22: 3 (Spring 1989), p. 288.

study be "microscopic,"[14] but the precision of Gaskell's focus presents similar organizational difficulties. This tension between the microscopic detail of observation and the organization of those details into a significant organization is a constitutive problem for realism. Gaskell herself makes this point with characteristic frankness in "The Last Generation": "As for classing the details with which I am acquainted under any heads, that will be impossible from their heterogeneous nature; I must write them down as they arise in my memory."[15] The heterogeneity of everyday life will register itself in the discursive structure of *Cranford*; just as Gaskell's scientific, empirical writing at the start of "The Last Generation" does not admit classification of its objects, so her literary technique in *Cranford* resists customary formal arrangement.

"Everyday life is not cumulative"; its movement is recursive and fragmented, not developmental and narrative.[16] Time, in the daily life of Cranford, takes its shape and pace from small alterations of the domestic environment:

My next visit to Cranford was in the summer. There had been neither births, deaths, nor marriages since I was there last. Everybody lived in the same house, and wore pretty nearly the same well-preserved, old-fashioned clothes. The greatest event was, that [the] Miss Jenkynses had purchased a new carpet for the drawing-room.[17]

Gaskell gestures here towards a monumental time – one of the two temporal modes available to Kristeva's hysteric – but her central discursive impulse is cyclical: the momentous rhythms of life – birth, death, and marriage – quickly give way to the minutiae of the drawing-room. Time there moves in small segments, and is registered in the objects which furnish daily existence. A propulsive narrative cannot easily be built about a world in which, as the *Athenaeum* commented, "there is hardly a solitary incident which is not of every-day occurrence."[18]

14  *Gentleman's Magazine* 40 (Nov. 1853), p. 494; Clifford Geertz, *Interpretation of Culture* (New York, Basic Books, 1973), p. 21.
15  Gaskell, "Last Generation," pp. 161–2.
16  Henri Lefebvre, *Everyday Life in the Modern World*, trans. Sach Rabinowitch (London, Penguin, 1971), p. 61.
17  Elizabeth Gaskell, *Cranford* (London, Oxford University Press, 1972), p. 13. All further references will be noted parenthetically in the text.
18  *Athenaeum*, no. 1339 (25 June 1853), p. 765.

A glance at Gaskell's own household makes plain her experience of this fragmentary, everyday time. In 1845, before she started writing professionally, Gaskell described the quotidian routine of her children and their maid, Hearn, to a friend:

1/2 7 I get up, 8 Flora goes down to her sisters & Daddy, & Hearn to her breakfast. While I in my dressing gown dress Willie. 1/2 p. 8 I go to breakfast with parlor people ... 3 p.m. go up again & I have two hours to kick my heels in (to be elegant & explicit). 5 Marianne & Meta from lessons & Florence from upstairs & Papa when he can comes in drawing room to "Lily a hornpipe", i.e. dance while Mama plays, & make all the noise they can. Daddy reads, writes or does what she [sic] likes in dining room ... 1/2 p. 5 Margaret (nursemaid) brings Florence's supper, which Marianne gives her, being answerable for slops, dirty pinafores & untidy misbehaviours while Meta goes up stairs to get ready and fold up Willie's basket of clothes while he is undressed (this by way of feminine & family duties). Meta is so neat and so knowing, only, handles wet napkins very gingerly. 6 I carry Florence upstairs, nurse Willie; while she is tubbed & put to bed ... From 8 till 10 gape. We are so desperately punctual that now you may know what we are doing every hour.[19]

As even this excerpt suggests, the weight of the passage rests on routines built around domestic material culture – Meta's gingerly handling of wet napkins, Marianne's responsibility for dirty pinafores, the tubbing of Florence – and this is a novelistic trait Gaskell would retain in her books. The division of the day into half-hour sections suggests the busy fragmentation of Gaskell's quotidian routine. And her claim to being "desperately punctual" reminds her correspondent of the cyclical nature of everyday life, its parts repeated from day to day, the same fragments recurring: "you may know what we are doing every hour."

The fragmentation of domestic material culture and the repetition of Gaskell's household activities enter into her description of them: the inconsistent abbreviations, dropped articles, phrases interrupted for qualifications, and repeated sentence structures, all show, at the level of casual technique, the routine and division of the day described. As Gaskell herself writes, "[A]rticles & pronouns very useless part of speech to mothers with large families aren't they?"[20] In *Cranford*, characters such as the Grand Turk – whose English was "so broken that there was no cohesion

19  Elizabeth Gaskell, *The Letters of Mrs. Gaskell*, ed. J. A. V. Chapple and Arthur Pollard (Cambridge, Harvard University Press, 1967), pp. 823–4.
20  Gaskell, *Letters*, p. 823.

between the parts of his sentences" (p. 87) – and Matty – who "began many sentences without ending them, running them one into another, in much the same confused sort of way in which written words run together on blotting-paper" (p. 81) – abound. Gaskell maintains the integrity of her individual sentences and her words do not run together like those on blotting paper. The splintered, cyclical structure of everyday life, however, does remain in the larger units of her prose.

But material culture does not, finally, "hold" either Gaskell or the inhabitants of Cranford. Both pick up that culture and manipulate it to particular ends. The eccentricity of the characters in matters of dress makes ostentatious the active behavior of Cranford women. The most frequent images Gaskell presents of her characters' apparel are extravagant and comical: "Their dress is very independent of fashion; as they observe, 'What does it signify how we dress here at Cranford, where everybody knows us?' And if they go from home, their reason is equally cogent: 'What does it signify how we dress here, where nobody knows us'" (p. 2). The need for economy does not eradicate this eccentricity. Rather than wearing ensembles of unusual taste, women mark their individuality in the marginal, less costly details of ornamentation. They wear "old brooches for a permanent ornament, and new caps to suit the fashion of the day" (p. 74). But "the fashion of the day" is loosely construed, and the narrator continually attempts to restrain Matty's wayward sartorial imagination. Having heard they were in fashion, Matty asks Mary to bring her a sea-green turban when she visits, and is greatly disappointed when Mary presents her with a "neat, middle-aged cap" instead (p. 81).

Simultaneously pressed by economic constraints and genteel aesthetic and social codes, the residents of Cranford must practice an "elegant economy" that encourages attention to "fragments and small opportunities" (p. 15): caps rather than gowns allow self-expression, and "odd jobs" are the jobs in which they characteristically engage (p. 59):

I had often occasion to notice the use that was made of fragments and small opportunities in Cranford; the rose-leaves that were gathered ere they fell, to make into a pot-pourri for some one who had no garden; the little bundles of lavender-flowers sent to strew the drawers of some town-dweller, or to burn in the chamber of some invalid. Things that many would despise, and actions which it seemed scarcely worth while to perform, were all attended to in Cranford. (p. 15)

Cranford inhabitants tactically turn their small opportunities to advantage. A gift, an object offered without consideration of exchange and with particular attention to the needs of the recipient, may be nothing more than a pot pourri, but its significance exceeds its material value.

This tactical manipulation of small opportunities and fragments is, according to Michel de Certeau, the defining practice of everyday life. It is a "way of operating" characteristic of the unempowered – "an art of the weak" – within a larger, more powerful economy.[21] "Unrecognized producers, poets of their own affairs,"[22] the tacticians of the everyday "poach" on what that economy gives to them in order to effect minor subversions. These subversions are not radical reorganizations of the surrounding environment; the everyday does not easily accommodate such extensive, utopian aspirations. Instead these subversions are ways of "making do," as de Certeau says, attempts at adjusting circumstances in order to make them more inhabitable.[23]

The gifts of this economy are of a sort not to be found in the more cynical world of *Vanity Fair*. Given Johnson's dictionary, Becky famously dispatches it out the window of her coach; given his *Complete Works*, *Cranford*'s narrator, Mary Smith, treasures them. Thackeray insists on the impossibility of conferring enduring worth on objects, and the transient values he does allow are generally solipsistic. Gaskell describes the comic independence of her characters' understanding of material culture, but the collective attention to dress and furniture provides ground for communal understanding. Their "housekeeping hearts" (p. 76) share common interests. Thus, the exchange of goods and of social information proceed together and in the same sites:

Miss Pole ... was in the habit of spending the morning in rambling from shop to shop; not to purchase anything (except an occasional reel of cotton, or a piece of tape), but to see the new articles and report upon them, and to collect all the stray pieces of intelligence in the town. (p. 82)

21 Michel de Certeau, *The Practice of Everyday Life*, trans. Steven F. Rendall (Berkeley, University of California Press, 1984), p. 37.
22 de Certeau, *Practice*, p. 34.
23 de Certeau, *Practice*, p. 29.

While Gaskell can vitiate passion by foregrounding the material goods surrounding it – she gently notes, for instance, that Matty's mother, Mrs. Jenkyns, first expressed her love when her husband-to-be sent her a "whole box full of finery" (p. 43) – her satire is less acrid than Thackeray's. The clothes Mrs. Jenkyns desires are soon seen clothing her baby, but this transposition of vanity to maternal pride has none of the psychological complications I noted in discussing Amelia's possessive relationship to her son in *Vanity Fair*. Similarly, when we hear that Miss Betty Barker and her sister, once ladies' maids, have set up a milliner's shop, we are not inclined to suspect that they followed the commercial practices of Fifine, Becky Sharp's ladies' maid, who set up her milliner's shop in Paris with the proceeds she derived from selling the unpaid-for household items she stole from Becky. The Miss Barkers had engaged in the unThackerayan activity of saving.

The community of Cranford, aided by the exchange of goods, continues beyond the grave; death, rather than evacuating goods of meaning, marks the profundity of the ties gifts mark. On the day after Mrs. Jenkyns dies, a parcel comes for her from her son Peter in India. Matty reports:

"It was a large, soft, white India shawl, with just a little narrow border all round; just what my mother would have liked.

"We thought it might rouse my father, for he had sat with her hand in his all night long; so Deborah took it in to him ... and we tried to make a kind of light careless talk about the shawl, opening it out and admiring it. Then, suddenly, he got up, and spoke: – 'She shall be buried in it,' he said; 'Peter shall have that comfort; and she would have liked it.'" (p. 58)

Gaskell is careful to note that the shawl was a considered gift, "just what my mother would have liked." Rather than being for "light, careless talk," it provides comfort for the giver, and reflects the wishes of the woman who was to have received it. The shawl thus serves an entire range of meanings which are seen to extend beyond death: this shawl is buried with Mrs. Jenkyns, not auctioned off at an estate sale.[24]

24 When, early in the novel, the deaths of her brother and sister leave Jessie Brown in solitude, she is threatened with the sale of her furniture and household goods; but her old lover, Major Gordon, providentially returns to prevent this fate. Later, Matty does suffer the sale of her goods, but as we shall see this becomes an occasion for the thoughtful generosity of her friends.

Like the goods used by characters, language is a *donée* in *Cranford*, structuring behavior while, at the same time, being available for manipulation. De Certeau has suggested that everyday life is one realm of "enunciation," a space like that of Geertz's "said," where languages (such as those of fashion) are exploited for individual purposes; this linguistic experience is congruent with the economic experience of goods previously discussed:

> Indissociable from the present *instant*, from particular circumstances and from a *faire* (a peculiar way of doing things, of producing language and modifying the dynamics of a relation), the speech act is at the same time a use *of* language and an operation performed *on* it. We can attempt to apply this model to many non-linguistic operations by taking as our hypothesis that all these uses concern consumption.[25]

The tactical actions of individuals modify the given language, acting on it and with it. Like a good, language is consumed and meaning is produced by idiosyncratic people in particular situations, taking "advantage of 'opportunities.'"[26]

In this way, Gaskell's text consumes its linguistic material, gathering together and transforming tales "handed down to me by older relations" as well as "observed by myself." A number of the interpolated tales in *Cranford* were the communal property of Knutsford inhabitants, and after the stories were published several articles noted the accuracy of Gaskell's recollections.[27] Gaskell, a narrative *bricoleuse*, drew up the fragmentary, received narratives of Knutsford to articulate them in her larger work; as the inhabitants use the received fashions of the day to form their own society, so the writer uses these fragmentary tales. Schor has described the ways in which *Cranford* critiques preexistent literary forms – those of Dickens and Johnson most clearly: "As elsewhere in her fiction, Gaskell begins by placing herself in an inherited literary tradition, but here it is one of parody and subversion, a tradition she can use to rewrite the novel."[28] And we have seen, in the opening of "The Last Generation of England," that Gaskell consciously identifies with a particular convention (of which

---

25  de Certeau, *Practice*, p. 33.      26  de Certeau, *Practice*, p. 37.
27  For examples see Alice Brown, "Later-Day Cranford," *The Atlantic Monthly* 77 (April 1896) and Beatrix L. Tollemache, "Cranford Souvenirs," *Temple Bar* 105 (August 1895).
28  Schor, "Affairs of the Alphabet," p. 289.

Southey's proposed history is the representative), which she then develops and modifies independently. The "history" she produces is, in the end, not shaped by the narrative conventions of historical writing, but by the more recursive form I have described.

The fragments and small opportunities of *Cranford* are reassembled constantly to produce the larger, fragmentary form of the episodic novel. Themes and events are repeated, developing a sense of character and community. It can be argued, from a more strictly sociological and empirical vantage, that the fragmentation of the text derives from its publishing history: Gaskell published the first two chapters in *Household Words* as a complete unit, without intending to write more. The success of that fragment encouraged her to continue writing the episodes irregularly across the next two years. This argument, however, does not explain the fragmentation within particular episodes of the text. I would suggest that the fragmentary form of Gaskell's writing allowed her to continue publishing the tales; she was able to expand the initial fragment because her writing imposed few formal constraints.

Joseph Boone has commented on the repetition of scenes of male intrusion, and of passages exemplifying the theme of "elegant economy" in *Cranford*; and below we will attend to scenes of cross-dressing which contribute to the text's recursive organization. This recursive fragmentation, however, and the tactical impulse it embodies, does not define the formal structure of the entire text. Opposing it are moments of propulsive narration, when the novel is not captivated by the trimming of bonnets, but registers that kind of static, microscopic attention only with frustration. Two subplots constitute this more fully linear structure. One, describing the failure of the Town and Country Bank, is a characteristically Victorian story of economic failure; the other describes Mary's search for Matty's brother Peter, and it is partially shaped by the detective story, that emergent and aggressively teleological form which, as we have seen, is particularly compatible with domestic history. One could argue that the teleological mode of these subplots takes up the fragmentary units of the digressive mode previously discussed and arranges them into a seamless whole: the heterogeneous details of everyday life would then be "classified" in its form. Conversely, one could claim that the teleological form of the detective story and the familiar Victorian tale of commercial failure are themselves received literary models that Gaskell tactically manipulated as her characters manipulate received fragments in their daily routines. But the novel does not admit absolute determinations; it vibrates between forms, not resting in one mode for any length of time.

When Signora Brunoni, describing her trip from India, reports that she was taken in by "that good kind Aga Jenkyns," Mary Smith wonders if this could be Matty's brother, last heard from in India:

An idea had flashed through my head: could the Aga Jenkyns be the lost Peter? True, he was reported by many to be dead. But, equally true, some had said that he had arrived at the dignity of the great Lama of Thibet [sic]. Miss Matty thought he was alive. I would make further inquiry. (pp. 110–11)

The available narratives are not to be trusted, and Mary sets out to construct one based on "facts." This project is conducted with the secrecy and discretion of a private detective: "I was tired of being called indiscreet and incautious; and I determined for once to prove myself a model of prudence and wisdom. I would not even hint my suspicions respecting the Aga" (p. 111). Discretely, then, Mary acts as a sleuth, assembling evidence with a particular end in mind, arranging fragments into a pattern of coherence defined by her goal. In *Mary Barton*, Gaskell had described the satisfactions of detective work:

There is always a pleasure in unravelling a mystery, in catching at the gossamer clue which will guide to certainty. This feeling, I am sure, gives much impetus to the police. Their senses are ever and always on the qui-vive, and they enjoy the collecting and collating evidence, and the life of adventure they experience.[29]

In her earlier novel, however, Gaskell deprecated this pleasure, associating it with "the vulgar and uneducated mind" and with popular "Jack Sheppard" narratives.[30] In *Cranford*, however, the search is not for a murderer but a brother, and the narrative which results is comic and redemptive rather than sensational. No aunt has expired on the sofa.

29  Elizabeth Gaskell, *Mary Barton* (Harmondsworth, Penguin, 1970, p. 273.
30  Gaskell, *Mary Barton*, p. 273.

The "pleasure in unravelling a mystery" quietly draws attention away from the routines of everyday life:

I suppose all these inquiries of mine, and the consequent curiosity excited in the minds of my friends, made us blind and deaf to what was going on around us. It seemed to me as if the sun rose and shone, and as if the rain rained on Cranford just as usual. (pp. 112–13)

But the process of Mary's investigation is thwarted by the digressive, fragmentary habits of Cranford, here exemplified by Miss Pole and Mrs. Forrester:

I asked Miss Pole what was the very last thing they had ever heard about [Peter]; and then she named the absurd report to which I have alluded, about his having been elected the great Lama of Thibet [sic]; and this was a signal for each lady to go off on her separate idea. Mrs. Forrester's start was made on the Veiled Prophet in Lalla Rookh – whether I thought he was meant for the Great Lama, though Peter was not so ugly, indeed rather handsome if he had not been freckled. I was thankful to see her double upon Peter; but, in a moment, the delusive lady was off upon Rowland's Kalydor, and the merits of cosmetics and hair oils in general, and holding forth so fluently that I turned to listen to Miss Pole, who (through the llamas, the beasts of burden) had got to Peruvian bonds, and the Share Market, and her poor opinion of joint-stock banks in general, and of that one in particular in which Miss Matty's money was invested. In vain I put in, "When was it – in what year was it, that you heard that Mr. Peter was the Great Lama?" They only joined issue to dispute whether llamas were carnivorous animals or not. (pp. 121–2)

Mary's task, then, is to "make the account given by the Signora of the Aga Jenkyns tally with that of 'poor Peter,' his appearance and disappearance," which she had "winnowed out of the conversation of Miss Pole and Mrs. Forrester" (p. 118). The process again is one of articulating narratives, but here it is done with a specific end in mind, namely the discovery of Matty's brother.

Gaskell suggests that these two discursive patterns – fragmentary and teleological, cyclical and linear – are gendered. The wayward, repetitive causerie of Miss Pole and Mrs. Forrester is particularly female, the directed detective investigation particularly male. And our glance at Gaskell's own daily routine as a housewife indirectly supports the idea that some types of women's experience encourage episodic narration. Similarly, Dorothy Smith writes:

A housewife, holding in place the simultaneous and divergent schedules and activities of a family, depends upon a diffuse and open organization of consciousness available to the various strands [of household activity], which are coordinated only in her head and by her work ... Over a life-time and in the daily routines, women's lives tend to show a loose, episodic structure that reflects the ways in which their lives are orga-nized and determined external to them.[31]

And Smith goes on to suggest, briefly, that such episodic experi-ence encourages episodic narratives. Conversely, when acting as detective, Mary plans not to solve the mystery of the lost Peter herself; that task, evidently, is a man's: "I would collect evidence and carry it home to lay before my father, as the family friend of the two Miss Jenkyns" (p. 111). He then will serve as the final agent in this case, implicitly governing its development; his role, as masculine advisor to the "two Miss Jenkyns" puts him in a place to approve the discovery of Peter and conclude this particu-lar narrative.

But, as is suggested by Mary's role in this subplot (as both its central actress and its narrator), Gaskell takes this easy gendering of discursive patterns and inverts it:

In my search after facts, I was often reminded of a description my father had once given of a Ladies' Committee that he had had to preside over. He said he could not help thinking of a passage in Dickens, which spoke of a chorus in which every man took the tune he knew best, and sang it to his own satisfaction. So, at this charitable committee, every lady took the subject uppermost in her mind, and talked about it to her own great contentment, but not much to the advancement of the subject they had met to discuss. But even that committee could have been nothing to the Cranford ladies when I attempted to gain some clear and definite infor-mation as to poor Peter's height, appearance, and when and where he was seen and heard of last. (p. 111)

Dickens has been associated in the text with a vigorous, intrusive masculinity since Captain Brown championed him over Deborah Jenkyns' favorite, Johnson. The exclusive, male society to which Mr. Smith refers – the discordant tenors are singing in Bob Sawyer's room in *The Pickwick Papers* during the masculine ritual of drinking brandy after dinner – underscores the gendered insu-larity of Dickens' passage. Replacing Pickwick as the presiding

31 Dorothy Smith, *Everyday Life as Problematic: A Feminist Sociology* (Boston, Northeastern University Press, 1987), p. 66.

officer, Mr. Smith assumes a dubious role when called upon to preside over the similarly discordant Ladies' Committee; he is, throughout the text, seen as the counselor to women, his daughter and the Misses Jenkyns in particular. As the men of Bob Sawyer's drinking party become the women of Mr. Smith's committee and then become Miss Pole and Mrs. Forrester, so Mr. Smith's role as managing figure is adopted by his daughter. What was, in Dickens, an exclusively male society becomes one exclusively female. If *Pickwick* describes the cacophony of men in their cups, *Cranford* rewrites this into a scene of particularly female digressiveness.

This rewriting is seen not as a simple process of willful manipulation but as the universal fate of fathers. Gaskell's scenes of reading suggest that all patriarchs – and not only "The Inimitable" – are displaced by their imitative readers. With Mrs. Forrester, Gaskell understands that every child of Adam suffers from linguistic illegitimacy: "'she had always understood that Fitz meant something aristocratic; there was Fitz-Roy – she thought that some of the King's children had been called Fitz-Roy ... Fitz-Adam! – it was a pretty name; and she thought it very probably meant "Child of Adam"'" (p. 64). Misbegotten aristocratic children are replaced by Mrs. Forrester's misbegotten reading, the swerve of patriarchal lines replicated by the swerve of interpretation – a move which ironically erases the illegitimacy of the bloodlines while demonstrating that illegitimacy to be an inescapable condition of all claiming descent from the first father.

In describing Mary's "search after facts," Gaskell has taken up a received story – a few sentences from *Pickwick* – and has tactically incorporated it into her own tale, rewriting it as she does so. The mode I have described as teleological, pushing towards its resolution and end, here converges with its digressive and tactical counterpart. Comically digressive women are common features in Victorian novels – nowhere more common than in Dickens – and in rewriting the men of Bob Sawyer's dinner into women, Gaskell is, to a degree, substituting the conventional comedy of incoherent women for that of drunken men. But the act of substitution itself is significant, a transposition of worlds suggesting that gender-characteristics are potentially exchangeable. The masculine role Mary adopts further emphasizes this kind of substitution: to the extent that anyone acts as presiding figure in this scene, governing the frenetic conversation of Miss Pole and Mrs. Forrester, it is she. And, although she has said she will present the evidence she discovers to her father, she does not do so. Mary sends her letter to Aga Jenkyns and makes the various narratives "tally" on her own. When Peter returns, he asks for Mary Smith (p. 150).

In the midst of Miss Pole's drifting, seemingly pointless conversation, a point significant for the financial subplot is made: Miss Pole has a "poor opinion of joint-stock banks in general, and of that one in particular in which Miss Matty's money was invested." The narrative mode has its eye on this clue, which the digressive mode has tossed off as comedy; the failure of the Town and Country Bank is the crisis towards which the financial plot of the novel has been moving. And, when the news of the bank's failure is finally received, the two discursive patterns intersect again. Here, however, Mary herself adopts the dilatory manner which, when exhibited by Miss Pole and Mrs. Forrester, made her impatient: "The very Tuesday morning on which Mr. Johnson was going to show the fashions, the post-woman brought two letters to the house. I say the post-woman, but I should say the postman's wife. He was a lame shoemaker ... "(p. 118). We discover, a long paragraph later, that the postman's wife has brought news intimating the approaching collapse of Matty's bank. Instead of immediately revealing this information – which would direct the narrative towards its crisis – Mary veers into a description of the postman and his relationship to various Cranford characters. When the postman brings the mail, which Mary tells us he does only on special occasions, it comes late because he is habitually delayed by conversation with the people on his route. Yet we, as readers, must impatiently wait out exactly this delay ourselves. Rather than bringing us the information contained in the letters – rather than continuing on the route of her plot – Mary is delayed by the individuals within it. Her attention pivots from the letters to the postman who conveys them. And this pivot again reverses the gender-categories which shape the circulation of writing: unlike her husband, the postman's wife brings the mail directly.

"I have wandered a long way from the two letters" (p. 119). Mary underscores her participation in the dilatory habits of Cranford conversation before turning back to the letters; and, as if to counterpoise the digressive style she has temporarily adopted with its opposite, she remarks, "My father's was just a man's letter; I mean it was very dull, and gave no information beyond that he was well, that they had had a good deal of rain, that trade was very stagnant, and there were many disagreeable rumors afloat" (p. 119). We do not read Mr. Smith's letter, but Mary's flat description suggests its bare, catalogue form, sharply opposed to her own digressive patter. The clear contrast of men's speech and women's seems established. Except that Mary's description of her father's note is disingenuous: the "dull man's letter" proves, in fact, to be of great interest to her as it suggests the imminent failure of the bank, about which, her father says, "there were very unpleasant reports" (p. 119).

Narratives by women in *Cranford* tactically arrange masculine knowledge and rationality – the dull man's letter – for their own purposes, enunciating the said, refashioning language while using it. We learn the news, but also about the way it is conveyed. At the same time, by giving us the information from Drumble, Mary furthers the propulsive narrative movement of her detective story, which, as she repeatedly notes, is based on "facts" like those contained in her father's letter. The insistent swerves and reversals of Gaskell's narratives produce a collection of speech habits which remains resolutely, wittily indeterminate.

## II

With the next morning's post, which brings the official news that the Town and Country has stopped payment, the financial plot of *Cranford* comes to a head, its denouement brought by the postman's wife. Though shaken, Matty immediately looks after her responsibilities, beginning by breaking the news to her servant, Martha. "While she went down to speak to Martha," Mary writes, "I stole out with my letter to the Aga Jenkyns, and went to the Signora's lodging to obtain the exact address" (p. 128). Gaskell carefully interlaces the two subplots of the novel with two letters, the crisis of one being announced while its resolution is furthered in the other:

At last I got the address, spelt by sound; and very queer it looked! I dropped it in the post on my way home; and then for a minute I stood looking at the wooden pane, with a gaping slit, which divided me from the letter, but a moment ago in my hand. It was gone from me like life –

never to be recalled. It would get tossed about on the sea, and stained with sea-waves perhaps; and be carried among palm-trees, and scented with all tropical fragrance; – the little piece of paper, but an hour ago so familiar and commonplace, had set out on its race to the strange wild countries beyond the Ganges. (p. 128)

Gaskell marks the distance between life in a rural village and the distant reaches of the empire, while at the same time suggesting that these locales are interconnected. Schor has imaginatively placed *Cranford* in the midst of the developments in railway travel which we charted in the last chapter: the novel describes the dangerous power of the new trains in its first chapter; Mary most likely moves back and forth from Cranford to Drumble on the railway; and the conclusion of the novel is effected with the help of colonial rails in India (pp. 85; 95–7). As we have seen, by the time of the Exhibition (which took place during the summer prior to the appearance of *Cranford*'s first episode), the distance from familiar letter-boxes to the "strange wild countries beyond the Ganges" would seem miraculously reduced, accessible by means of the space of exchange created through spectacles such as the Crystal Palace. For a reader in 1853, ensconced in the world that had been emerging in Drumble, the countries beyond the Ganges would have been more familiar than they are for Mary. (More strange to them than these countries, perhaps, is Mary's wonder at colonial communication. Rather than imagining the distant reaches of the globe, Gaskell's readers are called upon to imagine a time when recipients paid for the privilege to read a letter, and when there were no postage stamps or envelopes like those mechanically made at the Great Exhibition. "Much will appear strange," Gaskell suggests, "which yet occurred only in the generation immediately preceding ours"; the past, and not merely letters sent across the world, seems "gone like life.") For Mary, the ability to communicate across a great distance briefly suggests the limitations of life in Cranford, the town's prosaic familiarity. "But," she says, "I could not afford to lose much time on this speculation" (p. 128). The economy of her narrative limits the imaginative digressions she can "afford"; the vivid description of the letter's future extends her detective plot, but Mary (and the reader) must return to Matty's financial affairs.

What plots exist in *Cranford* end in character – and, in particular, in the return of Matty's brother, Peter. With the help of her friends in Cranford and Mr. Smith in Drumble, Matty constructs a new life for herself, but the comic resolution of the novel requires Peter's reappearance, awakened, as it were, from the dead. His arrival and the conclusion of the detective plot solves the novel's financial story as well: the last mention in the novel of "economy" has Peter and Matty distributing gifts through the town. Early reviews of the novel implicitly opposed the development of character and plot, and saw that its point was in the establishment of individuals in a community rather than the delineation of events. The "great charm" of *Cranford*, *Graham's Magazine* told its readers, "is its felicitous representation of character. The incidents are few."[32] Similarly, *The Examiner* wrote, "if we told you it contained a story, that would be hardly true – yet read only a dozen pages, and you are among real people."[33]

Peter provides the conclusion to the novel not only because he brings to a close these subplots, but also because his character is the culmination of particularly important, recurrent themes in the novel's recursive, fragmentary structure. Boone notes that Peter provides the final instance of male intrusion in the novel and, additionally, that he is *Cranford*'s last practitioner of "elegant economy." Peter, a "foe of male privilege and a willing accomplice of female harmony,"[34] also provides the culminating instances of gender-substitution in the novel, and it is this practice that allows him to settle so easily into the community at the novel's end.

The opening of *Cranford* derives its ironic humor from the play between socially accepted gender roles: "In the first place, Cranford is in possession of the Amazons; all the holders of houses, above a certain rent, are women." The description of the Cranford women as Amazons gives to the inhabitants of this female society the martial characteristics of the sex it banishes. Later, during "the panic," when all Cranford believes itself threatened by a band of robbers, one of the imaginary thieves is "masculine-looking – a perfect virago; most probably a man dressed in woman's clothes: afterwards we heard of a beard on

32 *Graham's Magazine* 43: 4 (October 1853), p. 448.
33 Reprinted in *Littell's Living Age* 2 (10 September 1853), p. 667.
34 Joseph Allen Boone, *Tradition Counter Tradition: Love and the Form of Fiction* (University of Chicago Press, 1987), pp. 301–2.

her chin, and a manly voice and stride" (p. 95). The substitution of the postman's wife for the postman, of Miss Pole and Mrs. Forrester for Dickens' inebriated diners, and of Mary for her father, are successive variations on a pattern which can be said to begin with Gaskell's conscious adoption in "The Last Generation" of Southey's position as domestic historian. But Peter's character is, in *Cranford*, the most significant instance of this structuring pattern.

We have been told that Peter's "career lay before him rather pleasantly mapped out by kind friends," a familiar linear narrative, one traditionally reserved for boys and men, which was to include honors at public school and at Cambridge, and then a clerical living presented as a gift from his godfather (p. 49). Peter, however, does not accept his role in this paternal narrative. As Patricia Wolfe notes,[35] Peter is associated with and formed by his mother rather than his father: "He was the darling of his mother, who seemed to dote on all her children, though she was, perhaps, a little afraid of Deborah's superior acquirements. Deborah was the favorite of her father, and when Peter disappointed him, she became his pride" (*Cranford*, p. 50). The "disappointment" leading to Deborah's becoming her father's pride was a result of Peter's "hoaxing," his satirical revelations of the (especially masculine) pretensions of those around him: "'He ... took in my father once, by dressing himself up as a lady that was passing through the town and wished to see the Rector of Cranford, "who had published that admirable Assize Sermon"'" (pp. 50–1). Mr. Jenkyns' pride in his sermons, elsewhere made the subject of gentle humor, here is the subject of satire: "I could hardly keep from laughing at the little curtsies Peter kept making, quite slyly, whenever my father spoke of the lady's excellent taste and sound discrimination" (51). In narrating this tale, Matty herself has difficulty keeping Peter's gender straight: "her – him, I mean – no, her, for Peter was a lady then" (p. 51).

For this ruse Peter receives an appropriate punishment: he is told by his father to copy out the sermons for the lady, and is unable to escape the task without revealing his deception. But when Peter next dresses as a woman, the punishment is more

---

35 Patricia Wolfe, "Structure and Movement in *Cranford*," *Nineteenth-Century Fiction* 33: 2 (September 1968), p. 175.

severe. Walking home from visiting his parishioners, Mr. Jenkyns discovers a crowd in his yard admiring, he imagines, a new rhododendron he has planted: "He walked slower, that they might have more time to admire. And he wondered if he could make out a sermon from the occasion, and thought, perhaps, there was some relation between the rhododendrons and the lilies of the field" (p. 52). Finally among them, he discovers Peter dressed in Deborah's clothes and carrying a pillow as if it were her baby. Peter's joke harshly deflates the Rector's idea that the crowd was admiring his "beautiful vegetable production" (p. 52) and his assumption that daily events can readily be transformed into occasions for the "grand, latinized, Johnsonian style" of his sermons. Given Peter's dress, the lilies of the field must no longer have appeared an appropriate text: "even Solomon in all his glory was not arrayed like one of these."[36]

For Peter to suggest that Deborah is a mother with a child reminds her of the femininity which she, adopting her father's characteristics, has sought to hide. His transvestitism parodies and inverts her adoption of a masculine role. But it does not prevent that exchange: Deborah, not Peter, from this point acts as their father's amanuensis. Like Mary, Peter oscillates between accepted gender-roles; he uses the habits of Cranford – the idiosyncratic manipulation of fashion, of caps and shawls – to create a graphic parody of those habits.

After being severely punished for his transvestitism, Peter leaves Cranford, withdraws from the masculine narrative he was to inhabit, and flees to the ocean and India. Gaskell portrays India conventionally, as a permissive world where transgressions are not answered by sermons and punishment; more significantly, however, she also portrays the colony as an essentially feminine space. The one extensive representation we have of India is given by Mrs. Brown, who describes the subcontinent as a realm shaped by determined maternal generosity in the face of extreme natural hardship. After six of her children die, Mrs. Brown insists to her husband that she take the last child back to England. While she was on this solitary trek, Mrs. Brown says, "the natives were very kind. We could not understand one another; but they saw my baby on my breast, and they came out

36  Matthew, 6, 29.

to me and brought me rice and milk" (p. 109). Moreover, Mrs. Brown is sustained as she goes by a picture of the Madonna, painted by "'a Catholic foreigner,'" and given to her by the wife of an officer for whom she worked as a washerwoman (p. 109). In the incidental details of this story, then, Gaskell maintains with great deliberation that maternity is associated with divine solicitude and that it transcends the boundaries of language, culture, religious creed, nationality, class, and, finally, gender, as well. At Chunderabaddad "that good kind Aga Jenkyns" takes Mrs. Brown and her daughter into his home. Peter is inserted into a narrative of maternal heroism, extending his association with his own mother and providing a space where that association can serve nurturing ends.

After Mrs. Brown's story, Gaskell gives us no picture of India other than the fabulous tales Peter provides at the novel's conclusion; in these, the colony appears primarily as an occasion for fantastic narration. Pat Brantlinger, who claims that Peter's tales are "a paradigm of the imperial adventure tale in Victorian society,"[37] argues that Gaskell sees these Indian narratives as the antithesis of the placid domestic realism of Cranford. The adventures Peter relates are obviously opposed to the daily life of the town, where no mountains are scaled and no cherubim shot; we have seen Mary imagine "the strange wild countries beyond the Ganges" (p. 128) and contrast those countries with her own provincial world. But more significant than this difference is the suggestion that the narrative behaviors associated with the two realms are on a spectrum; Peter's exaggeration is continuous with the patterns of sympathetic lying which make up the fabric of Cranford social relations. Although Peter appears to enter the text from afar and to be "'so very Oriental'" (p. 154), his stories are merely ostentatious demonstrations of the more gentle deceit practiced throughout *Cranford*. The physical transvestitism he enjoyed as a boy has been textualized, now approximating the verbal deceptions practiced by Cranford's women; as Peter's cross-dressing was the culminating instance of that theme in *Cranford*, so his fantastic stories provide the concluding examples of the novel's deceptions.

37 Patrick Brantlinger, *The Rule of Darkness: British Culture and Imperialism, 1830–1914* (Ithaca, Cornell University Press, 1988), p. 12.

This deceit encourages a communal spirit: "We had tacitly agreed to ignore that any with whom we associated on terms of visiting equality could ever be prevented by poverty from doing anything that they wished" (p. 4). "Tacitly agreed to ignore": silence is encased within silence, indirection within indirection. But the collective agreement to avoid certain conversations, particularly those concerning "mutual want[s]" (p. 78), forms Cranford's community: *We* tacitly agreed.[38] Peter's lies, similarly, encourage a communal spirit. But they are not required by "want." As a boy, Peter thought his jokes would provide the Cranford women "something to talk about," and at the novel's close they do exactly this, not upsetting the society, but providing it collective entertainment. His "wonderful tales" of distant life and adventure hold Cranford rapt and, more importantly, amuse and reconcile the feuding Miss Jamieson and Mrs. Hoggins, establishing the comic social unity of the novel's conclusion. In spinning his tales, Peter seems aware that such "hoaxing" might offend. He says to Mary: "'Don't be shocked, prim little Mary, at all my wonderful stories; I consider Mrs. Jamieson fair game, and besides, I am bent on propitiating her, and the first step towards it is keeping her well awake ... I shall go at it again by-and-by'" (pp. 159–60). Mary and the reader are here invited to sacrifice a strict and moralistic notion of truth to the interests of the community.

That Gaskell chooses Peter as her final narrator and as the figure who effects the conclusion of her plot establishes the significance of masculinity for the text: it is a man, after all, a lost brother like Gaskell's own, who is raised from the dead, not an aunt. But the novel as a whole, in its final paragraphs, ends by reflecting on Matty and the ways that she, without the bold actions of men, influences her community. More significantly, the novel's conception of identity is worked out most fully not through the few male characters like Peter, but through the development of its women. The sacrifice of narrow notions of truth described above is central to the novel's conception of identity and is most striking in Gaskell's representation of her main character, Matty.

38  On *Cranford* and deceit, see Nina Auerbach, *Communities of Women: An Idea in Fiction* (Cambridge, Harvard University Press, 1978).

When the Town and Country fails, economy takes over from elegance, "commerce and trade" enter Matty's vocabulary and daily life, an auctioneer must be hired, and Matty must be supported through the kindness of others. Matty is too proud to accept charity, and so, "'in consideration of the feelings of delicate independence existing in the mind of every refined female'" (p. 137), the contributions of her friends are delivered clandestinely to Mary's father in his role as Matty's financial advisor. Matty herself is told nothing precise about the state of her finances. But Miss Matty's friends do not hide her financial state from her only to preserve her feeling of independence. They also hide her resources because they have different ideas about how those resources should be maintained. When Matty discovers she is ruined, she feels responsible, as a stock-holder in the bank, for people who were not members but who held the bank's now worthless notes. She gives the five pounds she was going to use to buy a silk gown to a farmer who, at the same moment, discovered his notes were of no value. The principle of limited liability – legislated two years after *Cranford* appeared – does not govern Matty's ethical code. Gaskell wants to see Matty's gesture as heroic, the assertion of a communal ethos in the face of a bewildering and impersonal process. But, at the same time, she recognizes that it is an impractical way to live in a world increasingly dominated by such processes; if Matty were to continue paying those whom her bank has ruined, she herself would become destitute. "It is necessary," Derrida writes, "to limit the excess of the gift and of generosity, to limit them by economy, profitability, work, exchange. And first of all by reason or by the principle of reason."[39] It is the ethical tension produced by this undecidable relation between gift and economic rationality that Gaskell addresses in this narrative line. By limiting Matty's knowledge of the extent of her finances, Gaskell allows her to maintain her strict moral code (which requires her to pay back the bank's debts as far as she is able), and her feeling of independence, while remaining financially comfortable. This "occasioned a few evasions of truth and white lies (all of which I think very wrong indeed – in theory – and would rather not put them

39 Jacques Derrida, *Given Time I: Counterfit Money*, trans. Peggy Kamuf (University of Chicago Press, 1992), pp. 62–3.

in practice)" (p. 145). Lies mark the limitation of one person's autonomy, but, at the same time, mark the community's support of its members.

More incidentally, I should note that, in order to maintain Matty, her maid Martha takes over the rent of Matty's house and accepts Matty as a lodger. From the novel's beginning houses have been sites of the daily routines which have defined the lives of the characters, and "possession" of a house has been a mark of social status. (For all its precision about social status, however, *Cranford* never mentions the landowners to whom rent is due.) Again, comparison with Thackeray is telling. In *Pendennis*, when Morgan becomes the landlord of the house in which his master, Major Pendennis, lives, Thackeray registers only menace: it is a sign of domestic insurrection and individual rapacity. When Martha becomes Matty's landlady it is an act of generosity and submission, a final, paradoxical, affirmation of loyalty.

The conflict between Matty's moral code and that imposed by the commercial world becomes more explicitly an economic concern when Matty opens a tea shop to support herself. Here the issues of narrative structure and, especially, of characterization most clearly meet the novel's representation of material culture. Like the Crystal Palace, albeit on a somewhat smaller scale, this tea shop displays goods from across the world, from realms as far away as those to which Mary sent her letter. Unlike the Exhibition, however, Matty's tea shop tactically subverts the space of exchange; it is resolutely domestic, located in the front parlor of Matty's house, and it bases its economy on gifts rather than on financial gain. Matty makes sure selling tea will not harm the business of Mr. Johnson, the town's established tea-vendor; she entreats young customers not to buy green tea, which she believes injurious; and she gives to children an extra comfit for each ounce they buy, making "every sale into a loss" (p. 148). But this good faith and generosity, rather than losing Matty money, encourages the same in others: when her shop opens, "the whole country round seemed to be all out of tea at once" (p. 146); Mr. Johnson thereafter sends her customers; and other people regularly bring her gifts. Gaskell both says that financial gain is insignificant, and recognizes that it is, in fact, of great importance. So she has Matty, not out of cunning but out of "'simplicity,'" ignore gain and make a profit (p. 145). This is explicitly contrasted with the economy operative elsewhere: Perhaps, Mary says,

"it would not have done in Drumble, but in Cranford it answered very well...My father says 'such simplicity might be very well in Cranford, but would never do in the world.' And I fancy the world must be very bad, for with all my father's suspicion of every one with whom he has dealings, and in spite of all his many precautions, he lost upwards of a thousand pounds by roguery only last year." (pp. 144–5)

And, with precise irony, Gaskell has Mr. Smith wonder "'how tradespeople were to get on if there was to be a continual consulting of each others' interest, which would put a stop to all competition directly'" (p. 144).

Matty's "weakness," in an economy where the interests of others are generously consulted, is, in fact, a strength: "There was nothing she could teach to the rising generation of Cranford; unless they had been quick learners and ready imitators of her patience, her humility, her sweetness, her quiet contentment with all that she could not do" (p. 132). The defensiveness of the sentence – a little bristly in its sarcasm – reveals Gaskell's understanding that she is resisting an emergent understanding of virtue. Matty's weakness, whether in managing her finances or in running her tea shop, brings out the benevolence of this community. Even Mr. Smith, representative of the masculine and mercantile world, is moved: "'See, Mary, how a good innocent life makes friends all around. Confound it! I could make a good lesson out of it if I were a parson; but, as it is, I can't get a tail to my sentences – only I'm sure you feel what I want to say'" (p. 141). With a gesture towards Matty's father, the parson, Gaskell dresses Mr. Smith as a Cranford woman, unable to say what he means, relying on the unspoken communication of feeling to form a communal bond. By the novel's end, Matty becomes a moral agent for everyone, unconsciously, inarticulately spreading goodness through her society: "it was really very pleasant to see how her unselfishness, and simple sense of justice, called out the same good qualities in others" (p. 145). And the novel closes, "we all love Miss Matty, and I somehow think we are all of us better when she is near us" (p. 160).

The characters and, most strikingly, the women we saw in *Vanity Fair* were self-enclosed and isolated, fungible units of exchange analogous to the commodities they stole, pawned, and lost. Using terms derived from Elizabeth Abel, Boone notes that *Cranford* characters are "'fluid, open, and nonhierarchical'";[40] they exist in an economy of character exemplified by the relations of Matty's tea shop rather than Mr. Smith's business in Drumble. They are everyday characters. As de Certeau writes, "no delimitation of an exteriority ... provides [the tactics of everyday life] with the condition necessary for autonomy. The space of a tactic is the space of the other."[41] The moral code in such an economy of everyday characters places communal relations above the individual, and the unity of the social body over the "mercantile verities" of a reified notion of truth and falsehood.[42] The "deceptions" in the novel are not seen negatively by the text; instead they are instances of communal behavior and affirmations that no individual either can or need stand autonomously.

But the dangers of condescending to these characters – seeing them as "so inane and so frivolous" – remain great.[43] The attention to the everyday in *Cranford*, in which objects are fragmented and opportunities small, encourages a perception of character that is similarly limited. Matty and the reader of *Cranford* both make do with fragments and turn those fragments to advantage – but in order to praise this ingenuity, to affirm the small opportunities of life in Cranford, those opportunities must first be acknowledged small. This narrative and moral pattern, like the novel's understanding of character, is necessarily divided by its situation in an economy dominated by institutions like the Town and Country Bank. The residual social world, "rescued" in a fragmentary form from the rapidly shifting phases of society, exists as a critique of the mores of the world which succeeded it. At the same time, however, the social and subjective characteristics which allow the generosity Gaskell endorses appear to be limitations and, indeed, have the consequences of limitations: Matty's tea shop would not succeed in Drumble. I do not think this opposition can be reconciled; but unresolved issues and open relationships are characteristic of the everyday. As Smith writes, "the everyday world [i]s that in which questions originate,"[44] and it is in the world of everyday material culture that *Cranford* finds its home.

40  Boone, *Tradition*, p. 282.        41  de Certeau, *Practice*, p. 37.
42  Boone, *Tradition*, p. 300.      43  *The Athenaeum* 1339 (25 June 1853), p. 765.
44  Dorothy Smith, *Everyday Life*, p. 91.

# 4

# Rearranging the furniture of *Our Mutual Friend*

"Keep things in their places," Charles Dickens wrote to his wife, Catherine; "I can't bear to picture them otherwise."[1] The quotidian world of the Dickens household appears to have progressed on principles opposed to those characterizing Cranford. Instead of communal practices and everyday characters, the life of the Dickens household seems to have been dominated largely by Charles' solitary will. "If it is the property of a domestic nature to be personally interested in every detail," writes John Forster,

> the smallest as the greatest, of the four walls within which one lives, then no man had it so essentially as Dickens, no man was so inclined naturally to derive his happiness from home concerns. Even the kind of interest in a house which is commonly confined to women, he was full of. Not to speak of changes of importance, there was not an additional hook put up wherever he inhabited, without his knowledge, or otherwise than as part of some small ingenuity of his own. Nothing was too minute for his personal superintendence.[2]

Forster's phrase, "even the kind of interest in a house which is commonly confined to women, he was full of," seen along with Dickens' injunction to his wife, supports the idea that the routines of the Dickens household proceeded according to Charles' dictates rather than Catherine's. This was not transgressive gender-bending – none of Peter Jenkyns' hoaxing here; Dickens mans this home like a fort. For Catherine to have managed their home, she would have had to manage Charles as well, to collaborate with his "domestic nature," and to check with him before placing new hooks on the wall. Arranging objects, especially around Dickens, cannot be separated from arranging people; and

1 Charles Dickens, *The Letters of Charles Dickens*, 7 vols., ed. Madelaine House, Graham Storey, et al. (Oxford, Clarendon, 1965–), vol. IV, p. 216.
2 John Forster, *The Life of Charles Dickens*, 3 vols. (London, Chapman and Hall, 1874), vol. III, pp. 473–4.

when Dickens writes Catherine to tell her not to move the things among which she is living, so that he, from a distance, can imagine them in their familiar places, he is imagining a familiar place for her as well. In this context, Mamie Dickens' description of her father's daily domestic inspections is not surprising. Each morning, she writes, Dickens toured the house before beginning his work, a policeman on his beat, checking on the arrangement of each of the children's rooms: "If a chair was out of its place, or a blind not quite straight, or a crumb left on the floor, woe betide the offender."[3]

Mamie's story suggests that the images Dickens creates of "good" housekeepers – Esther Summerson, Amy Dorrit, Bella Wilfer, each of them soundlessly dusting and tidying, their keys jingling in their baskets – do not describe his own "domestic nature." He seems to be closer to another type, which includes Mrs. Joe Gargery, and Mrs. MacStinger, who have what Freud called "housewife's psychosis." Speaking briefly about (his) Dora's mother, Freud writes that she "was occupied all day long in cleaning the house with its furniture and utensils and in keeping them clean – to such an extent as to make it almost impossible to use or enjoy them."[4]

When, after attending to the arrangement of his children's rooms, Dickens sat down to write, it was in the central room of a swiss chalet, a small building on his property given to him by an admirer. Dickens had carefully arranged the chalet's interior: five mirrors reflected the surrounding trees, corn fields, and, in the distance, the "sail-dotted" Medway; nearer, on his desk, were his "indispensable little accompaniments of work," a collection of objects (including the stuffed, duelling frogs which turn up in Venus' workshop) which served as approving familiars for his writing. The novels he wrote there, and *Our Mutual Friend* in particular, describe an urban landscape composed of the detritus sloughed off in the heat of capitalist transformation.[5] Entering

3 Mamie Dickens, *My Father as I Recall Him* (New York, E. P. Dutton & Co., 1898), pp. 12–13.

4 Sigmund Freud, "Fragment of an Analysis of a Case of Hysteria," in *Dora: The Analysis of a Case of Hysteria* (New York, Macmillan, 1963), pp. 34–5.

5 Dickens had begun the novel at a friend's house but the furniture there appears to have gotten in the way: this "odious little house," he wrote, "seems to have stifled and darkened my invention." Forster, *Life*, vol. III, p. 339.

imaginatively into the destructive energy of this volatile material world, Dickens also constructs imaginary enclaves from it. Two of these are especially significant: the household, like that he arranged at Gadshill, where his will could master the objects and people around him and "picture" them as he desired; and the space of writing itself, like that he arranged in the chalet, where his will could mold characters and language into determinate shapes. The precarious interplay between these enclaves and the desiccating environment of dust-heaps shapes Dickens' construction of material culture and subjectivity in *Our Mutual Friend* and his other writing from the mid-1860s.

# I

In the memoranda book he kept in the 1850s and 60s, Dickens writes:

English landscape. The beautiful prospect, trim fields, clipped hedges, everything so neat and orderly – gardens, houses, roads. Where are the people who do all this? There must be a great many of them, to do it. Where are they all? And are *they*, too, so well kept and so fair to see?[6]

In the art of formal landscape, Dickens recognizes both the physical labor required to create and maintain an orderly perspective, and the deliberate attempt to make the prospect appear free from the traces of that labor. In spite of the rhetorical finale (written with a self-conscious cadence, an audience before Dickens' eye), the question posed here retains its force: people are treated with less concern than the objects they produce, and remain hidden behind the material culture they build and maintain. In Chapter 2, we saw *Punch* raise a similar question regarding the Exhibition: "Shall we ostentatiously show off all manner of articles of comfort and luxury, and be ashamed to disclose the condition of those whom we have to thank for them?"[7]

The disposition to connect objects with their production is what Raymond Williams calls a "way of seeing" which perceives relations that the transformation of use-value into exchange-value hides. Dickens' landscape, and the points he makes about

6 Charles Dickens, *Charles Dickens' Book of Memoranda*, transcribed by Fred Kaplan (New York, New York Public Library, 1981), p. 10.
7 *Punch* 20 (1851), p. 42.

it, are duplicated by Williams' description of the "pleasant prospects" of the century prior to Dickens':

It can be said of these eighteenth-century arranged landscapes not only, as is just, that this was the high point of agrarian bourgeois art, but that they succeeded in creating in the land below their windows and terrace what Jonson at Penshurst had ideally imagined: a rural landscape emptied of rural labour and labourers ... [it is] an effective and still imposing mystification.[8]

Apparently unaware of Dickens' memorandum, Williams later claims for him the power to see beyond this kind mystification: "this is [one] aspect of Dickens' originality. He is able to dramatise those social institutions and consequences which are not accessible to ordinary physical observation."[9]

This process of occlusion did not only define the representation of labor in the pastoral scene described in the memorandum book; the growing geographical and social segregation of producer and consumer encouraged a similar mystification in the material life of Victorian London. Within middle-class households, for instance, an analogous segregation of servants' quarters from those of their masters was achieved; and the patterns of servants' daily routines were arranged so they skirted those of the masters.[10] Wordsworth's description of London as the "nation's emporium" (a phrase Dickens used in his letters) presents the city as a display window stocked with attractive articles of consumption. In emporia, as we have seen, the "technocracy of sensuality" governs the display of objects: objects are at their most captivating, exhibited in aesthetically appealing guises, the

8  Raymond Williams, *Country and City* (New York, Oxford University Press, 1973), pp. 124–5.
9  Williams, *Country and City*, p. 156.
10 See Gareth Stedman Jones, *Outcast London: A Study in the Relationship Between Classes in Victorian Society* (Oxford University Press, 1971), pp. 19–32; Donald J. Olsen, "Victorian London: Specialization, Segregation, and Privacy," *Victorian Studies* 17:3 (March 1974), pp. 265–78; Friedrich Engels, *The Condition of The Working Class in England*, trans. W. O. Henderson and W. H. Chaloner (Stanford University Press, 1968), pp. 53ff; for the arrangement of domestic space, see Adrian Forty, *Objects of Desire: Design and Society from Wedgwood to IBM* (New York, Pantheon, 1986), pp. 82–6; and see Barbara Dennis and David Skilton, eds., *Reform and Intellectual Debate in Victorian England* (Beckenham, Croom Helm, 1987), pp. 71–3; finally, on the relationship between aesthetics and marketing see Wolfgang Haug, *Commodity Aesthetics*.

signs of their origins and labor stripped from them.[11] In London, the West End achieved this mystification most successfully; there, even a *memento mori* could have its "shop-window quality" marketed: "You may go and buy a skeleton at the West End if you like, and pay the West End price, but it'll be my putting together," Venus remarks from the vantage of his Clerkenwell workshop.[12] Elaborated, of course, this becomes the structure of *Our Mutual Friend* as a whole: beneath the finished surface of West-End society lie the watery depths of the East End.

The habit of mind that sees in objects the labor required for their manufacture produced the many articles in *Household Words* and *All The Year Round* (among other periodicals) that explain to readers the manufacture of common objects; during the Great Exhibition, for instance, Dickens wrote an essay on the making of plate glass. This interest in manufacture was part of a more general Victorian enthusiasm for, and pride in, the industry of the nation. But, as Dickens (like Ruskin) shows, this habit of mind could serve a critical purpose as well; the pride in work could be part of a coherent, discriminating social practice.

Dickens' response to the process of occluding labor, however, was contradictory. At times he praises exactly the process of concealing labor that we have seen him criticize:

That mysterious paper currency which circulates in London when the wind blows, gyrated here and there and everywhere. Whence can it come, whither can it go? It hangs on every bush, flutters in every tree, is caught flying by the electric wires, haunts every enclosure, drinks at every pump, cowers at every grating, shudders upon every plot of grass, seeks rest in vain behind the legions of iron rails. (*Our Mutual Friend*, p. 191)

This "paper currency," febrile and mysterious, circulates in a prospect neither neat nor well trimmed. The city is a fissiparous totality without aesthetic order; like the Great Exhibition it is available only to the catalogue.[13] Dickens continues:

11  Haug, *Commodity Aesthetics*, p. 45.
12  Charles Dickens, *Our Mutual Friend* (London, Penguin, 1971), p. 127. All future references will be given parenthetically in the body of the text.
13  Dorothy Van Ghent writes: "assuming that there is coherence in a world visibly disintegrated into things, one way to find it is to mention everything. Hence the indefatigable attention to detail. No thing must be lost as it is doubtless essential to the mysterious organization of the system." Dorothy Van Ghent, "The Dickens World: the View from Todgers," in Martin Price, ed., *Dickens* (Englewood Cliffs, Prentice Hall, 1967).

In Paris, where nothing is wasted, costly and luxurious city though it be, but where wonderful human ants creep out of holes and pick up every scrap, there is no such thing. There, it blows nothing but dust. There, sharp eyes and sharp stomachs reap even the east wind, and get something out of it. (p. 191)

The form of this volatile passage is identical to that of Dickens' indignant interrogation of the clipped hedges and trim fields, turning on the contrast between visible order and concealed work: he still recognizes that orderly and pleasing prospects require the unseen labor of unvalued workers, ants in holes. But the significance of that form contends with Dickens' affirmation of resourceful waste reclamation. Efficiency and economy are praised, and the reference to the workers carries, instead of critical force, a kind of grotesque insensitivity. As John Carey writes, "the implication is that a little starvation wonderfully improves a city's appearance."[14] Dickens simultaneously treats people as elements of a larger and determinant inhuman order and criticizes such treatment.

This rhetorical gesture – by which Dickens indignantly condemns the actions he is performing – has its psychological analogue in what Freud calls *Verneinung*.[15] Some ideas, Freud suggests, can be admitted into consciousness only by first being negated. Intellectual judgment denies what the unconscious desires; satisfied by this opposition, the subject can then act on the desires negated. I think a case could be made for *Verneinung* as a defining characteristic of Dickens' psyche, but it should be understood that Dickens' contradictory investment in both order and fragmentation is not only a product of his psychology; the contradiction was also indigenous to (and supported by) the social formation within which he wrote. The "isolation and fragmentation" of urban capitalist life, writes Lukács, are

only apparent. The movement of commodities on the market, the birth of their value ... is not merely subject to strict laws but also presupposes

14  John Carey, *The Violent Effigy: A Study of Dickens' Imagination* (London, Faber and Faber, 1973), p. 31.
15  Freud, "Negation," *The Standard Edition of the Complete Psychological Works of Sigmund Freud*, 24 vols. (London, Hogarth Press, 1953–74), vol. XIX, pp. 235–9. See also Jean Hippolyte, "A Spoken Commentary on Freud's *Verneinung*," in Jacques Lacan, *The Seminar of Jacques Lacan: Freud's Papers on Technique, 1953–54*, trans. John Forrester, ed. Jacques-Alain Miller (New York, Norton, 1988), pp. 289–97.

the strict ordering of all that happens. The atomization is, then, only the reflex in consciousness of the fact that the "natural laws" of capitalist production have been extended to cover every manifestation of life in society.[16]

Atomization and the circulation of commodities, dramatically rendered by the mysterious paper currency circulating throughout London, was the complementary moment of the increasingly ordered arrangement of urban society; Dickens saw rationalization as the remedy for fragmentation, whereas, as Lukács suggests, it can also be seen as its cause.

The greatest emblem of fragmentation in the novel – the desiccated dust-heap – thus is an element in the economic rationalization of the society, bringing in, as Dickens notes, great profits. Trash – material that the industrial system casts off and cannot use – is recycled as revenue, providing a vivid illustration of the inclusive activity of capitalist economics. Dickens' final validation of the dust-heap (and other images of what *Household Words* called "important rubbish") presents the possibility that revolutionary change is unnecessary: if the potential of what we discard is actually used, then a fundamental restructuring of the economy will not be required.[17] While this validation marks Dickens' reformist attitude towards the possibilities of changing the order of society generally, it is most vividly present, as I will argue, in his style; there we can see again the useless put to productive work.

On an ideological level, the contradiction between fragment and structure exists as the opposition between an individualist morality and politics, on the one hand, and a governing, authoritarian impulse on the other. Few mediating structures seem to exist between the individual and the central institutional order. Responsibility remains with the individual who exists in an increasingly structured system, where the crucial decisions are made at a distance, determined, as Mr. Dolls haltingly puts it, by "circumstances over which [one has] no control" (p. 293). Humphry House has noticed Dickens' participation in both

16 Lukács, *History*, p. 91.
17 Dickens' understanding of the production of value in waste can be contextualized usefully by reference to Michael Thompson, *Rubbish Theory: The Creation and Destruction of Value* (Oxford University Press, 1979).

moments of this social dialectic: "There was ... a strong authoritarian strain in him which has often been overlooked. In an age of predominantly individualistic thinking, when the individualistic case plainly breaks down ... a man of passion and feeling is likely to rush to the opposite extreme, and assume that highly concentrated central power is the only cure."[18] The play back and forth between these two extremes is various and intricate, but its general shape can be described: the period entertained conscious political and moral philosophies centered on a particular and strong individualism, and, simultaneously, experienced the increasing permeation of an ordering, systemic routine into the corners of daily experience.

The relationship between a rationalized order and atomization defines not only the material environment we have considered so far, but also the institutional patterns and the routines of characters enmeshed in those institutions. "We all know this hotel," Dickens writes in the *Uncommercial Traveller*,

in which we can get anything we want, after its kind, for money; but where nobody is glad to see us, or sorry to see us, or minds (our bills paid) whether we come or go, or how, or when, or why, or cares about us. We all know this hotel, where we have no individuality, but put ourselves into the general post, as it were, and are sorted and disposed of according to our division.[19]

"We all know ... the great station hotel belonging to the company of proprietors, which has suddenly sprung up in the back outskirts of anyplace we like to name" because there are many of them, all identical.[20] The desultory inhabitants of this hotel have become like the "mysterious paper currency" that blows through London, inscrutable to the few who care to wonder, coming and going without apparent purpose. The people who wait on us "wish they had never come, and ... (inevitable result) wish *we* had never come"; our waiter is "thankful to say he is an entire stranger in that part of the country, and is going back to his own connexion [sic]" – doubtless by train – "on Saturday."[21] The sig-

18  Humphry House, *The Dickens World* (London: Oxford University Press, 1942), p. 201.
19  Charles Dickens, *Uncommercial Traveller and Reprinted Pieces* (Oxford University Press, 1958), p. 60.
20  Charles Dickens, *Uncommercial Traveller*, p. 60.
21  Charles Dickens, *Uncommercial Traveller*, pp. 59–60.

nificant "connexion" is now between these hotels rather than between the people who work or stay in them; and the institutions that allow movement and change for individuals (the variety of travel and extended communication) simultaneously install a more systemic homogeneity. No one is visibly constrained to remain, but each person seems to be acting against his or her will. The hotel – public travesty of the private home – is governed by the logic of commerce rather than by desires. Dickens is careful to locate this development with some historical precision: these are "new people," with "new furniture," and "walls that are too new," all in this "new hotel"; it has sprung up with the railway (these are railway hotels), and the penny post, which provides one model for the system.[22] In this pallid utopia, individuality has been posted away under the order of a routine developed around money.

Dickens claims this process is hegemonic, dominating much of the mental and imaginative life of society. After seeing the English section of an international exhibition of art he wrote to Forster:

There is a horrid respectability about most of the best of them – a little, finite, systematic routine in them, strangely expressive to me of the state of England itself ... Don't think it a part of my despondency about public affairs, and my fear that our national glory is on the decline, when I say that mere form and conventionalities usurp, in English art, as in English government and social relations, the place of living force and truth.[23]

"A little, finite, systematic routine," has become increasingly restrictive, making art, government, social relations, daily habits, the hotels, food, and postal service conform to its schedule. Podsnap, proud Britannia personified, has his art, as everything else, "respectfully descriptive of getting up at eight, shaving close at a quarter-past, breakfasting at nine, going to the City at ten, coming home at half-past five, and dining at seven" (*Our Mutual Friend*, p. 174).

22  Schivelbusch conducts a lucid investigation of the simultaneous homogenization and diversification of experience caused by the development of railways; one description of the experience of railway travel – used by Ruskin for instance – was that it turned people into "parcels" for posting. *Railway Journey*, pp. 38–9.
23  Quoted in Forster, *Life*, vol. III, pp. 123–4.

And yet Dickens' own routine, described by his son, was as mechanical as Podsnap's: "No city clerk was ever more methodical or orderly than he; no humdrum, monotonous, mechanical task could ever have been discharged with more punctuality or with more business-like regularity, than he gave to the work of his imagination and fancy."[24] Dickens' relation to social institutions and their effects on the individuals within them is as conflicted as his response to the material landscapes he sees those institutions producing. He saw the rationalizing process in most institutions (in schools, like that to which Charlie Hexam daily repairs in *Our Mutual Friend*, as well as in hotels and the production of art) as unambiguously negative; and yet he validated the same process in the police. While he opposes "systematic routine" when discussing the "State of England," Dickens uncritically praises it among detectives at the time of the Exhibition:

Although the Metropolitan Police Force consists of nineteen superintendents, one hundred and twenty-four inspectors, five hundred and eighty-five serjeants [sic], and four thousand seven hundred and ninety-seven constables, doing duty at twenty-five stations; yet, so uniform is the order of proceeding in all ... [that] the description of what is done at one station [can] be taken as a specimen of what is done at the others.[25]

Multiplicity again is reduced to unity, but here the process is applauded. In the police office of *Our Mutual Friend*, "the lower passions and vices were regularly ticked off in the books, warehoused in the cells, carted away as per accompanying invoice" (p. 833), sorted, inscribed, and disposed of according to division.

Detective work allows Dickens the pleasures both of routinized, systematic organization and of individual achievement, the exercise of individual will; it mediates in a satisfying way between a centralized power and individual activity. The policeman on his beat and the detective stalking a criminal through the city are the heroes of their own tales while, simultaneously, they are elements within a larger ordering force. Both Dickens' pleasure in the impersonal system of the police force and his identification with individual policemen – his "curious and almost morbid partiality for communing with and entertaining

24  Quoted in Philip Collins, *Dickens and Crime* (London, Macmillan & Co., 1962), p. 216.
25  Dickens and Wills, "Metropolitan Protectives," p. 256.

police officers" – are disturbing.[26] Dickens strongly identifies with the ability of policemen to enter public and private places, intimidate the inhabitants, and reduce them to an obedient audience:

Inspector Field is the bustling speaker. Inspector Field's eye is the roving eye that searches every corner of the cellar as he talks. Inspector Field's hand is the well known hand that has collared half the people here, and motioned their brothers, sisters, fathers, mothers, male and female friends inexorably to New South Wales. Yet Inspector Field stands in this den, the Sultan of the place. Every thief here cowers before him, like a schoolboy before his schoolmaster. All watch him, all answer when addressed, all laugh at his jokes, all seek to propitiate him.[27]

The prose focuses relentlessly on Field, his body-parts are fetishized, hand, eye, and voice accruing an independent and awe-inspiring power, the talismanic repetition of his name and the involuted phrasing ("Mr. Field's eye is the roving eye ... Mr. Field's hand is the well known hand") allowing Dickens and the reader to dwell on and in his strength. The narrative voice of this essay is radically unstable; free indirect discourse gives Dickens great license, and he shifts silently from his own voice, to Field's, to that of his subordinate, Detective Sergeant Rogers: "Clear the street here, half a thousand of you! Cut it Mrs. Stalker – none of that – we don't want you! Rogers of the flaming eye, lead on to the tramps' lodging house!"[28] There are no quotation marks; this is Dickens, imagining himself into a policeman's role. By the mid-sixties, Dickens has written: "it is my habit to regard my walk as my beat, and myself as a higher sort of police-constable."[29]

The less flamboyant Inspector in *Our Mutual Friend* combines the mechanical and impersonal with the aggressive and energetic. He is said to be "meditatively active in this chronicle" (p. 830); contemplation – the attitude Lukács sees determining the experience of alienated individuals in a routinized society – combines with an active, individual existence. When we first see "our imperturbable friend," as Mortimer calls him (p. 203), the Inspector is in his office "with a pen and ink, and ruler, posting up his books in a whitewashed office, as studiously as if he were

26  G. A. Sala, quoted in Collins, *Dickens and Crime*, p. 196.
27  Charles Dickens, *Uncommercial Traveller*, p. 516.
28  Charles Dickens, *Uncommercial Traveller*, p. 517.
29  Charles Dickens, *Uncommercial Traveller*, p. 345.

in a monastery on top of a mountain, and no howling fury of a drunken woman were banging herself against a cell-door in the back-yard at his elbow" (p. 66). Dickens underlines the distance that the routine of pen and ink and ruler imposes between the Inspector and the rest of a feminized, frenzied society: his is a mountaintop monastic life. Even the space of his office is monkish: the adjacent "cell" suggests a homologous architectural atomization and Weberian asceticism, reminding the reader that Weber was to see the monk as the "first human being who lives rationally, who works methodically and by rational means towards a goal" – and that Erasmus thought the city a huge monastery.[30]

Simmel noted the tendency of urban existence to develop the purely rational elements of the psyche at the expense of the sympathetic; man is a "differentiating creature," and "the rapid crowding of changing images, the sharp discontinuity in the grasp of a single glance, and the unexpectedness of the onrushing impressions" encourages a "predominance of intelligence in metropolitan man." This cognitive stance is clearly related to the development of the detective and detective fiction, in which the pursuing policeman rationally traces the marks of crime through the fragmented city.[31] Detectives, as Dickens writes, live "lives of strong mental excitement."[32] The drunken, bestial woman – one of Dickens' extraordinary figures of female rage, more extraordinary for her casual, gratuitous appearance in the text – represents all that is irrational, emotional, on the other side of the wall from order and duty. "Emotion," Dickens tells us, "is no part of a policeman's duty."[33]

In *Cranford*, we saw Mary Smith pull away from her community as she became absorbed in her detective work; and, here, Dickens' description of the Inspector's monastic office places the

30 Max Weber, *General Economic History* (New Brunswick, Transaction Books, 1981), p. 365.
31 Georg Simmel, "The Metropolis and Mental Life," in *The Sociology of Georg Simmel*, trans. Kurt H. Wolff (Glencoe, Illinois, The Free Press, 1950), p. 410. See also Philip Fisher, "City Matters: City Minds," in J. H. Buckley, ed., *The Worlds of Victorian Fiction* (Cambridge, Harvard University Press, 1975), pp. 371–89.
32 Charles Dickens, *Uncommercial Traveller*, p. 487.
33 Dickens and Wills, "Metropolitan Protectives," p. 258.

detective at a distance from the society he regulates. But detectives were simultaneously implicated in the object of their study. One of the questions posed about both the Bow Street runners and their successors, the Metropolitan Detectives, concerned their relationship to the criminals they policed; corruption was, if not a frequent occurrence, at least an obvious threat, and the Detectives needed to make a conscious attempt to distinguish themselves from both criminals and informers.[34] The policeman must project himself into the mind of "perverted ingenuity," and adapt himself to "every variety of circumstances," becoming as protean as he is regular and mechanical.[35] While detectives illustrate the rationalization of occupations, they also illustrate the doubling and dividing of character that attends such rationalization.[36]

Mr. Inspector, whose split relation to the fluctuations of social life makes him observer and participant at once, recognizes in Eugene someone similarly divided. "Singular and entertaining combination, sir, your friend," says the Inspector to Mortimer (p. 224). Eugene and Mr. Inspector are both singularly "combined" men, engaged and aloof from society, enmeshed in and fragmented by it while simultaneously isolated at a distance. Lounging in Mortimer's office, having just finished dinner, Eugene remarks:

"The wind sounds up here ... as if we were keeping a lighthouse. I wish we were."

"Don't you think it would bore us?" Lightwood asked.

"Not more than any other place ... It would be exciting to look out for wrecks."

"But otherwise," suggested Lightwood, "there might be a degree of sameness in the life."

"I have thought of that also," said Eugene, as if he really had been considering the subject in its various bearings with an eye to the business; "but it would be a defined and limited monotony. It would not extend beyond two people. Now, it is a question with me, Mortimer, whether a monotony defined with that precision and limited to that extent, might not be more endurable than the unlimited monotony of one's fellow-creatures." (p. 192)

---

34  Collins, *Dickens and Crime*, pp. 200–2.
35  Charles Dickens, *Uncommercial Traveller*, p. 502.
36  John Kucich offers a more lengthy discussion of the psychological partitioning of the men in *Our Mutual Friend* in *Repression in Victorian Fiction*, pp. 220–2.

Instead of enduring the tedium of urban plenitude (a plenitude like that of the dystopian railway hotel, where anything may be had, of its kind), Eugene fabricates the isolation and limited monotony of this lighthouse, his cellular and fictional equivalent of the Inspector's monastic mountaintop.

Unlike the Inspector, Eugene is not alienated by participation in a particular occupation. Instead, Dickens suggests that Eugene is cynical and isolated because he was born to upper-middle-class privilege: "'My own small income,'" Mortimer tells Eugene, "'has been an effective Something, in the way of preventing me from turning to at Anything. And I think yours has been much the same'" (p. 885). Mortimer intimates that the advantages Eugene rejects produce the attitude which leads to that rejection. But another source, more important but unstated, is the anomie of city life. In his journal, the poet William Allingham commented:

In London is a crowd, a press, a torrent of people and things far too much for clear sensation, much less thought, to grapple with discriminately. Individuality is cheap, the check of public opinion almost disappears. Evil tendencies expand, men grow reckless, or *blazé* [sic], put a low valuation on the best things in life, nay on humanity itself, acquire a greed for passing pleasures, at any cost or risk.[37]

*Nil admirari*, a feeling produced by the miscellaneous press of things and people at the Great Exhibition, becomes a characteristic of life outside the crystal walls of the Palace.[38] Working from an understanding of the city as a place of continual change, Simmel later developed the idea of an attitude which he, like Allingham, called *blasé*:

The essence of the *blasé* attitude consists in the blunting of discrimination. This does not mean that the objects are not perceived ... but rather that the meaning and differing values of things, and thereby the things themselves are experienced as insubstantial. They appear to the *blasé* person in an evenly flat and grey tone.[39]

Although the *blasé* attitude seems antithetical to the stance of the detective, they are both supported by the rapidly changing psy-

---

37 William Allingham, *By the Way: Verses, Fragments, and Notes* (London, Longman's Green, & Co., 1912), p. 143.

38 *Illustrated London News* 18 (28 June 1851), p. 628.

39 Simmel, "Metropolis," p. 414.

chological and physical agitation characteristic of urban life. Where Mr. Inspector's energies of discrimination are engaged and honed, however, Eugene's are alienated and blunted. The variety of stimulations casually encountered in the city jade metropolitan inhabitants and encourage a kind of monochromatic and banal dandyism. What was the mannered stance of particular and recognizable individuals, of Jos and Major Pendennis, has been diffused through the perceptual habits of a larger part of the population. "Ennui," Jameson writes, "which is ... one of the most characteristic and emblematic experiences of the modern world, can now be seen to presuppose the rift between intention and act as a precondition of its own existence: to know spleen, the sufferer must be able to see activity as pure technical performance without intrinsic purpose or value."[40] The paradox of this ennui – or the blasé attitude – is, as Jameson notes, that it comes into its own during the extraordinary activity of Victorian urban life; the "pure technical performance" of the Inspector, who pursues his profession without suggesting that its effects are related to his actions, and Eugene's professional inertia only emblematize this more general phenomenon.

Eugene justifies his casual alienation by claiming that the leisure of people like himself is necessary for society because it provides a market for others' goods. "'If we were all as industrious as you, little Busy-Body,'" he says to Jenny Wren,

"we should begin to work as soon as we could crawl, and there would be a bad thing ... If we all set to work as soon as we could use our hands, it would be all over with the dolls' dressmakers."
"There's something in that," replied Miss Wren. (p. 289)

This theory rationalizes loitering, objectless, non-productive impulses by claiming that they provide work for the productive members of society. But Jenny's acquiescence to Eugene's argument is half-hearted, and Dickens himself remained divided on this matter. His contradictory response to the arduous, labored effacement of labor in the various landscapes discussed above reemerges here: he simultaneously wants to allow Eugene his unproductive loitering and to claim that he is, after all, a productive element of society.

40 Fredric Jameson, "Vanishing Mediator: Or Max Weber as Storyteller," in *Ideologies of Theory*, vol. II, p. 10.

Unlike Jenny, Bradley Headstone does not acquiesce to Eugene; he jealously resents Eugene's leisure. Their chases through the nocturnal streets of London provide a graphic image of Dickens' conflicted attitudes towards work and leisure: Eugene is at ease, a dandy out for an aimless stroll, while Bradley walks with straining determination towards a goal and end. This tension, written on the bodies of Eugene and Bradley as they traverse the streets of the city, was written no less legibly on the body of their author. The ambulatory habits of the two men were Dickens' own:

My walking is of two kinds: one, straight on end to a definite goal at a round pace; one, objectless, loitering, and purely vagabond. In the latter state, no gipsy on earth is a greater vagabond than myself; it is so natural to me, and strong with me, that I think I must be the descendent, at no great distance, of some irreclaimable tramp.[41]

In spite of Dickens' pleasure in the leisurely and pointless, Eugene must be inducted into the Victorian virtues of earnestness and engagement. Men of leisure live uneasily in an age that understands work as a defining virtue, and Eugene must be educated away from the residual languor and ennui of the dandy and into the values of earnestness, engagement, and industry. His redemption begins when he first sees Lizzie Hexam: "'Do you,'" Eugene asks Mortimer, "'feel like a dark combination of traitor and pickpocket when you think of that girl?'" (p. 210). That Eugene has not, in fact, *done* anything to cause him this guilt – he has not, for instance, stolen food for an escaped convict, or invested unwisely in shares – marks this as a significant development in Dickens' thinking about individual responsibility in society. In *Little Dorrit* Dickens satirizes the social consequences of bureaucratic amorality; here, in *Our Mutual Friend*, he notes the obscure psychological consequences of a rationalized existence. The feeling of culpability appears simply to permeate Eugene's way of life, as an indictment of his whole manner in and purchase on his community. His guilt can only be understood as a historically new and contradictory emotional response to a particular social situation, in which the responsibility for social injustice is lodged not only in individual actions but also in a diffuse, involuntary complicity with social actions that are beyond indi-

41  Charles Dickens, *Uncommercial Traveller*, p. 95.

vidual control. Eugene's position within a social structure radically in need of attention, and not any particular action he commits, produces his contrition.

To see this more precisely, we can compare Eugene's guilt with that which Matty Jenkyns feels in *Cranford*. In Chapter 3, we saw that Matty's bank, the Town and Country, represented even in its name the growing distance between the sources of social power and the individuals like Matty over whom that power was exercised. Gaskell carefully notes how opaque this power is to Matty, how little she understands the distant institution. When Matty discovers that the bank has failed, she redeems with her last pounds the notes held by a non-member. The face-to-face ethics which prompt this act are explicitly seen in the novel as residual, part of an obsolete way of relating to institutions; no limited liability act had yet legislated restrictions on Matty's moral responsibility. According to her code, Matty remains responsible for the actions of an institution with which she feels only a slight and obscure financial connection. In *Our Mutual Friend*, social relations have been further clouded, and questions of responsibility have become more cryptic. Eugene's guilt – arising not from any particular action but from an enigmatic complicity in a guilty system – has the same source as Matty's, but that source is more occluded.

Across the course of the novel, Eugene's love for Lizzie interpellates him into the public virtues of responsibility; his guilt before her turns Lizzie into an agent of social redemption. This process is opposed, however, by Bradley Headstone. The antagonism of the two men, graphically illustrated in their walks, is compounded by a spectacular triangulation of desire, in which the desired object, Lizzie, drops out of the narrative, leaving only the hatred of the two men. While they move through the urban, de Chirico streets, the object of their admiration is nowhere to be found; she is hiding in the pastoral suburbs. The structure of this triangular relationship is that of the commercial system, in which an object is valued not for its use but its value in exchange. Becky Sharp continually recommodified and circulated herself to maintain her value; Bradley and Eugene do not actually exchange Lizzie (although this was an obvious fear: "'Do you design to capture and desert this girl?'" Mortimer asks Eugene), but her value does lie, in part, in the possibility that she might be passed between men.

Luce Irigaray describes the potential exchange of women producing "an essentially *economic* pleasure" for men; there is only
desire, no pleasure, in the relationship between Eugene and
Bradley, but theirs remains a libidinal economy based on the circulation of women considered as goods.[42] Although Eve
Sedgwick argues that Irigaray elides both history and sex itself in
her analysis of the exchange of women, the terminology Irigaray
uses – that of commodity fetishism – is contemporaneous with
*Our Mutual Friend*, and historically appropriate if abstract.[43]
Sedgwick's own attention to sexuality is necessary and radical,
but part of Irigaray's point is exactly the absence of sex in a dominant phallocentric discourse: "The value of symbolic and imaginary productions is superimposed upon, and even substituted
for, the value of relations of material, natural, and corporal
(re)production."[44] Erotic desire for Lizzie or between the two
men is not absent in *Our Mutual Friend*, but the text presents
Lizzie most fully as a symbol for qualities unrelated to sexuality:
for Eugene, salvation; for Bradley, a danger to his status; for the
pair of them, an occasion for competition.

The women of the novel recognize the use to which Lizzie is
being put: Lizzie herself rightly tells Bradley that it is not she but
Eugene who engages his passion (pp. 457–8). And when Eugene
treats Lizzie as a commodity – as his potential mistress – Jenny
Wren slaps him down:

> "I think of setting up a doll, Miss Jenny."
> "You had better not," replied the dressmaker.
> "Why not?"
> "You are sure to break it. All you children do."

Later he repeats the request, asking Jenny to serve as a pander:

> "And so, Miss Wren," said Mr. Eugene Wrayburn, "I cannot persuade
> you to dress me a doll?"
> "No," replied Miss Wren snappishly; "if you want one, go and buy
> one at the shop." (p. 594)

In treating her as a commodity, Eugene handles Lizzie in the
manner Dickens himself handles other women characters. As he

---

42  Irigaray, *This Sex*, p. 184.
43  Eve Kosofsky Sedgwick, *Between Men: English Literature and Male Homosocial
     Desire* (New York, Columbia University Press, 1985), p. 26.
44  Irigaray, *This Sex*, p. 171.

placed and arranged Catherine in the domestic space at Gadshill, so his representation of the women of his novels displays the pleasures of treating others as objects. Miss Peecher, the school-teacher sharing duties with Bradley, is an obvious example: "Small, shining, neat, methodical, and buxom was Miss Peecher; cherry-cheeked and tuneful of voice. A little pin-cushion, a little housewife, a little book, a little work-box, a little set of tables and weights and measures, and a little woman, all in one" (p. 268). Miss Peecher struggles through the course of the sentence to emerge as a sentient being from her material environment. The language of the sentence, its tripping rhythms and self-satisfied repetition, insures that the reader will not consider Miss Peecher human.

Dickens earlier castigated Podsnap for his inability to perceive that his daughter might resist being "put away like the plate, brought out like the plate, polished like the plate, counted, weighed, and valued like the plate" (pp. 189–90). But here, in a diminutive version of that handy regularity – similar even in the repetitive quality of the prose – emerge Miss Peecher's cherry cheeks and buxomness, eroticized investments by Dickens in this character whom he brings out, polishes, and puts away. Dickens' eroticization of Miss Peecher first displays her, setting her up as a doll (exactly the process he refused Eugene), and wheeling her out like the plate. And then this is followed by obvious sexual violence: she is a little pin-cushion full of pins.

This reduction of women to objects conversely gives to the space they then inhabit an erotic content; Dickens, as I noted in Chapter 2, has an obsessive fascination with drawers and corners, nooks, "snug-spaces" and a whole range of three-dimensional representations of an inside-outside dialectic. "It appeared to me," Pip says, that Pumblechook "must be a very happy man indeed, to have so many little drawers in his shop."[45] In *The Poetics of Space*, Bachelard writes frankly:

I feel more at home in miniature worlds, which, for me, are dominated worlds ... To have experienced miniature sincerely detaches me from the surrounding world, and helps me resist dissolution of the surrounding atmosphere.

---

45 Charles Dickens, *Great Expectations* (Oxford, Oxford Illustrated Press, 1953), p. 49. See also Carey, *Violent Effigy*, p. 45.

Miniature is an exercise that has metaphysical freshness; it allows us to be world conscious at slight risk. And how restful this exercise on a dominated world can be![46]

The representation of the miniature – like the representation of women – creates an imaginary space away from fragmenting urban environment in which one feels "more at home." In the atomized environment of *Our Mutual Friend*, the dividing and divided world of the dust-heap, this diminished, dominated space is fashioned with great attention and energy. The orderly manipulation of reduced, fetishized others is thus one response to the fragmenting urban environment – as Wendy Graham notes, fetishization is "the subject's method for coping with isolation, the sense of separateness which is continually reinforced by contact with 'alien' objects."[47] Dickens' representation of women and the domestic provides a site for the volatile interplay between rationalization – the injunction to "keep things in their places," the desire to arrange women into a protecting home – and the "dissolution of the surrounding atmosphere." Thus, even when the domestic life of his heroines appears busily fragmented – like the domestic activity we saw in Gaskell – the enthusiastic, chipper diminution of Dickens' representations suggests firm control rather than disarray: "Such weighing and mixing and chopping and grating, such dusting and washing and polishing, such snipping and weeding and trowelling and other small gardening … !" (p. 749). As Alexander Welsh writes, "if the problem that besets him [Dickens] can be called the city, his answer can be named the hearth."[48]

## II

Building and furnishing the Swiss chalet in which he wrote, like fashioning the domestic space of the household, provided Dickens with the pleasures of a "dominated world," a managed realm of the imaginary:

46 Gaston Bachelard, *The Poetics of Space*, trans. Maria Jolas (Boston, Beacon Press, 1969), p. 161.
47 Wendy Graham, "A Narrative History of Class Consciousness," *Boundary 2* 15: 1/2 (Fall 1986/Winter 1987), p. 48.
48 Alexander Welsh, *The City of Dickens* (Cambridge, Harvard University Press, 1986), p. 142.

In the setting up of the said châlet, after the manner of a child's architectural toy, Charles had found the greatest amusement, for he was indeed
one of those who find "A child's keen delight in little things," and the
hanging of his pictures, the arranging his furniture [sic], the annexation
of a tiny conservatory, and the construction of an underground tunnel,
which connected the area round the house with a small plantation of
lofty cedars, under the shade of which he had erected his châlet, were all
sources to him of intense interest.[49]

Like the household, the space of writing is free from the desiccating environment; its satisfactions can be controlled and managed.
"The writing table," Dickens wrote a friend while on vacation, "is
set forth with a neatness peculiar to your estimable friend; and
the furniture in all the rooms has been entirely re-arranged by the
same extraordinary character."[50]

Discussing *David Copperfield*, Mary Poovey similarly claims
that housekeeping and writing are uniquely related in Dickens:
"Like a good housekeeper, the good writer works invisibly, quietly, without calling attention to his labor; both master dirt and
misery by putting things in their proper places; both create a
sphere to which one can retreat – a literal or imaginative hearth
where anxiety and competition subside."[51] In addition to providing a space free from competition, both provide a space where
Dickens can exercise his will, managing all that is around him
without obstruction. Fiction and housekeeping both are done
without strain, as gifts produced easily: "the two images – of
effortless housekeeping and effortless writing – are interdepen-
dent at every level."[52] Dickens' memorandum regarding formal
landscape and his more ambivalent representation of urban
scenes criticized the occlusion of labor in material culture; writing and domesticity appear to be free from this mystification:
labor is not oppressive and its products are not occlusions.

---

49  Philip Collins, ed., *Dickens: Interviews and Recollections*, 2 vols. (London,
    Macmillan, 1981), vol. I, p. 86.
50  Dickens *Letters*, vol. II, p. 77. "*Before* I tasted a bit or drop yesterday," he wrote
    Forster, "I set out my writing table with extreme taste and neatness, and
    improved the disposition of the furniture generally," *Letters*, vol. II, p. 78.
51  Poovey, *Uneven Developments*, p. 122.
52  Poovey, *Uneven Developments*, p. 101. In "Cookery, not Rookery: Family and
    Class in *David Copperfield*," *Dickens Studies Annual* 15 (1986), Chris R. Vanden
    Bossche earlier observed that "Dickens was always most at home when he
    was at work" (p. 105).

In *Our Mutual Friend*, the history of John Rokesmith's relation-ship with Boffin exemplifies the idea of effortless verbal produc-tivity. When Rokesmith first arrives at Boffin's Bower to discuss the possibility of his being employed as a secretary, Boffin asks:

"It was Secretary that you named; wasn't it?"

"I said Secretary," assented Mr. Rokesmith.

"It rather puzzled me at the time," said Mr. Boffin, "and it rather puz-zled me and Mrs. Boffin when we spoke of it afterwards, because (not to make a mystery of our belief) we have always believed a Secretary to be a piece of furniture, mostly of mahogany, lined with green baize or leather, with a lot of little drawers in it. Now, you won't think I take a lib-erty when I mention that you certainly ain't *that*."

Certainly not, said Mr. Rokesmith. But he had used the word in the sense of Steward.

"Why, as to Steward, you see," returned Mr. Boffin, with his hand still to his chin, "the odds are that Mrs. Boffin and me may never go upon the water. Being both bad sailors, we should want a Steward if we did; but there's generally one provided."

Mr. Rokesmith again explained; defining the duties he sought to undertake, as those of general superintendent, or manager, or over-looker, or man of business.

"Now, for instance – come!" said Mr. Boffin, in his pouncing way. "If you entered my employment, what would you do?" (p. 227)

Boffin's habits as a manager of materials and Rokesmith's as an incipient manager of words are neatly opposed here: Boffin cata-logues the chief characteristics of a Secretary, as he understands them, with the professional eye of a man who has spent his life evaluating goods and their various parts. He thinks of language as an object and tool – more like the baize-lined desk than a gen-erous element – valuable only to the degree that it does work, that it has a function and an end. Rokesmith, by contrast, under-stands language to be copious play, an activity which effortlessly and without waste creates redundance: secretary, steward, super-intendent, manager, overlooker, man of business – the language is not large enough, a single word will not do for the expansive imagination. In explaining his understanding of the term "Secretary," Rokesmith demonstrates the verbal facility that will be required of him when he becomes one. And, to the extent that readers are interested in giving themselves over to it, this playful style produces a vertiginous hilarity, an exultant and utopian vision of possibilities: there appear to be no psychological or societal obstacles for this prose. Dickens' verbal freedom, which Rokesmith here represents rather tamely, is a flagrant violation of the predictability that Weber (and after him Lukács) saw as the characteristic anodyne of reified life, a violation of a "contemplative" stance, and a jolting into action of the passive reader.

These modes of language are tangled throughout *Our Mutual Friend* and rarely so clearly delineated as they are here: Rokesmith's first task as secretary, for instance, is to take a letter to himself, and this underscores both Boffin's playfulness and his belief that writing is something faintly ridiculous. Nonetheless, in the same way that he wants Eugene's loitering, leisurely manner to be socially productive, Dickens wants writing – his "day's no-business" as he called it – to be both play and work.[53] Ideally, writing, like walking, is an "objectless, loitering, and purely vagabond" activity, and one that "moves straight on, to a definite goal at a round pace." The reconciliation of these opposed modes of language is anticipated when Boffin, trying to discover what Rokesmith will *do*, asks him to arrange his papers. "No sooner said than done," Dickens writes: speech and productivity are united; writing and its consequences, we can imagine, will be similarly joined as Rokesmith takes on his job.

The complete integration of saying and doing, however, comes in the fiction of Boffin's own miserliness, where the redundant play of language educates Bella out of her avarice. At the climax of this story, Rokesmith tells Boffin he has tried to "win her affections and possess her heart."

> "Win her affections," retorted Mr. Boffin, with ineffable contempt, "and possess her heart! Mew says the cat, Quack-quack says the duck, Bow-wow-wow says the dog! Win her affections and possess her heart! Mew, Quack-quack, Bow-wow!"
> John Rokesmith stared at him in his outburst, as if with some faint idea that he had gone mad. (p. 660)

Boffin later recalls this moment with Bella, now enlightened, at hand:

> "On the celebrated day when I made what has since been agreed upon to be my grandest demonstration – I allude to Mew says the cat, Quack quack says the duck, and Bow-wow-wow says the dog – I assure you, my dear, that on that celebrated day, them flinty and unbelieving words

53  Charles Dickens, *Uncommercial Traveller*, p. 18.

hit my old lady so hard on my account, that I had to hold her, to prevent her running out after you, and defending me by saying I was playing a part."

Mrs. Boffin laughed heartily again, and her eyes glistened again, and it then appeared, not only that in that burst of sarcastic eloquence Mr. Boffin was considered by his two fellow-conspirators to have outdone himself, but that in his own opinion it was a remarkable achievement. "Never thought of it afore the moment, my dear!" he observed to Bella ... "I couldn't tell you how it come into my head or where from, but it had so much the sound of a rasper that I own to you it astonished myself." (pp. 847–8)

This description of the creative process and its pleasures can be seen as a reflection at the end of Dickens' career on the characteristic form of his comedy, the initial source of his achievement. The scene enacts his own writing and the response to it, even his bewilderment: "I couldn't tell you how it come into my head or where from." Boffin's Bow-wow, Quack-quack triumphantly leads Bella out of her mercenary desires, and frees her from her libidinal engagement with the movement of commodities. Effortless, useless, and even nonsensical fiction here does work, namely leading Bella into a household with John, where she can begin to work herself, quietly putting and keeping things in their places, effortlessly performing domestic labor.

In *Cranford* we saw "hoaxes" like this used to create a communal spirit; Peter's tales of India educated the women around him out of their anger and into a social group. I noted there the danger of appearing to condescend to these characters; because deception limits the autonomy of individuals, stealing the free-will they own like a possession, even benevolent lies can patronize and belittle characters. Gaskell largely avoided this condescension because her everyday characters were open and fluid, living in the "space of the tactic"; autonomy was not privileged and its loss was not degrading. Because subjectivity and female subjectivity in particular is not fluid and non-hierarchical in *Our Mutual Friend* but commodified and self-enclosed, Dickens' representation of Bella is heavily patronizing. The hoax offered here limits her autonomy; effortless fiction does the work of education by deception. Although he has effectively reconciled the demands of play and work, creating an effortless style which produces change, he does so at the expense of women and Bella in particular.

The imaginary space of a fiction without tensions is not, how-ever, entirely distinguished from the symbolic environment described above; if this effortless style has its end in the house-hold, it too, like the problems it is to solve, can be said to have its beginning in the city. Steven Marcus suggests, speaking of Dickens' earlier novels, that Dickens' self-surprised style was reinforced if not created by his experience as a stenographer. Such training subordinated the conscious thought of the writer to the speeches Dickens heard, and created a style both propulsive and spatial:

What I am suggesting is that this experience of an alternative, quasi-graphic way of representing speech had among other things the effect upon Dickens of loosening up the rigid relations between speech and writing that prevail in our linguistic and cultural system ... it allowed the spoken language to enter into his writing with a parity it had never enjoyed before in English fictional prose. Speech here was not the tradi-tional subordinate of its written representation; it could appear now in writing with a freedom and spontaneity that made it virtually, if momentarily, writing's equal.[54]

The rational hierarchies of the symbolic are replaced by a more nearly imaginary speech, a shifting play of signifiers unmoored from signification. When Rokesmith demonstrates the pleasures of effortless speech in his conversation with Boffin, we can see these as typical of all Dickensian verbal play – written as well as spoken. Rokesmith takes down words as Dickens did, transform-ing the spoken into the written with ease. That Rokesmith's speech initially seems to mystify Boffin, however, that it serves no purpose other than to demonstrate linguistic play, suggests the limitations of the imaginary as a space for communication. Although critics have rarely discerned so precise a relationship between the city and Dickens' style, the significance of Dickens' career as a metropolitan journalist has been noted ever since Bagehot observed that Dickens described London "like a special correspondent for posterity."[55] Just as newspapers retrained urban readers for life in cities, so Dickens' urban novels ade-quated city-dwellers' modes of perception – taught them to "reperceive," as Philip Fisher has it – to the new environment

54 Steven Marcus, "Language into Structure," *Daedalus* 101: 1 (Winter 1972), p. 193.
55 Bagehot, "Charles Dickens," in *Collected Works*, vol. II, p. 87.

which surrounded them and which had produced his own writing.

Eugene shares with the journalist and the police their habit of telling tales, but he also suffers from its liabilities. Throughout the text, he develops a particularly Dickensian voice, treating people as minor characters in a novel he is casually writing. When, for instance, he calls Riderhood, "our friend of the perspiring brow" (p. 214), he has picked up Riderhood's voice in a typically Dickensian fashion. And, when Mr. Inspector trades his books and pens for drinks at the Jolly Porters, and (to disguise their surveillance activities) creates a little story about lime, Eugene immediately falls in with the tale: "You can't do better," the Inspector says, "than be interested in some lime."

> "You hear Eugene?" said Lightwood, over his shoulder. "You are deeply interested in lime."
> "Without lime," returned that unmoved barrister-at-law, "my existence would be unilluminated by a ray of hope." (p. 207)

There is no lime, of course, and Eugene's existence has, at this point, no hope to illuminate it. The Inspector's occupational cynicism – "it was always more likely that a man had done a bad thing than that he hadn't" (p. 206) – is fully equaled by Eugene's private and less productive variety. And both are freed by this psychological distance into a verbal facetiousness, a playful attitude towards language and referentiality:

> "Speaking as a shipper of lime — " began Eugene.
> "Which no man has a better right to do than yourself, you know," said Mr. Inspector.
> "I hope not," said Eugene; "my father having been a shipper of lime before me, and my grandfather before him – in fact we having been a family immersed to the crowns of our heads in lime during several generations." (p. 208)

Eugene and the Inspector play this game with a shared sense of its rules and of the necessary tone: the Inspector is "imperturbable," Eugene "unmoved." The story Eugene tells, in fact, is a veiled description of his own alienation as well as a symptom of it. His has been a "family immersed to the crowns of [their] heads in lime during several generations," and he too is deeply immersed. The lime that covers Eugene's deceased relatives in their graves covers him; he is a realistic descendant of the roman-

tic death-in-life figure, grandnephew to Major Pendennis, spending his days in a monotonous and enervating routine. "Eugene,
friend of Mortimer; buried alive in the back of his chair" (p. 53):
this is our introduction to his character.

Eugene's metaphoric death is both an image of the fate of tale
tellers and one of the occupation's prerequisites: he is able to give
himself up to character-roles because he has so fully absented himself from his own life. What prevents Dickens from the same fate is
the extraordinary power of his ego. Dickens is, in spite of the parodic impersonation of others, always present in his writing: "the
narrator," writes Kucich, "willingly and, one might almost say, lovingly becomes and acts out what he parodies."[56] Kucich goes on to
read Hegel's master-slave dialectic through Bataille in order to
explain the sense of authority and "sovereignty" Dickens' prose
conveys: by violating limits, launching himself into the dizzying
world of speech free from restraint, by expending himself fully
into his texts, Dickens' narrative voice demonstrates its willingness
to risk death, to proclaim itself as a master. But this Hegelian
understanding of Dickensian power also can be traced in another
direction, through Lukács rather than Bataille, in order to discover
not the authentic mastery of Dickens' prose, but the way that mastery is dialectically upended by its own power.

Forster gives a telling description of Dickens' ego and its history which suggests the connection between its strength and the
process of writing:

[Dickens'] early sufferings brought with them the healing powers of
energy, will, and persistence, and taught him the inexpressible value of a
determined resolve to live down difficulties; but the habit, in small as in
great things, of renunciation and self-sacrifice, they did not teach; and,
by his sudden leap into a world-wide popularity and influence, he
became master of everything that might seem to be attainable in life,
before he had mastered what a man must undergo to be equal to its
hardest trials.[57]

If schematic, this biographical explanation seems accurate: it
explains the principal sources of Dickens' will and the significant
moment when that will is confirmed as authorial power. Again,

56 John Kucich, *Excess and Restraint in Charles Dickens* (Athens, University of
    Georgia Press, 1981), p. 234.
57 Forster, *Life*, vol. III, p. 154.

comparison with Thackeray is useful. Thackeray's crucial experience, as he was defining an adult personality, was of loss; I described in the first chapter how this experience encouraged a dynamic of desire and disenchantment, and produced a deeply ambivalent attitude towards the author's project. For Dickens, the crucial experience, again at the moment when his adult personality was being formed, is of acquisition and confirmation, producing, as Forster elsewhere writes, "a too great confidence in himself, a sense that everything was possible to the will that would make it so."[58] Objective events in Dickens' history – the early trauma developing his determination, his overpowering desire for social acceptance and his sensitivity to social humiliation, the young success confirming his will in its apparent ability to transform material into a determinate shape – provide both the content of later fiction, the autobiographical elements frequently detailed, and also a central aspect of its form and procedure, the shaping, reifying process that sees the shape of the world emanating from Dickens' own actions. His success contributes significantly to the production of Dickens' *habitus*, the congeries of conscious and unconscious dispositions which structure the apparent improvisations of his texts.[59] "It is true," Lukács writes,

for the capitalist also there is the same doubling of personality, the same splitting up of man into an element of the movement of commodities and an (objective and impotent) observer of that movement. But for his consciousness it necessarily appears as an activity … in which effects emanate from himself. This illusion blinds him to the true state of affairs, whereas the worker, who is denied the scope for such illusory activity, perceives the split in his [own] being.[60]

Conventional understanding associates Dickens with popular entertainment and lower-class interests; Thackeray, by contrast, traditionally has been affiliated with more residual literary forms, eighteenth-century satire in particular, and an aristocratic world. I'm suggesting, however, that Dickens can be seen as Lukács'

---

58 Forster, *Life*, vol. I, p. 52. Similarly, George Ford writes, "It can be plausibly argued that a conquest of the public made at the age of twenty-four was too easy and premature, and that Dickens never recovered from its intoxication." *Dickens and His Readers* (Princeton University Press, 1955), p. 20.

59 On the *habitus* as a structure of subjectivity producing improvisation, see Pierre Bourdieu, *Outline of a Theory of Practice*, trans. Richard Nice (Cambridge University Press, 1977), pp. 78 87.

60 Lukács, *History*, p. 166.

capitalist and Thackeray as his worker. The sense of presence one feels reading Dickens – and the imaginary verbal freedom from utility – are sharply limited when understood in the larger context of Dickens' own history and the social formation from which that history emerged. To the extent that the success of *Pickwick* was due to changes in the literary mode of production, the development of what N. N. Feltes calls the "commodity-text," Dickens' ego was validated by the increasing rationalization of form in the novel.[61] Indeed, the sense of presence in the Dickensian text can be seen as a compensation for the increasing routinization of the author's task, his increasing distance from the readers whose proximity is now interpellated on a largely ideological level [62] The Bataillian excess of Dickens' writing thus can be said to emerge from Dickens' "technique," as Benjamin would call it, his position in a shifting social formation.

The submission of Dickens' rational thought to fundamental activities of language is a linguistic equivalent of the equally "fundamental and primitive" spatial fascination I noticed before, the idiosyncratic nature of Dickensian space. And, indeed, the space in which Dickens wrote was itself constructed in such a way that it allowed the combination of self-abnegation (losing himself in his characters) and self-assertion (impressing his will on his linguistic materials) which I have been describing. His daughter Mamie describes secretly watching him act out his characters in front of mirrors – like the five installed at Gads Hill – while he wrote: "For the time being he had not only lost sight of his surroundings, but had actually become in action, as in imagination, the creature of his pen."[63] It is tempting to see these doublings as emblematic of a specular structure of the novels in which the space created – like that created by the mirror – is a three-dimensional world which Dickens can simultaneously be inside and outside of. Mirrors double the interiority of a room, make there more of an interior space than the dimensions initially allow; and, at the same time, they allow the observer an exteriority and control over the mirrored body and the created space – exactly the control that Thackeray, looking through plate-

61  Feltes, *Modes of Production*, p. 8.
62  Poovey, *Uneven Developments*, p. 104.
63  Mamie Dickens, *My Father*, p. 50.

glass windows, lacked. If Thackeray is in his texts, but uneasy there, continually suggesting that responsibility for writing is elsewhere, pointing to some other realm, the objects on the other side of the glass, Dickens is present twice over, on both sides of the mirror. Where the discursive structure of *Vanity Fair* is a monument to the sustaining frustrations of the fetish, Dickens presents a fantasy of narcissistic transumption, where all objects / causes of desire are achieved and identified with the self.

In Dickens' simultaneous absorption into his characters and his pleased self-promotion as their creator we can see two forms of authorial identification, imaginary and symbolic. "Imaginary identification," Slavoj Žižek writes, "is identification with the image in which we appear likeable to ourselves, with the image representing 'what we would like to be,' and symbolic identification, identification with the very place *from where* we are being observed, *from where* we look at ourselves so that we appear to ourselves likeable, worthy of love."[64] In this light, Dickens' association with his characters, his imaginary identification in which he appears to lose himself, is allowed by a second identification, his identification in the symbolic register – his identification, that is, with the managing powers of rationalization. Indeed, Žižek rather surprisingly uses Dickens to illustrate exactly this difference between imaginary and symbolic identifications: he presents

the Dickensian admiration of the "good common people," the imaginary identification with their poor but happy, close, unspoiled world, free of the cruel struggle for power and money. But (and therein lies the falsity of Dickens) from where is the Dickensian gaze peering at the "good common people" so that they appear likeable; from where if not from the point of view of the corrupted world of power and money?[65]

Dickensian imaginary identification – not only with the "good common people," but with all "happy, close, unspoiled" worlds and spaces – is supported by a simultaneous identification with that point in the symbolic register which creates and shapes this space, which allows his presence there. Just as we have seen the imaginary freedom of Dickens' writing to have its beginning in the spaces of the city, so this imaginary identification is allowed

64  Slavoj Žižek, *The Sublime Object of Ideology* (London, Verso, 1989), p. 105.
65  Žižek, *Sublime Object*, p. 107.

by the symbolic: "It is the symbolic identification ... which domi-
nates and determines the image, the imaginary form in which we
appear to ourselves likeable."[66]

In *Our Mutual Friend*, these identifications can be seen most
strikingly, perhaps, in the "cosy" of the Jolly Porters, when
Eugene Wrayburn, Mortimer Lightwood, and the Inspector
jointly imagine being members of the trade in lime. Having first
visually constructed this space – which "seemed to leap out of a
dark sleep and embrace them warmly" – and its contents,
Dickens remarks:

It may be here in confidence admitted that, the room being close shut ...
there had not appeared to be the slightest reason for the elaborate maintenance of this same lime fiction. Only it had been regarded by
Mr. Inspector as so uncommonly satisfactory, and so fraught with mysterious virtues, that neither of his clients had presumed to question it.
(p. 209)

Admitted "in confidence"; if there is no reason to maintain the
secret fiction within the Jolly Porters, there certainly is no cause
to pretend to secrecy in the pages of this serialized novel. But
Dickens has joined the creatures of his pen in the snugness of the
bar, fraternizing with them in their isolation. The desire to identify with the symbolic position of these characters (with the polic-
ing Inspector and his temporary assistants) encourages Dickens'
imaginary fraternization. The creation of fictions appears to
develop in distance and secrecy, in the closely shut room and the
mysterious virtues of the "happy, close, unspoiled world" where
the self can adopt roles and create characters: one writes in a
monastery, a lighthouse, a mirrored chalet.

## III

The verbal representation of visual space, of the three-dimensional,
imaginary spaces I have been describing, finally proves impossible; the mirrored space of writing cannot provide a secure enclave
because language and the subjects attempting to use it suffer from
the bleaching and fragmentation of the environment.

In the novel's opening paragraphs, Lizzie and Gaffer steer
their boat across London's blighted landscape towards

---

66  Žižek, *Sublime Object*, p. 108.

Limehouse to drop off the body which lies on the floor of the boat between them. Dickens writes: "Lizzie took her right hand from the scull it held, and touched her lips with it, and for a moment held it out lovingly towards" her father (p. 46). The phrasing here is not extraordinary when seen in isolation, but is the first sign of what will become, across the course of the novel, a more pronounced and extraordinary pattern. Lizzie's hand is, syntactically, the object of this sentence, on which the subject, Lizzie acts: "Lizzie took her right hand from the scull it held." As this phrasing recurs in the novel, the use of body parts as objects slides from the syntactic to the ontological: people act on their own bodies as if these bodies were objects. They develop, as Dorothy Van Ghent writes, a "me-half" and an "it-half" (p. 26). Thus, when Rogue Riderhood and John Rokesmith meet, Dickens writes: "At first Riderhood had sat with his footless glass extended at arm's length for filling, while the very deliberate stranger [Rokesmith] seemed absorbed in his preparations. But, gradually his arm reverted home to him, and his glass was lowered and lowered until he rested it upside down upon the table" (p. 414). Riderhood is no longer the agent guiding the activities of this wayward hand; he is merely a convenient haven when it is at rest.

This process of dismemberment is significantly transformed during the first conversations between Silas Wegg and Mr. Venus. The chapter in which these conversations take place – "Mr. Wegg Looks After Himself" – begins with Dickens being unusually mysterious: "'If I get on with him as I expect to get on ... it wouldn't become me to leave it here,'" Wegg thinks; 'It wouldn't be respectable.'" The "him" is Boffin, the "it" is Wegg's leg, and the "here" is Venus' shop, but we know none of this (p. 121). We are introduced to Venus by means of a kind of verbal inventory of his parts and appurtenances without being told, for instance, that he is a taxidermist. After some preliminary conversation, Wegg asks:

> "And how have I been going on, this long time, Mr. Venus?"
> "Very bad," says Mr. Venus, uncompromisingly.
> "What? Am I still at home?" asks Wegg with an air of surprise.
> "Always at home." (p. 124)

We are given no points of reference by which to comprehend this dialogue. We later come to understand that Wegg is talking

about his leg: he no longer wants to be "'what I may call dis-
persed, a part of me here, and a part of me there'"; he would like
instead to collect himself "'like a genteel person'" (p. 127). But
further mysteries arise. Dickens, more here than in other chapters, absents himself, providing no comprehensive consciousness
through which to understand the conversation. From the reader's
perspective the language of the novel, like its character's limbs,
has become resistant, an object on its own. If in the last section I
showed Dickens' vexed attempt to see writing as an imaginary
space free from the capitalist exchange and the fragmentation of
urban capitalism with which he, nonetheless, identified, in this
concluding section I will suggest the entrance of fragmentation
and reification not only into the body, but into the very substance
and material of language itself.

Dickens implies that language is material in obvious and
comic ways. He performs a kind of verbal amputation on the
names of his characters, reducing them to their initials: R.W.,
MRF, T and P, WMP, and her husband, MP. Henrietty Boffin
receives her name as the genetic offspring of the names of her
mother and father. And Wegg must get his name not only, as
many critics have noted, from Hood's "Mrs. Killmansegg and
Her Precious Leg," but from the cutting and pasting of his own
"w[ooden l]eg" – "that timber fiction" as it is called (p. 357).
Finally, in his notes for the novel, Dickens wrote of Chapter 10:
"this chapter transferred bodily from No. 2," the second monthly
serial. Editing is a surgical process of grafting inanimate body-
parts. Eugene at one point holds "his pen ready to reduce him
[Riderhood] to more writing" (p. 197). Perhaps, as Boffin insists,
everything does not turn to rags (p. 136), but Mr. Dolls does
explicitly: strapped down after his collapse he is "rendered a
harmless bundle of torn rags" (p. 800). And perhaps it is to such
rags that Eugene reduces Riderhood: rags, of course, were
retrieved from dust heaps to make paper. The fracturing of the
material world creates such improbable rhetorical relationships –
metaphorical, indexical, iconic – of its own accord.

More soberly, the materiality of language becomes a matter of
explicit commentary later in the novel. When Rokesmith leaves
Riderhood's house, he recalls to himself (author and reader of his
own text) the attempt which was made on his life while he lay
drugged, in an enclosed room, perched over the water:

"I dropped down. Lying helpless on the ground, I was turned over by a foot. I was dragged by the neck into a corner. I heard men speak together. I was turned over by other feet. I saw a figure like myself lying dressed in my clothes on a bed ... The figure like myself was assailed, and my valise was in its hand. I was trodden upon and fallen over." (p. 426)

And then he asks himself: "'This is still correct? Still correct, with the exception that I cannot possibly express it to myself without using the word I. But it was not I. There was no such thing as I, within my knowledge'" (p. 426). The fragmentation of character (and the body) and the alienation of language into an object come together here in a complicated tangle: "I cannot express it to myself without using the word I."

Rokesmith – who cannot express his simultaneous existence and non-existence adequately within his "knowledge" – is confronted with his mirror-image in a "figure" across the room. How would Dickens have acted out this nonexistent, divided, and doubled character for his five mirrors? How could he represent both Rokesmith and the figure like him, George Radfoot? The symbolic register with which Dickens identifies as he constructs spaces for his imaginary seems not to easily accommodate this combined and absent subjectivity. Indeed, in order to attempt this representation, Dickens had to create a figure rather than use the literal language which was his initial impulse. The final text of the novel reads, "'I saw a figure like myself lying dressed in my clothes on the bed'"; but in both the manuscript and the proofs there is no "figure" – no simile – of or for Radfoot. The early versions have, more simply, "'I saw myself lying dressed in my clothes on a bed.'" The conflict between the final text and the earlier versions represents a struggle between Dickens' imaginary and symbolic identifications, and, in this instance, the symbolic register rejects Dickens' attempts to represent Harmon's subjectivity: Rokesmith was not lying on the bed; a figure like him (George Radfoot) was. Syntactic structures do not encourage us to think of doppelgänger subjects becoming objects, and the "it-half" returns to the "me-half," leaving a "figure" supine across the room. Dickens' strong will and imaginary desires cannot fully manage the symbolic order of language.

Dickens struggles here to represent a particular type of character, whose interiority is divided and fragmented through the course of his narrative development; as we have seen, this is a novel populated by such "combinations." The novelist can either attend fully to the subjective perceptions of her or his characters, detailing with precision their responses to an environment which (because language resists the necessary transmutations) no longer can be registered simultaneously with assurance; or she or he can attend to what seem to be objective structures (if only the objective structures of language), while uncertainly registering the position of characters and him or herself within them.[67] John Rokesmith states to himself fully the impressions of his experience, but that statement is bewildering, and the language he uses is tortured in the attempt. The other central plot of the novel, that involving Eugene and Lizzie, faces this narrative problem even more fully; its crisis is displayed not in retrospect (as the crisis of the Rokesmith/Wilfer plot is), but within the progress of the narrative action. In that crisis, set in a rural landscape, we see again the dramatic dissolution of Dickens' narrative technique:

In the rosy evening, one might watch the ever-widening beauty of the landscape – beyond the newly-released workers wending home – beyond the silver river – beyond the deep green fields of corn, so prospering, that the loiterers in their narrow threads of pathway seemed to float immersed breast-high – beyond the hedgerows and clumps of trees – beyond the windmills on the ridge – away to where the sky appeared to meet the earth, as if there were no immensity of space between mankind and Heaven. (p. 757)

In this "English landscape" there are workers, but the drudgery of their work has been diffused by the distance and by the muted focus of Dickens' prose; this can be seen as another compromise in his understanding of work and art. In the mystified beauty of this leisurely, loitering narrative, only the word "released" contains submerged within it a suggestion of the conditions of the millworker's labor. What does it mean that this landscape is "ever-widening"? That the eye of the perceiver gradually takes

---

67 Raymond Williams provides a clear representation of this marxist history of the novel in both his *The English Novel: From Dickens to Lawrence* (London, Hogarth Press, 1984), pp. 119–39, and *Country and City*, pp. 164–81; Fredric Jameson extends it in "Cognitive Mapping," in Cary Nelson and Lawrence Grossberg, eds., *Marxism and the Interpretation of Culture* (Urbana, University of Illinois Press, 1988), pp. 348–50.

in more of the image, moving from foreground to sky? That the thickening light of evening illuminates a growing field of vision? Both, perhaps, but more than either the sentence connotes its own ever-widening, encircling movement, including each element, the corn and trees and hedgerows, in a unity bordered visibly and conceptually by Heaven. Although Dickens attempts to present the landscape as an image of natural continuity and integration, the widening of the scene is the register of the author's activity, the arrangement and ordering of this view into an aesthetic whole; it is a landscape no less arranged than the formal landscapes of the previous century. In a self-amusing way Dickens' presence perhaps is registered by the fact that it is a paper mill that these workers are leaving, having produced the material on which they are being described; but more assuredly it is found in the qualifications Dickens makes that register this as a *willed* exercise: "one might watch ... as if there were no immensity of space between earth and heaven." And, further, Dickens' ordering hand is here in the self-conscious literariness of the description, the mannered reference to a romantic landscape tradition. It is, as Dickens himself says, a "living picture" (p. 757): beauty is denoted by reference to art; "nature" itself carries the traces of its representation, the signs of the author's hand at work. This is a total image, but one which nonetheless shows that its totality has been achieved by the conscious and individual activity of the author.

In this picture, then, we find Eugene, after his conversation with Lizzie, walking:

The rippling of the river seemed to cause a correspondent stir in his [Eugene's] uneasy reflections. He would have laid them asleep if he could, but they were in movement, like the stream, and all tending one way with a strong current. As the ripple under the moon broke unexpectedly now and then, and palely flashed in a new shape and with a new sound, so parts of his thoughts started, unbidden, from the rest, and revealed their wickedness. "Out of the question to marry her," said Eugene, "and out of the question to leave her. The crisis!" (p. 766)

Wordsworth provided Dickens the most familiar and powerful description of imaginary unity in the face of alienating possibilities when he described the collaboration of the body and spirit with the natural world:

For I, methought, while the sweet breath of heaven
Was blowing on my body, felt within
A correspondent breeze, that gently moved
With quickening virtue, but is now become
A tempest, a redundant energy,
Vexing its own creation[68]

Integral, but vexed, a disturbed lull unsettles Wordsworth, the breeze, Eugene and the river. That the Wordsworthian integrity is described in terms of the relationship between the body and its material environment suits Dickens' purposes; and that Dickens, in his prose, as Wordsworth in his poetry, attempts to develop a stylistic equivalent of this relationship – a vexed lull, regular rhythms and redundant energy – underscores the linguistic participation in the anxiously balanced correspondence. But the musing sentences Eugene speaks – "'Out of the question to marry her ... and out of the question to leave her'" – have no subject. The moral and social paradox in which he finds himself, damned if he does and if he doesn't, seems to bear down upon a seemingly absent subject. "He had sauntered far enough. Before turning to retrace his steps, he stopped upon the margin, to look down at the reflected night" (p. 766). Dickens is careful to place Eugene at the midpoint of his walk, and between the night and its reflection. "In an instant, with a dreadful crash, the reflected night turned crooked, flames shot jaggedly across the air, and the moon and stars came bursting from the sky" (pp. 766–7). The earlier oscillation between "living" landscape and the picturing perceiver has broken down, and we have here only Eugene's perceptions without any larger aesthetic or logical frame into which we can put them. Unlike the landscape scene, there are no suggestions that this is to be understood as a willed representation of the writer (no "as if," for instance); the relationship between objective phenomena and their perception is violently disturbed, and the only narrative possibility is to represent the perspective of the individual. If in the sections between Wegg and Venus, language became something from which we as readers were estranged, total perhaps, but alien, here it has receded almost entirely into the imaginary of the isolated subject.

68  William Wordsworth, *The Prelude* (1850), Book I, lines 33–8, in *The Prelude: A Parallel text* (New Haven, Yale University Press, 1971), p. 37.

The moment passes. Dickens has, from the scene's beginning, suggested that Bradley has been following Eugene; and immediately after this crisis, the detective mode of Dickens' narrative disposition takes over: "Was he struck by lightning? With some incoherent half-formed thought to that effect, he turned under the blows that were blinding him and mashing his life, and closed with a murderer, whom he caught by a red neckerchief – unless the raining down of his own blood gave it that hue" (p. 767). The red neckerchief is given to the reader as a clue; but the suggestion that the neckerchief could be red because saturated with Eugene's blood is a moment of melodrama which reminds us of the violent, bodily rupture of subject and object, the coloring given by people to things.

Paul De Man has written of the "dependence of any perception" in Wordsworth's poetry "on the totalizing power of language. It heralds this dependency as 'the first/Poetic spirit of our human life.' The possibility of any contact between mind and nature depends on this spirit manifested by and in language."[69] In this scene from *Our Mutual Friend*, only linguistic failure suggests to us the (lost) possibility of any totality; this moment is the crisis not only of the novel's plot but of the subject's position within the orders which produce that narrative, the linguistic conditions of possibility for a totalized understanding. That this was an emergent technique in a historical development is suggested by reference to Conrad, for whom it became an authorial trademark. Ian Watt notes that Conrad's "literary impressionism implies a field of vision which is not merely limited to the individual observer, but is also controlled by whatever conditions – internal and external – prevail at the moment of observation."[70] Understood in the largest sense, this technique is a register of the retreat of the individual in the face of "circumstances over which no control." Those circumstances, as I have tried to show, are not abstract or timeless ontological difficulties but social and

69  Paul de Man, *The Rhetoric of Romanticism* (New York, Columbia University Press, 1984), p. 91.
70  "One of the devices that he [Conrad] hit on was to present a sense impression and to withhold naming it or explaining its meaning until later; as readers we witness every step by which the gap between the individual perception and its cause is belatedly closed within the consciousness of the protagonist." Ian Watt, *Conrad in the Nineteenth Century* (London, Chatto and Windus, 1980), p. 178.

psychological processes particular to the fragmentation resultant from a routinized life.

Eugene is saved from the water and the fluctuations of his fluid subjectivity by Lizzie, and the novel closes with her bringing him into the orderliness of her household. Through the course of *Our Mutual Friend*, Dickens has attempted to construct discursive spaces which allow the process of imaginary identification to go forward unimpeded. Riven by a routinized, fragmenting symbolic environment, language and the space of writing prove to be unsatisfactory enclaves; the domestic arrangement of mute objects appears to be a more satisfying and coherent structural resolution to the narrative problems Dickens experienced than the arrangement of words. Domestic material culture, associated with the non-verbal processes of the imaginary more fully than the symbolic processes associated with language, offers Dickens the most satisfying space in which subjectivity can reside. The sentimentalized space of the feminized household into which the novel recedes saves the writer from the fragmentation of his professional medium.[71]

But this separation of the domestic and the linguistic cannot be maintained for any length of time. Their interconnection is suggested comically by Dickens himself when he describes an early (and uncharacteristically dusty) set of rooms in the *Uncommercial Traveller*:

I could take off the distinctest impression of my figure on any article of furniture by merely lounging upon it for a few moments; and it used to be a private amusement of mine to print myself off – if I may use the expression – all over the rooms. It was the first large circulation I had.[72]

Printing and circulation are, in this surreal image, impressed on the material culture of the home, formed by the bodily force of Dickens' domestic nature. More generally, the home was inscribed into a broad cultural discourse of moralizing domesticity, one that saw the organization of household objects as active elements in a narrative of improvement. Dickens' "domestic

---

71 Of *David Copperfield*, Vanden Bossche similarly notes that "the form of David's autobiography reinforces the division of the world into public and private realms, constraining the autobiography within the realm of the domestic and private...while excluding his [David's] writing activity ... to discuss his writings would be to bring his commercial activity into the home" (p. 106).

72 Charles Dickens, *Uncommercial Traveller*, p. 139.

nature," attentive to the hooks on the walls and the crumbs on the floor, would have approved Southwood Smith's belief that "a clean, fresh, well-ordered house exercises over its inmates a moral, no less than a physical influence."[73] One early sign of Eugene's increasing attention to "the domestic virtues," for instance, is the kitchen he has built for the rooms he shares with Mortimer: "See! ... miniature flour-barrel, rolling-pin, spice-box, shelf of brown jars, chopping board, coffee-mill, dresser elegantly furnished with crockery, saucepans and pans, roasting jack, a charming kettle, an armoury of dish-covers. The moral influence of these objects, in forming the domestic virtues, may have an immense influence upon me" (p. 337). That Eugene here mocks the moral tale written through domestic objects does not prevent this narrative from shaping the novel's conclusion. The installation of Bella and John Harmon into Boffin's richly appointed Bower "makes a pretty and a promising picter" (p. 849), a culminating image at once aesthetic and moral. The arrangement of domestic objects, as Baudrillard writes

is the "spontaneous" middle class representation of culture ... Polish and varnish (like framing and symmetry) are the exaltation of a "trivial" cultural mode which is not that of beauty and ornamentation but the moral one of cleanliness and correction. The objects here are entirely equivalent to children in whom one must first instill good manners, who must be "civilized" by submitting them to the formal imperatives of politeness.[74]

In "civilizing" his own domestic space, as we have seen, Dickens impressed his will on the idealized world of the home by patrolling it: the morning tours of the domestic policeman, the attention to the hooks on the walls, and the displacement and, finally, ridicule of Catherine. The creation of the home, this imaginary space, must be rigorously defended, its order maintained so that the sovereign will residing within it can exercise its desires and picture things in their places.

73  Quoted in Forty, *Objects of Desire*, pp. 108–9.
74  Baudrillard, *Political Economy of the Sign*, p. 45.

# 5

# Owning up: possessive individualism in Trollope's *Autobiography* and *The Eustace Diamonds*

The images of Eugene Wrayburn perched within his imaginary lighthouse, of Dickens writing in his mirrored chalet, and of the pair of them together spinning tales in the Jolly Porters' "cosy" gave us, in the last chapter, emblems of the mid-Victorian male writer protected from the increasingly pervasive pressures of modern urban society, able in these enclaves to let his imagination play with some freedom. Moving from those images to the concerns of the present chapter immediately recalls Henry James' queasy admiration of Trollope aboard the *Bothnia*, producing his daily quota of work as steadily as if he had been at his desk in London, while his shipmates lurched to the privacy of their rooms. Trollope's careful maintenance of his famous accounting books, ruled into weeks at work and pages written, his precise calibration of words to a page and pages to an hour, his unembarrassed belief that sentences should be accommodated within the same rational economy as hours and shillings, all these habits appear to locate him firmly within a buffering Weberian scheme of bureaucratized subjectivity. Like that of a faithful employee assigned to the novel-producing division of the firm, Trollope's career demonstrates the enormously enabling energy provided by the routines of commodity production for those who enter into them and make them their own. All of the other Victorian novelists I am considering resisted the commodity form; Trollope seems to have embraced it and in it found his authority and a sheltering structure.

For all their calculated effrontery, Trollope's notorious comparisons of himself with various artisans and workers – shoemakers, upholsterers and coffin-makers – do underscore his unabashed understanding of himself as a producer of "marketable commodit[ies]";[1] and his letters reveal his thorough understanding of himself as a man earning his "bread by writing," a "literary labourer ... worthy of his hire" and attentive always to "pounds, shillings and pence."[2] More significant even than his aggressive defense of his mercenary interests, however, is the silent absorption into his work of this economy which exchanges words for shillings; through the course of his career, the routines of commodity production came to be an internal, assumed part of Trollope's activity and thought, shaping his "task-work" (*Autobiography*, p. 118). As Mary Hamer has argued, "Trollope discovered form not as an ideal abstract but as a practical problem. It was contemporary publishing conditions which first imposed form of the simplest kind on the novelist's work."[3] And, as he developed as a writer, Trollope incorporated the loose strictures of part-publishing into the habits of his labor.

Trollope's own appreciation of "the things of this world" and his pride in his novels as wares make it all the more odd to discover, when we turn to the actual pile of commodities Trollope produced, that the representation of material culture there is extraordinarily thin. Trollope sees the novels he produced as objects subject to the circulation of goods – goods which the novels themselves appear to find of little interest. Even *The Eustace Diamonds*, the novel one might most expect to attend to material culture, is austerely furnished; the most remarkable thing about the titular diamonds themselves is how rarely we see them. Lizzie Eustace, the novel's central character and an "opulent and aristocratic Becky Sharp," allows Trollope an opportunity to confront many of the concerns we first saw in *Vanity Fair*; but where Thackeray clutters his novel with descriptions of goods, Trollope takes the material for granted.[4]

1 Anthony Trollope, *An Autobiography* (Oxford University Press, 1950), p. 109. All further references will be included parenthetically in the text.
2 Anthony Trollope, *The Letters of Anthony Trollope*, ed. N. John Hall, 2 vols. (Stanford University Press, 1983), vol. I, p. 194.
3 Mary Hamer, *Writing by Numbers: Trollope's Serial Fiction* (Cambridge University Press, 1987), p. 46.
4 That this book is in some degree a refashioning of *Vanity Fair* has been assumed by critics since it was first published – and, indeed, even Trollope's characters understand their actions in the terms laid out by Thackeray's book. Lizzie, for instance, sanctimoniously avers that "she had had her day of pleasure, and found how vain it was" (vol. II, p. 333) – thus using the narrative of vanity circulated by Thackeray to her own (vain) ends. Anthony Trollope, *The Eustace Diamonds* (Oxford University Press, 1983).

What Trollope does study, however, is the social activity stimulated by goods, the desires, social exchanges, intrigue, and expense which blow around the absent jewels. The diamonds first enter the tale as a sort of afterthought, at the end of a passage in which various members of the Eustace family worry about the behavior of the novel's heroine, Sir Florian Eustace's widow, and the mother of the family heir:

In that matter of the great family diamond necklace, – which certainly should not have been taken [by Lizzie] to Naples at all, and as to which the jeweller had told the lawyer and the lawyer had told John Eustace that it certainly should not now be detained among the widow's own private property, – the bishop strongly recommended that nothing should be said at present. (vol. I, p.12)

Although "nothing should be said at present" to Lizzie, a good deal is, in fact, said here about the necklace; while the jewels themselves are as notably absent from the story as they are from the Eustace family vaults, they nonetheless prompt a metonymical verbal exchange engaging the jeweller, the Eustace family lawyer, Mr. Camperdown, John Eustace, and the Bishop. When the Eustace family claims ownership of the diamonds and attempts to prosecute Lizzie for their return, the absent jewels become central to the development of the novel's plot; like a Hitchcockian Macguffin, they are absent from the narrative but serve, nonetheless, as the pretext for its exfoliation.

If the object which Lizzie possesses is most visible in its effects, the language of possession itself percolates through the novel, defining characters' moral and psychological identities as well as their relation to the material environment. In this novel as elsewhere in his work, Trollope understands identity in terms derived from the market; he is squarely in the British tradition of possessive individualism, defining the individual as "essentially the proprietor of his own person and capacities."[5] C. B. Macpherson, who has defined this Lockean tradition most fully, traces the several ways that the concept of property narrowed from the late seventeenth century to the present; most significantly, for my purposes, he describes the movement from a notion of property that includes "one's own person, one's capaci-

---

5 C. B. Macpherson, *The Political Theory of Possessive Individualism: Hobbes to Locke* (Oxford, Clarendon Press, 1962), p. 263.

ties, [and] one's rights and liberties," to one limited to "property in material things or revenues."[6] In tracing this history, Macpherson argues that the erosion of the notion of the subject as a possession was a result of the growing awareness in the nineteenth century among the working classes that "full individuality for some was produced by consuming the individuality of others."[7] In what follows I will be exploring the notion of possessive individualism and the contradictions of its logic by attending not to changes in class-consciousness but to the commodity form. Defining subjectivity as a thing possessed became a problematic enterprise when possession in general was dominated by the experience of commodities; as we saw while considering Thackeray's writing, commodities elude their owners, circulating from hand to hand, thwarting those who want to arrest their movement. In *The Eustace Diamonds* Trollope repeatedly satirizes attempts to check this circulation: the immense energies spent in forming public opinion, in imposing legal measures, and in physically protecting the Eustace diamonds from theft all prove futile. As the language of property spirals out to shape the self, the futility of possession accrues new pathos: just as the possession of commodified goods is a vexed enterprise, so the possession of the self becomes troubled in the novel.

Because his own identity as an author was proudly bound up in the production of circulating commodities, establishing a secure means by which their ownership could be assessed was, in spite of its difficulties, of great importance for Trollope. The significance of establishing a proper understanding of ownership was not unique to Trollope, of course – the various debates over copyright are the most salient sign of the broad significance of the issue – but in Trollope the need to clarify this relation is particularly pressing. Because the tension between the satirical representation of circulating commodities and his own identity as a producer of them was so fully rooted in the conditions of his literary production and self-understanding, Trollope could not resolve it in any enduring fashion. In his recurrent attempts to ease this tension, Trollope developed a moral vocabulary centering on the

---

6 C. B. Macpherson, "Human Rights as Property Rights," *Dissent* 24 (Winter 1977), p. 72.
7 Macpherson, *Political Theory*, p. 261.

terms of honesty; he worked to define an honest understanding of ownership.

# I

As if to publish his decision to avoid representing the Eustace diamonds, Trollope has his heroine fashion a cumbersome iron box for their safekeeping; this box becomes a visible emblem of the diamonds' narrative invisibility, an object frequently offered up for the reader's inspection. With the construction of the box, and with Trollope's frequent allusions to it, the diamonds become not only missing from the text but visibly missing from it. When, halfway through the novel, an attempt on the diamonds is made and Lizzie's iron box stolen, the jewels' figurative absence is literalized: the theft of the diamonds would appear to make unnecessary Trollope's scrupulous reminders of their narrative absence. With this theft, then, the diamonds do not merely appear to be missing from the text, they actually are missing from it. Except that, by a sort of authorial legerdemain, Trollope had removed the diamonds from the iron emblem of their absence before the robbery and placed them under his heroine's pillow for the night. For some sixty pages, then, the characters of the novel think that the diamonds are missing while they are, in fact, still in Lizzie's hands; and, if readers are told soon after the robbery that the diamonds have not in fact been stolen, nonetheless we still do not have them described for us. They remain missing from the narrative, unannounced, undescribed, unrepresented. Only after a successful, second robbery are the missing diamonds finally stolen (for good, one is tempted to say) and secreted away, outside the parameters of the novel's society to weigh upon the chest of a Russian princess.

In this involuted history of the diamonds, their presence and absence, we can see that even the attempt to hide the jewels merely reinvigorates the interest they provoke, making attention to the fugitive diamonds more fervid than it otherwise would be. The presence of the iron box, signifying the diamonds' absence, can only heighten characters' curiosity about its contents: when Lizzie attempts to take the necklace with her to her castle in Scotland, for instance, we are told that the iron box, "small, and so far portable that a strong man might carry it without much trouble," was, nonetheless, "so heavy that it could not be taken with her without attracting attention" (vol. I, p. 184). Banishing the diamonds to Russia thus appears as the only means of eliminating both the jewels and the attention they attract; Trollope's opinion about the diamonds' history appears to agree with that of the lawyer Mr. Dove, who, frustrated by the inability of the law to legislate ownership of the necklace, remarks that, "it is, upon the whole, well for the world, that property so fictitious as diamonds should be subject to the risk of such annihilation" (vol. II, p. 298).[8]

By insisting that this fictitious property was a gift given to her by her dead husband, Lizzie enters the jewels into a matrimonial circuit of gift-exchange. Metonymically affiliated with her body from the novel's beginning – the young Lizzie, we are told, "went about everywhere with jewels on her fingers, and red gems hanging around her neck, and yellow gems pendant from her ears, and white gems shining in her black hair" (vol. I, p. 2) – jewelry carries a conventional erotic significance which Lizzie extends and manipulates. She implicitly proposes marriage to her cousin by asking him to take the diamonds; she refuses to marry Lord Fawn because he will not accept them; and, of Lord George she thinks, "If he would only tell her that he loved her, then he would be bound to her, – then he must share with her the burthen of the diamonds – then must he be true to her" (vol. II, p. 104). Giving the jewels, she would give herself. These matrimonial designs are written by Lizzie as romantic tales, each man a potential Corsair, each development in her imagined history "a proper Corsair arrangement" (vol. II, p. 210), each scene an occasion to "indulge her passion for romance and poetry" (vol. I, p. 99). She says:

"I do feel so like some naughty person in the 'Arabian Nights,' who has got some great treasure that always brings him into trouble; but he can't get rid of it, because some spirit has given it to him. At last, some morning it turns into slate stones, and then he has to be a water-carrier, and is happy ever afterwards, and marries the king's daughter." (vol. I, pp. 286–7)

8 As D. A. Miller notes, the final burglary makes what had been, in Lizzie's case, a theft of dubious legality a firmly, unambiguously illegal action; across the course of the novel, then, theft thus moves from the drawing-room world of gentlemen to the realm of delinquency and becomes a matter which we as readers can comfortably leave to the police. See Miller's *Novel and the Police* (Berkeley, University of California Press, 1988), pp. 11–16.

"This thing of the gift," writes Derrida, "will be linked to the – internal – necessity of a certain narrative [*récit*] or of a certain poetics of narrative ... The thing as given thing, the given of the gift arrives, if it arrives, only in narrative."[9]

Once the diamonds become notorious – once Lizzie's legal right to them has been challenged by the Eustace family – and the jewels become troublesome to her, Lizzie's romantic tales run aground; but the greater the demands that she return the jewels, the greater is her insistence that she keep them. Like her figure from the *Arabian Nights*, she soon discovers that she is incapable of giving the diamonds up. Unable to unload them onto a suspicious market or to give them away to her wary suitors, she becomes unwilling to do so: at one point prior to her tacit proposal of marriage to her cousin Frank, she thinks of asking him to take charge of them, "but she could not bring herself to let them out of her own hands" (vol. I, p. 185); although she wishes "that she had never seen the diamonds," nonetheless, we are told that "it was almost impossible that she should part with them" (vol. I, p. 187). Her insistence on keeping the diamonds increasingly appears, I think, as a perverse and oddly modern form of pride, pride at work in a culture that defines identity through possession: the necklace, gained by marriage, comes to define its owner, to be felt as an essential part of her nature.[10]

Lizzie, then, gives us one set of attitudes towards ownership in the novel: she understands the necklace as a sacred gift, an instrument in her erotic negotiations, a crucial prop in the narratives that define her identity. Against these vigorously

9 Derrida, *Given Time*, p. 41. Derrida's text is an analysis of Marcel Mauss, *The Gift: Forms and Functions of Exchange in Archaic Societies*, trans. Ian Cunnison (London, Cohen, 1954), which has also shaped my thinking about the social consequences of gift exchange; among the many other commentators on Mauss' text, see the first volume of George Bataille's *The Accursed Share: An Essay on General Economy*, 3 vols., trans. Robert Hurley (New York, Zone Books, 1988) and William Miller's *Humiliation* (Ithaca, Cornell University Press, 1993), p.10.

10 "Some sort of 'gathering,'" writes James Clifford, "around the self and the group – the assemblage of a material 'world,' the marking-off of a subjective domain that is not 'other' – is probably universal. All such collections embody hierarchies of value, exclusions, rule-governed territories of the self. But the notion that this gathering involves the accumulation of possessions, the idea that identity is a kind of wealth (of objects, knowledge, memories, experience), is surely not universal." "On Collecting," p. 143.

imaginative assertions of ownership, the Eustace family, in the person of their lawyer, Mr. Camperdown, argues that the jewels are inalienable heirlooms embodying a complex and enduring relationship between the family and its members. Because families as historical entities do not fully exist at any one moment, they cannot be embodied by any one person. Heirlooms, by contrast, endure across generations, and can be in this way more adequate representations of a family than any member. As a result, a particular member of the family may possess an heirloom but does not have all the legal rights of property over it – most importantly, she or, more usually, he cannot alienate it by sale or gift. By borrowing he may raise money with it – the Eustace diamonds are said thus to be worth £500 a year – and may do as he wishes with the money raised, but the diamonds may not be exchanged or given away. The necklace could not have been presented to Lizzie and she, in now attempting to give it away, attempts to give what she does not have.[11]

Working on the assumption that the diamonds are heirlooms, Mr. Camperdown feels confident that he can legally retrieve them from Lizzie and return them to the family vaults. On asking for an opinion on the case from his colleague Mr. Dove, however, Camperdown discovers that the Eustace diamonds are probably not heirlooms at all, that this particular case is not governed by the general law regarding such property. As Dove explains it, just as the individual member of the family, who is mortal and alterable, cannot be the full representative of the family, so a particular object, unless it is unalterable, cannot represent the family as heirloom. Although Lizzie has not altered the diamonds, the possibility of their being altered legally prevents them from being claimed by the family as an heirloom. A diamond in a star of honour, writes Dove, could form part of an heirloom, "because a star of honour, unless tampered with by fraud, would naturally

---

11 Readers of Lacan will recognize this as the role of the woman seen from the vantage of the phallus and its law: "the phallus of the signifier," he says, "constitutes her precisely as giving in love what she does not have." Lacan's comments on the necessity of the phallus being veiled and the consequent production of female masquerade speak to both the odd occlusion of the jewels in the novel and the theatricality which Lizzie shares with Becky Sharp. Jacques Lacan, "The Meaning of Phallus," in *Feminine Sexuality*, ed. Juliet Mitchell and Jacques Rose (New York, Norton, 1982), p. 84.

be maintained in its original form" (vol. I, p. 258). By contrast, "the setting of a necklace will probably be altered from genera- tion to generation" (vol. I, p. 258). In this view, it is not the mater- ial nature of the heirloom but its form that represents the family; and an object with an alterable form cannot represent the ostensi- bly unalterable family.

The importance of enduring form in the laws concerning heir- looms links them with narratives and the recounting of stories:

The system of heirlooms, if there can be said to be such a system, was not devised for ... [the] protection of property ... It was devised with the more picturesque idea of maintaining chivalric associations. Heirlooms have become so, not that the future owners of them may be assured of so much wealth, whatever the value of the thing so settled may be, – but that the son or grandson or descendant may enjoy the satisfaction which is derived from saying, my father or my grandfather or my ancestor sat in that chair. (vol. I, pp. 258–59)

One has property in stories as much as in material assets and, as far as heirlooms are concerned, ownership is defined by "chival- ric" narratives which displace the materiality of heirlooms behind their historical associations.

Dove presents the law on heirlooms as a romantic deviation from normal legal activity, a transgression into the realms usually governed by writers of romance: "The Law, which, in general, concerns itself with our property or lives and our liberties," he says, "has in this matter bowed gracefully to the spirit of chivalry and has lent its aid to romance" (vol. I, p. 259). In attending to these objects the law gives itself up to fiction and becomes a chivalric figure itself, lending its aid as if to the distressed maiden of romance, interesting itself in affecting tales. Failing as heirlooms, the jewels (and, with them, Trollope's narrative of their history) escape this romantic tale. But for the worldly Mr. Camperdown, Mr. Dove's speeches on the law "almost lent poetry to the subject," and infused "a certain amount of poetic spirit" into the lawyer's bosom (vol. I, p. 259). Like Lizzie, Camperdown is swayed by the charms of romance, and Dove, unlikely as it may seem, becomes something of a dusty legal Corsair for his friend.

Having established the opposition between Lizzie's grasping need for the necklace and the family's assumption of legal right, and having used the energy of that opposition to initiate the movement of his narrative, Trollope characteristically refuses to adjudicate between their claims. That he esteems Mr. Camperdown infinitely more than he does Lizzie makes it all the more striking that he does not allow the lawyer the satisfaction of prosecuting her. Instead, as we've seen, Trollope simply relieves his narrative of the jewels by orchestrating the second, successful robbery and secreting them off his narrative stage. This empty resolution of the necklace's story, complains one minor figure, is "a most unworthy conclusion to such a plot." But such unsatisfactory endings are characteristic of Trollopian realism: here, as elsewhere, Trollope defines his realistic mode in a conventional and negative fashion as the open-ended frustration of romantic expectation, the flat shoreline exposed by the receding tide of immature romantic desires. Neither Lizzie's romantic notions nor Mr. Camperdown's will be satisfied.[12]

## II

With the diamonds' departure, however, ownership is not annihilated as a concern; from the novel's beginning the absence of the goods has appeared only to stimulate the dissemination of the language of property through the text. In scenes that are otherwise inconsequential, Trollope recurs to issues of ownership: the obscure parliamentary debate over the Sawab of Mygawb, for instance, turns on an undefined question of property rights. "'I think the prince is being used very ill,'" says Lucy Morris, "'that he is being deprived of his own property, – that he is kept out of his rights just because he is weak'" (vol. I, p. 65). Similarly, Trollope concludes his description of the hunt at Lizzie's Scottish estate by revealing that Frank Greystock has mistakenly ridden

---

12 Trollope's comment on Lady Glencora's later career characterizes his attitude towards the relationship of realism and romance generally: "the romance of her life was gone, but there remains a rich reality of which she is fully able to taste the flavor" (*Autobiography*, p. 183). On the problems and complexities of Trollope's negative definition of realism see Levine, *Realistic Imagination*; Walter M. Kendrick, *The Novel Machine: The Theory and Fiction of Anthony Trollope* (Baltimore, The Johns Hopkins University Press, 1980), especially chapter 6; and Christopher Herbert, *Trollope and Comic Pleasure* (University of Chicago Press, 1987). The last of these critics notes, in a passage typical of this view, that realism is "always an ironic, adversarial mode, but almost by definition has a strong symbiotic relationship with the conventions that it purports to do away with" (p. 107).

the horse belonging to someone else; in a few pages, this "theft" raises questions of finance, integrity, rank, and etiquette while depicting the perverse resistance to reason that issues of possession can produce (pp. 358–61).

More generally, the language of property is diffused through the tropes of the novel so that "ownership" comes to be a part of the novel's atmosphere, a barely perceived, almost invisible aspect of the narrative element. What Derrida says of "to give" is as true of "to own": "all the figures of this tropic are difficult to contain within the limits of a rhetoric the margins or 'terms' of which can no longer, in principle and in all rigor, be fixed."[13] Speaking of a letter to Lucy Morris, Trollope writes: "But by putting the letter into her pocket she could not put it out of her mind" (vol. II, p. 187). This zeugma allows Trollope to effect efficiently the exchange of the consequences of a good for the good itself, thus displacing the material by the immaterial and repeating in a brief space the larger logical movement of the novel. Here, as elsewhere, the object is of less interest than its psychological and social consequences. In the most complicated use of this figure, the diamonds are said to be "like a load upon her [Lizzie's] chest, a load as heavy as though she were compelled to sit with the iron box on her lap day and night" (vol. I, p. 187). Wearing the diamonds, having them weigh upon her chest, becomes a figure for the burden of owning these diamonds which Lizzie rarely wears; at the same time, this image allows Trollope to underscore the diamonds' erotic significance. Placing the heavy iron box and its jewels in Lizzie's lap suggests the trouble they caused for her while unblushingly equating them with sexuality. The physical weight of the box metaphorically represents the weight of Lizzie's burden while metonymically representing Lizzie's body and her genitalia specifically. Having escaped into the fugitive world of figure, objects leave their language to define all that is non-material: "The diamonds were at this moment locked up within Lizzie's desk. For the last three weeks they had been there, – if it may not be more truly said that they were lying heavily on her heart" (vol. II, p. 79).

With the figural permeation of this language through the novel, "to own" becomes the verb that shapes character, forms

13  Derrida, *Given Time*, p. 49.

social life, and molds what one knows of their relationship: Lizzie "was too young as yet to have become mistress of that persistent courage which was Lady Linlithgow's peculiar possession" (vol. I, pp. 50–1); Frank does not "possess the courage needed" to marry Lucy; "a huge, living, daily increasing grievance that does one no palpable harm," is seen to be "the happiest possession that a man can have" (vol. I, p. 34); Lizzie, who avers that Frank is the only person "belonging to me that I call my own" (vol. I, p. 98), later feels that Sir George has "robbed her of all that observance which was due to her as a woman and a lady" (vol. II, p. 223). Lizzie's honest companion, Miss Macnulty, we are told, "could not call these [personal] qualities by other names, even to the owners of them" (vol. I, p. 199). After the failed theft, the police become "sure that her ladyship was possessed ... of some guilty knowledge" (vol. II, p. 85) and soon discover that she had been possessed of the diamonds as well – at which stage, of course, the secret of Lizzie's ownership "was no longer quite her own" (vol. II, p. 114).

In a deliberate elaboration of this figure, Trollope offers his description of Lucy Morris, "truth itself," apparently jilted by her lover, Frank:

What did it matter now where she went? And yet she must go somewhere, and do something. There remained to her the wearisome possession of herself, and while she lived she must eat, and have clothes, and require shelter. She could not dawdle out a bitter existence under Lady Fawn's roof, eating the bread of charity, hanging about the rooms and shrubberies useless and idle. How bitter to her was that possession of herself, as she felt that there was nothing good to be done with the thing so possessed. (vol. II, p. 189)

Bereft of her desire for Frank, her proper due thus purloined, the anticipation of a contented future lost, Lucy's person now merely moves among objects – food, clothing, a house. In this way, while goods appear only infrequently on the stage of Trollope's text, the language of the novel transmutes what is there, even individual character, into goods whose properties and constitution are shaped by the codes of possession. And, with people given to us as goods, social life develops into a series of exchanges – thefts, losses, gifts, inheritances. Understanding the dissemination of this language of ownership through Trollope's moral and social vocabularies, we can now see that the adjudication of the dispute between Lizzie and Mr. Camperdown is a specific investigation into the general laws by which an individual may be said to own certain traits or a relationship said to possess certain qualities. The narrowly juridical issue here serves as a means of consolidating (and taming) the broader regulation of ownership through the social world.[14]

Trollope's representation of romantic interest provides an extended illustration of the permeation of possession throughout the vocabulary of social relations. As we've seen, Lizzie, covered with jewels as a child, is affiliated from the novel's opening with her possessions; in a trope which combines her dishonesty with her avarice, she is figured as counterfeit money: her "metal," Lucy Morris feels, does not "ring true" (vol. I, p. 21). One might expect that Lucy herself, the novel's principal figure of virtue, would escape the reified representation of character, but she is, we discover, "a treasure" (vol. I, p. 23; vol. I, p. 24), and Lizzie, at least, does not shy away from thinking of her in terms derived from the novel's central concern: "You may knock about a diamond, and not even scratch it; whereas paste in rough usage betrays itself. Lizzie, with all her self-assuring protestations, knew that she was paste, and knew that Lucy was real stone" (vol. II, p. 230). Figured as an object, Lucy then has her virtue represented as the proper attitude towards and behavior with possessions. She is neither covetous nor excessively proud: "what she had was her own, whether it was the old grey silk dress which she had bought with the money she had earned or the wit which nature had given her ... Lord Fawn's title was his own, and Lady Fawn's rank her own. She coveted no man's possessions, – and no woman's; but she was minded to hold by her own" (vol. I, pp. 25–6). Lucy, the most prepossessing figure in the book, may also be said to be its most self-possessed.

Having affiliated women with objects, Trollope then figures the romance of his novel as a negotiation over goods. Like other novelists, he represents marriage as a market: the extraordinary, gothic tale of Lucinda Roanoake and Sir Griffen Tewett, whose mercenary marriage drives Lucinda mad on the morning she is to

---

14 This regulation of property rights, broadly construed, thus serves as a central instance of that discipline which D. A. Miller sees permeating the world of the text. *Novel*, pp. 11–16.

be wed, is an unnerving dramatization in *The Eustace Diamonds* of the consequences of this way of thinking. But Trollope, more thoroughly than other writers, also represents marriage as a complex and uneven process of possessing, giving and sharing, as an economy which picks up and puts in motion the integrity, expectations, respect, and affective energies, as well as the financial wealth of those involved. Knowing Lucy, Frank "recognized the treasure, and had greatly desired to possess it" (vol. I, p. 165) and asks her to "share" his home (vol. I, p. 136). Indeed, Lucy understands that "he owed it to her to share" his home, and that "if he evaded his debt he would be a traitor and a miscreant" (vol. II, p. 174). Similarly, in the most extraordinary extension of this way of thinking, Trollope writes that "there are many men, and some women, who pass their lives without knowing what it is to be or to have been in love." Although these men – the passage drops its interest in women – may marry and live honest lives worthy of respect,

as men, they have lacked a something, the want of which has made them small and poor and dry. It has never been felt by such a one that there would be triumph in giving away everything belonging to him for one little, whispered, yielding word, in which there should be acknowledgement that he had succeeded in making himself master of a human heart. (vol. I, p. 120)

These men lack something the absence of which causes them to miss the truly masculine sacrifice of all they do possess; and they miss, therefore, the triumph which that sacrifice would bring when exchanged for a word acknowledging that they have mastered a woman's heart and can call it their own.

Marriage, as Trollope describes it here, centrally incorporates the circulation of a word, the entrance of language into a social economy. While the language of property disseminates through the text, transmuting intangible qualities of characters, social relations, and institutions into artifacts, language *as* property emerges as an equally significant textual force, an element circulated within its social economies. Some twenty-six letters, for instance, are transcribed through the course of the novel, and Trollope, taught by his day job at the Post Office to attend to the demands and consequences of letters' material nature, is careful to describe their effects in his novel. As they are circulated, however, their condition as artifacts is carefully noted. Frank's epistolary proposal to Lucy, for instance, lies in a pillar box for a day because of the Post Office's prohibition on Sunday deliveries. This delay causes Lucy to suffer a day's uncertainty about her future; more interestingly, as Trollope notes, it points out a curious state of ownership: though Lucy has not seen it and does not know of its existence, nonetheless, the letter "was already her own property, though lying in the pillar letter-box in Fleet Street" (vol. I, p. 132).

## III

Trollope's absorption in issues of ownership, so strong that it displaces attention from the material characteristics of the objects owned, emerges from an idiosyncratic investment in public reputation, a tacit but continual and emotional assertion that he owned the writing for which he was famous and which, at the same time, he was proud to sell. Before moving to consider Trollope's attempts to resolve the tension between ownership and exchange, I will trace out the particular way that he found his identity in the making of commodified novels.

Like Thackeray's life after the loss of his fortune, Trollope's childhood as an impoverished gentleman dramatized painful tensions between wealth and status in early Victorian England: separated from a mother for whom he appears to have had sharply mixed feelings, living with a melancholic father, so poor that "boots, waistcoats, and pocket-handkerchiefs ... were closed luxuries" to him, he could, as he entered adulthood, "appreciate at its full the misery of expulsion from all social intercourse" (*Autobiography*, p. 9; p. 11). We have seen that Thackeray, even as he moved away from this position of alienation, retained a fundamental disbelief in the forms of social intercourse and the narrative forms he used to satirize social practice; from this incomplete social and narrative interpellation Thackeray wrested a cynical and unhappy self-definition. Trollope, by contrast, found authority in the social forms from which he felt estranged as a young man; and the ownership of goods, luxuries or necessities, came to be intertwined with the "social intercourse" for which he longed.

Trollope's love of hunting – the strength of which seemed inexplicable even to the writer himself – can be illuminated, for instance, by the entrance it provided him into a social world from which he had felt estranged as a child; "to hunt," in Christopher Herbert's telling phrase, allowed Trollope "almost to become himself." At the same time, however, hunting also imposed on him a stylized image of that world's formal rules. In the field, "euphoric release and obedience to social formalities turn out ... to be identical."[15] As a postal surveyor Trollope similarly became himself through the formalities of his work, formalities which granted him authority. The apparently magical change from adolescent scapegrace to dutiful adult which came over Trollope as he entered his maturity must be linked to the access of authority and independence which came with his early move to the position of surveyor in Ireland. The frankly emotional language he uses to describe his later career – his passion, delight, love, anger, and bitterness – makes clear how thoroughly his sense of identity was "steeped ... as it were, in postal waters" (*Autobiography*, p. 283).

Describing his early job of reorganizing the network of rural deliveries in Ireland and England Trollope writes, "It was my special delight to take them [the postal carriers under his direction] by all short cuts," thus making the system as efficient as possible (*Autobiography*, pp. 89–90). Later, as Trollope travelled to Egypt, Malta, the West Indies, and America, he worked to rationalize the global postal network, harmonizing the demands of governments, commercial firms, and the particular people who worked within both institutions.[16] In Trollope the annihilation of space, which we saw effected by the Exhibition in Chapter 2, becomes a remunerative occupation and an occasion for individual identity; time, made tangible by the pages of his accounting books and the clock at St. Martin Le Grand, is the thick element through which both the civil servant and the novelist move.

Trollope's sleepless pursuit of efficiency did not produce a clerklike automaton similar to those now familiar from dystopian visions of bureaucratic existence, but an idiosyncratic man with

15 Herbert, *Trollope and Comic Pleasure*, p. 40 and p. 38.
16 Trollope's work throughout his postal career demanded that he attend to the peculiarities of individual people within the extensive bureaucratic world of the Post Office. It was a job which required "not only that the man doing it should know the nature of the postal arrangements, but also the characters and the peculiarities of the postmasters and their clerks" (*Autobiography*, p. 97); the attention to individuals enmeshed within institutions is a similarly defining and distinctive element of Trollope's writing.

eccentric behavior. Organizing his life so that he could hunt during the season, for instance, Trollope occasionally descended upon his bewildered rural customers, often women on farms in the west of Ireland, in his full hunting regalia. More striking in the present context, Trollope used the greatest symbol of Victorian efficiency – and the most effective means by which space was annihilated – in order to carry forth his activities as civil servant and as novelist simultaneously: "If I intended to make a profitable business out of my writing," he comments, "and, at the same time, to do my best for the Post Office, I must turn [my] hours to ... account ... I made for myself, therefore a tablet, and found after a few days' exercise that I could write as quickly in a railway-carriage as I could at my desk" (*Autobiography*, p. 103). Turning hours to account, making time into money, exchanging the progress of the clock for the columns of a financial diary and the lines in a novel, produces an appearance of "literary ostentation, to which," Trollope tells us, "I felt myself to be subject when going to work before four or five fellow-passengers. But I got used to it, as I had done to the amazement of the west country farmers' wives when asking them after their letters" in hunting clothes (*Autobiography*, p. 103). Following the demands of efficiency fully to their end will produce what appears to be anomalous behavior – but repetition and practice will inure one to the feeling.

The combination here – of a rationalized scheme of work and an idiosyncratic collection of personal activities and experiences – recurs in a more significant way in the practices of Trollope's writing. Consider this description of the effects of the accounting books Trollope devised, the material technology of self-regulation: "There has ever been the record before me, and a week passed with an insufficient number of pages has been a blister to my eye, and a month so disgraced would have been a sorrow to my heart" (*Autobiography*, p. 119). The conjunction of passionless, clerklike regularity with the vividly painful physical description of "a blister to my eye" is a brief indication of the general psychological situation. Turning the contradiction in the other direction, away from Trollope's biography and towards the commodities he produced, we can see the paradox of a faceless and depersonalized "novel-machine," as Walter Kendrick calls Trollope, producing novels dependent not on the mechanical plots which characterized the work of contemporaneous sensational novelists but on the representation of plausible but idiosyncratic characters.

Social formalities and rigid work schemes provided Trollope with routines through which he could "become himself"; his sense of identity and the apparently anonymous social practices through which he moved thus come together. This symbolic self-definition helps to explain the importance Trollope gives, in the *Autobiography*, to names and to publicity. His experiment with the anonymous publication of *Nina Balatka* and *Linda Tressel*, his attempt thus to obtain "a second identity," his belief that "it is a matter of course that in all things the public should trust to established reputation" (*Autobiography*, p. 206), all point to his careful attention to the proper definition of his public identity. "Over and above the money view of the question, I wished from the beginning to be something more than a clerk in the Post Office. To be known as somebody, – to be Anthony Trollope if it be no more – is to me much" (*Autobiography*, p. 107). Adherence to his scheme of work, the earnings that came with the production of "marketable commodities," and his strong desire to establish a "position among literary men" (*Autobiography*, p. 167), all come to be understood as issues of the circulation of names. When Longman refused his terms for *The Three Clerks*, Trollope tells us that the publisher said, "'it is for you ... to think whether our names on your title-page are not worth more to you than the increased payment.'" As Trollope remarks in the *Autobiography*, "I did think much of Messrs. Longman's name," but not circulating with his on a title-page; instead, he said, "I liked it best at the bottom of a cheque" (p. 109).

Trollope's concern over the use of his name and the shape of his own public reputation were not unique, certainly. Hilary Schor has shown, for instance, how Gaskell, while publishing *Cranford* in *Household Words*, had to contend with Dickens in exactly this matter of names: "Despite his professions of modesty, Dickens's name was everywhere in the journal (and in its publicity) – and his was, of course, the *only* name. All contributions to *Household Words* were anonymous – but Dickens's name ('conductor of Household Words') ran at the top of every leaf."[17]

---

17  Hilary Schor, *Scheherezade in the Marketplace: Elizabeth Gaskell and the Victorian Novel* (New York, Oxford University Press, 1992), p. 92.

Within the text of her novel as it ran in Dickens' journal, his name was omitted, and her references to *Pickwick* were taken out on his editorial authority. As Schor suggests, this move fixes Dickens as the conductor of the journal, outside of it and controlling its direction and movement – not as a figure to be located within its pages.

But if the issue of names and publicity was not Trollope's alone, he appears to have felt its tensions with particular force. As we shall see, his two desires – to make his name and to make money – are not easily or consistently distinguished in writing and thought. But in *The Eustace Diamonds* he does manage to parody the confusion between the circulation of names and of money at Matching Priory, where conversation revolves solely around two subjects. In discussing the mysterious disappearance of the diamonds, the circulation of names and their promiscuous mixing is a repeated tic of the conversation: Camperdown's name is forgotten and remembered, the name of a suspected thief is scrupulously avoided ("one mustn't mention names in such an affair without evidence" [vol. II, p. 143]), and Lord Fawn mournfully admits that his "name has, of course, been much mixed up with [Lizzie's]." In the second topic of conversation, we are explicitly told that "there is so much in a name ... such a great deal in a name' (vol. II, pp. 140–3); and, indeed, "the great question of the day" (vol. II, p. 141), the parliamentary issue which has been absorbing Plantagenet Palliser's enormous energies, turns on the question of names: "by what denomination should the fifth part of a penny be hereafter known?" (vol. II, p. 140). Here, as in Thackeray at his most mordant, "words represent money."

## IV

In "advocating the signature of the authors to periodical writing," a practice not much followed until the late 1860s, Trollope argues that "the name of the author does tend to honesty" (*Autobiography*, pp. 191–2); owning to having written a text helps ensure that the views represented are truly the author's. The relationship between honesty, ownership, and reputation finds its fullest representation in Trollope's discussion of his own literary practices, but it begins to unfold through the course of *The Eustace Diamonds* itself.

The novel opens with a set piece that displays the entrance of lies into a Thackerayan economy of debt, death, material culture, and sexual intrigue. Like Becky Sharp, Lizzie Eustace appears to have no mother, and when her father dies in the course of the novel's first paragraph she is dependent on her despised Aunt, Lady Linlithgow:

> There was literally nothing left for anybody, – and the [jewelers] Messrs. Harter and Benjamin of Old Bond Street condescended to call at Lady Linlithgow's house in Brook Street, and to beg that the jewels supplied during the last twelve months might be returned. Lizzie protested that there were no jewels, – nothing to signify, nothing worth restoring. Lady Linlithgow had seen the diamonds, and demanded an explanation. They had been "parted with," by the admiral's orders, – so said Lizzie, – for the payment of other debts. Of this Lady Linlithgow did not believe a word, but she could not get at any exact truth. At that moment the jewels were in very truth pawned for money which had been necessary for Lizzie's needs. (vol. I, p. 2)

In this scene, an early version of the later confrontations over the more valuable Eustace diamonds, Lizzie's lies get little credit; Lady Linlithgow, however, cannot get at the truth, and the jewelers soon see that it is in their interest to buy Lizzie's story. When we are told that "a proper use of her various charms" – the pawned jewels included – "will allow Lizzie to marry the immensely wealthy" and conveniently ill Sir Florian Eustace (vol. I, p. 4), the hermetic circularity of this economy is neatly traced: the jewelers take Lizzie at her word, renegotiate their terms, and extract the diamonds from hock for her; the jewels are then deployed, the marriage comes off, and the diamonds finally can be purchased from the jewelers by the man whom they beguiled. Lizzie emerges from this circuit of exchange with a noble name and a great deal of wealth reaped from the death of male relatives, the reification of her own "charms," and the shrewd merchandising of her dishonest tale.

This early investment in lies and theft, implicit in Lizzie's negotiation with Messrs. Harter and Benjamin, accrues interest as the novel continues. Manufactured as the occasion requires and entering into circuits of exchange, dishonest words are traded for goods: "the reader knows," as Trollope reminds us, that Lizzie "had stolen" the diamonds; even Lizzie herself "knew well enough" that, by claiming that they were a gift to her, "she was endeavoring to steal" them (vol. I, p. 252; p. 55). Recognizing that she "could invent any form of words she pleased as accompanying the gift" (vol. I, p. 42), she lies to retain her loot. Although she does lose the diamonds, the novel finally settles her appropriately in a marriage with Mr. Emelius, who, like Lizzie herself, lies about his property: "a man, to be a man in her eyes, should be able to swear that all his geese are swans; – should be able to reckon his swans by the dozen, though he have not a feather belonging to him" (vol. II, p. 314). The large movement of the narrative as it follows Lizzie's career takes us from the issues of property and possession to those of perjury and this movement indicates the structurally analogous positions of dishonesty and theft. "The end of it," says the sympathetic Lord George to Lizzie, "seems to be that you have lost your property, and sworn ever so many false oaths" (vol. II, p. 326); and the less sympathetic Lord Chiltern, providing a disgruntled summation of Lizzie's career, similarly remarks, "all that I can hear of her is, that she has told a lot of lies and lost a necklace" (vol. II, p. 375).

When Lizzie herself suffers the theft of the diamonds, we are told that she "felt that fresh trouble was certainly coming upon her. She had learned now that the crime for which she might be prosecuted and punished was that of perjury, – that even if everything was known, she could not be accused of stealing" (vol. II, p. 215). With this shift of interest Trollope juxtaposes Lizzie's thoughts about her two crimes – a theft which cannot be legally prosecuted, and a lie which can:

What had she done? She had stolen nothing. She had taken no person's property. She had, indeed, been wickedly robbed ... If it had not been for one word ... she could still have borne it well. She had told a lie; – perhaps two or three lies. She knew that she had lied. But then people lie every day. She would not have minded it much if she were simply to be called a liar, but ... she would be accused of – perjury. There was something frightful to her in the name. (vol. II, p. 260)

When Major Mackintosh finally tells her that she has "given incorrect versions" of the narrative of the robbery, Lizzie can still reply: "I know I have. But the necklace was my own. There was nothing dishonest" (vol. II, p. 264). "It could not be real, wicked perjury," she says elsewhere, "because the diamonds had been her own" (vol. II, p. 286). This conflation of honesty and possession, which we might simply attribute to the vagueness of

Lizzie's legal and moral thought, in fact pervades her society: "people," we are later told, "did not think so very much of perjury, – of perjury such as hers, committed in regards to one's own property" (vol. II, p. 293). "After all," remarks Mr. Dove, "she has only told a fib about her own property" (vol. II, p. 296). To own a good somehow also brings with it the right to lie about it: possession not only defines social relations, individual character, and behavior, it also seems to authorize representations of truth.[18]

But, by Trollope's lights, when words become elements of a material economy – when they are exchanged for diamonds, love, admiration, recognition – then dishonesty effects an unequal exchange, and becomes, practically and structurally speaking, a theft. When Lizzie lies about her possession of the diamonds, when she falsely says they are a gift from her husband for her to dispose of as she likes, she is no less a crook than the novel's later, more clumsy, burglars. To lie, in *The Eustace Diamonds*, is to steal and "to own" is, of course, to tell the truth: Frank was "frank enough in owning to himself" that he had been weak (vol. I, p. 113); Lucy, after claiming that Lord Fawn has spoken an untruth, "must own it" (vol. I, p. 262); Lizzie "thought it better to own" that she knows Mr. Benjamin, that she "had once owed him two or three hundred pounds" (vol. II, pp. 96–7). Indeed, we are told, Mr. Camperdown finally "owns that he was wrong" about the laws of heirlooms (vol. II, p. 149). Speaking of the diamonds, Lord Fawn insists that Lizzie must "own, with all deference and good feeling" that he had requested that she "give up the actual possession of the property" (vol. II, p. 250). Finally, after Lizzie has lost the jewels she thinks she owns and is sent to court as a witness against the men who made off with them, she is asked by the prosecuting barrister – who "seemed to possess for the occasion the blandest and most dulcet voice" – whether, after the first, unsuccessful robbery, she had announced the theft of her jewels "of her own will," even though "she knew that the jewels were

18  Similarly, Trollope apprehends the concerns which led him to write *The Way We Live Now* as a matter of honesty and opulent ownership: "A certain class of dishonesty, dishonesty magnificent in its proportions, and climbing into high places, has become at the same time so rampant and so splendid that there seems to be reason for fearing that men and women will be taught to feel that dishonesty, if it can become splendid, will cease to be abominable" (*Autobiography*, pp. 354–5).

actually in her own possession." In the court, forced to acknowl-
edge her lies, Lizzie is humiliated – and, thus, as Trollope writes,
"it must be owned that poor Lizzie did receive ... some of that
punishment which she certainly deserved" (vol. II, p. 320).

## V

This confusion – between ownership and truth – is not limited to
the world within Trollope's novel; it extends beyond that world to
impinge on the construction of novels like *The Eustace Diamonds*.
On one level, matters of representation themselves were presented
in terms which linked the honesty of representation with the status
of novels as commodities; on another level, Trollope's rigorous
attention to the production of his texts and their materiality – their
introduction into the economies of commodity exchange – made
him scrupulous about ethical matters of production and property.
Trollope's analysis of "true portraiture" is bound up explicitly with
the novel's status as a good produced according to laws of supply
and demand; and his understanding of authors as the producers of
commodities is written in terms of honesty and dishonesty.

The first of these two concerns – the honesty of representation
– is traced out in "Too Bad for Sympathy," the chapter in which
Trollope defends his designation of Frank Greystock as the
novel's hero. "A man," we are told, may be "untrue to his troth, –
and leave true love in pursuit of tinsel, and beauty, and false
words, and a large income. But why should one tell the story of
creatures so base?" (vol. I, p. 317). The reader Trollope constructs,
"not unnaturally imagines that a hero should be heroic" (vol. I,
p. 319). Trollope's reply to this criticism has been given, implicitly, in his representations of Lizzie: the desire for a hero of
romantic proportions, for a Corsair, is false, leads to a misunder-
standing of life's events, and, finally, encourages false actions.
"We cannot have heroes to dine with us. There are none" (vol. I,
p. 319). The domestic is the standard against which character is
evaluated, not the heroic achievements of romance; honest books
should concern those whom we love in daily life and with whom
we share our meals. "There is no gift which an author can have
more useful to him" than the ability to paint portraits effectively;
but those portraits should be of men as they are found in their
routine occupations (*Autobiography*, p. 99).

The pressures to represent life in dishonest ways, however, are various and strong. The criteria of an aesthetic tradition that delights to "paint the human face as perfect in beauty" have been espoused by critics and internalized by individual artists themselves, so that, Trollope argues, they would not themselves appreciate any work they performed which was more purely realistic (vol. I, p. 318). More forcibly, however, Trollope asserts that the pressures of the market encourage this dishonest representation:

> Go into the market, either to buy or sell, and name the thing you desire to part with or to get, as it is, and the market is closed against you. Middling oats are the sweepings of the granaries. A useful horse is a jade gone at every point. Good sound port is sloe juice. No assurance short of A 1. betokens even a pretence to merit. And yet in real life we are content with oats that are really middling, and very glad to have a useful horse, and know that if we drink port at all we must drink some that is neither good nor sound. In those delineations of life and character which we call novels a similarly superlative vein is desired. (vol. I, p. 319)

With less hesitation than Thackeray, Trollope locates novels firmly in the same economy as port, horses, and oats; not only are the claims made about books by advertisers superlative, the construction of character and plot is seen to be subject to the inflationary pressures of the market. This complaint, disingenuous from a man who had been both well-praised and well-paid for the realism of his portraits, allows Trollope to reassert the honesty of his descriptions, to distinguish his novels from mercenary romances, and, at the same time, to distinguish himself from his hero. Like Frank himself, novelists may leave truth in pursuit of false words and a large income, but Trollope will abjure feminized romantic characters and present "truth of description, truth of character, human truth as to men and women" (*Autobiography*, p. 229).

In describing Frank's weakness, prior to defending it and defending his representation of it, Trollope characteristically points out that people like his hero exempt themselves from the rigorous standards of behavior which apply to others: "they attempt to be merry without being wise, and have theories about truth and honesty with which they desire to shackle others, thinking that freedom from such trammels may be good for themselves" (vol. I, p. 317). The form of this argument is found frequently in Trollope's work, and he describes its venality in a range of degrees, from hypocrisy to honest self-deception. In *Phineas Finn*, for instance, Mr. Monk remarks that

"There are general laws current in the world, as to morality. 'Thou shalt not steal' for instance … But the first man you meet in the street will have ideas about theft so different from yours, that, if you knew them as you know your own, you would say that his law and yours were not even founded on the same principle. It is compatible with this man's honesty to cheat you in a matter of horseflesh, with that man's in a traffic of railway shares."[19]

But the most characteristic instance of this argument, this meditation on the relation of general law and individual behavior, is found in the *Autobiography*, where Trollope defends his own mercenary attitude towards writing.[20] If, at the level of representation Trollope decries the pressures of the market, at the level of production, he has little problem with them.

Those who preach the doctrine of the contempt of money, he writes,

require the practice of a so-called virtue which is contrary to nature, and which, in my eyes, would be no virtue if it were practiced. They are like clergymen who preach sermons against the love of money, but who know that the love of money is so distinctive a characteristic of humanity that such sermons are mere platitudes called for by customary but unintelligent piety. (*Autobiography*, p. 105)

"Honesty," in Mr. Monk's sense of the word, requires that mercenary desire be seen as a natural and beneficial quality. And, in naturalizing capitalist self-interest, Trollope characteristically uses the language of property: "Brains that are unbought," he insists, "will never serve the public much" (p. 107). This naturalization of the author's mercenary pursuits – "the natural bias of his interest" as Trollope calls it (p. 108) – seems to contravene the argument made in the novel against the forces of the market: on the one hand, Trollope suggests that the pressures of the market lead to "untrue portraiture"; on the other he suggests that pro-

19  Anthony Trollope, *Phineas Finn* (Harmondsworth, Penguin, 1972), p. 549.
20  In *Trollope and Comic Pleasure*, Herbert provides an extended analysis of this form of moral analysis in Trollope (pp. 158–63); he similarly finds it most fully tested in *The Eustace Diamonds* and most fully displayed in the passage I will consider from the *Autobiography*.

ducing commodities for financial gain is an honest and natural human practice.

The tension between honesty and the market, returning as the shaping problem of literary production, does not slacken; possession and perjury, owning and owning up remain uneasily juxtaposed in Trollope's mind. As a problem endemic to the mode of literary production in which he comfortably found himself, it required persistent attention and regulation. And, as result, Trollope returns to the issue again and again, revising his terms in accordance with particular circumstances. His continuing work on behalf of international copyright agreements – as a member of the Royal Commission on the subject in 1877–8, in his letters, and in his essays – provided one central occasion for such regulation. Victorian law regarding international copyright, like that regarding heirlooms and gifts in *The Eustace Diamonds*, was unable adequately to regulate the rights of ownership, and Trollope's abiding investment in matters of public identity made it virtually inevitable that he would become much involved in the issue. "To you and me," he wrote James Russell Lowell in an open letter published in the *Athenaeum*, "and to men, who, like us, earn our bread by writing, the question is, of course, one of pounds, shillings and pence, or of dollars and cents." Whatever the name of the coinage – whether pound, shilling, dollar, cent, or palliser – the issue was, for Trollope, one of honesty. "For myself," he wrote, "I profess that I regard my profession as I see other men regard theirs: I wish to earn by it what I may honestly earn"; as a result, he pleads "for the honest payment for goods supplied" by English writers to America and, similarly, "the honest payment for goods supplied" by American writers to England.[21]

As matters were regulated at the time Trollope wrote, American publishers were free to pirate editions of British writers without contracting with either the writer or with his or her publisher. Trollope had suffered in particular from Harpers in New York, which had published his works and undercut his attempts to negotiate with other American publishers; indeed, their publication of Trollope's work had become so regular that he was seen as one of their authors, his name appearing regularly

---

21  Trollope, *Letters*, p. 194

over theirs on the title-pages of books. "'You are Mr. Harper's property'" he was told by other American publishers; "it was in vain," Trollope writes, "that I declared that I had not made myself over to the Messrs. Harper."[22]

The most emblematic instance of the historical and personal dilemma that arises out of the troubled relations of possession, identity, and honesty as Trollope conceived them, remains his encounter with Charles Reade. In April 1872, while *The Eustace Diamonds* was appearing each month in *The Fortnightly Review*, *Shilly Shally*, the play Reade based on *Ralph the Heir*, appeared under both their names but without Trollope's authorization. Reade wrote to Trollope, then in Australia visiting his son, not to ask his permission nor to suggest a collaboration, but to announce the dramatization as a *fait accompli*; although improved postal communications had reduced the time letters took to cross the globe, the play was running on stage before Trollope received Reade's letter. Upon receiving it Trollope fired back an angry note to Reade, a second to his own publisher, George Smith, and one to *The Pall Mall Gazette*, publicly disavowing the play; a month later, when he discovered that the play had been accused of indecency, he wrote a fourth to *The Daily Telegraph*.

Domestic copyright law could, in this case, do nothing for Trollope, even if he were inclined to use it. In the following year, and not in reference to his own work, Trollope would argue that the plot of novels, as well as the particular words used, should be protected by copyright: "if a dramatist have a property in the plot of his play or a novelist in the words of his story, – why should not the novelist have a similar property in his

---

22 Trollope, *Letters*, p. 197. Given this frustration with the use by Americans of his name, consider what Trollope would make of the following advertisement appearing in *The New York Times* on 18 February 1979: under a heading "Original Autographs at Altman's," the New York department store B. Altman's listed for sale a series of autograph letters each accompanied by a fine, framed engraving: the autographs of John Tenniel ($35); Queen Victoria (initials only, $25); R. L. Stevenson ($500); William Wordsworth ($200); Florence Nightingale ($150); Abraham Lincoln and William Seward ($1750), and Zola ($275), were available to the interested public. Trollope's autograph letter, written on 20 August 1866 went for $275.00 – and all we are given of its contents is: "I take very great interest in the subject of International Copyright" (p. 46; see also Trollope, *Letters*, p. 350). Long after Trollope died Americans continued to profit from the sale of his name, on exhibition in a commercial palace.

plot?"[23] Not only should printed words be possessions, but the immaterial narrative form itself should become a commodity. But in 1872 Trollope was not wholly certain of the relevant legal points: "As to the plot you say you have law on your side," he wrote to Reade after the latter informed him of the play's existence. "I did think that the copyright law was against you, – but I take it for granted you are right. At any rate I should not trouble the lawyers."[24] "I think," he wrote later, "that one author should not require the law to protect him from such usage at the hands of another."[25]

But, "let the law be as it may," Trollope insisted, "I do not think it right that one man should put anothers man [sic] name on a play bill or a title page without the sanction of that other man, nor that a play writer should take the plot of a contemporary writer without his sanction."[26] Again, in the letter to the *Gazette*, Trollope wrote: "I wish to let it be known that though I was responsible for the novel, as was shown by my name on the title-page, I am in no way responsible for the play though my name has appeared on the play bills."[27] And in the *Telegraph*: "My name has been used without my sanction, and my plot adopted without my knowledge … [A]s I claim no share in the dramatic merits of the piece, so neither am I responsible for its faults, though it has been made to bear my name."[28] Reade's response to Trollope's complaints was to announce that he had "'decided to give Mr Trollope half the receipts of "Shilly-Shally," and, by the same rule, half the credit.'"[29] Reade could not understand that, in Trollope's eyes, "credit" and money do not follow the same rule: if Trollope "'objects to his name being connected with the play,'" Reade argued, then "'his only connection shall be with the receipts.'"[30] But having his name on a cheque, while generally pleasant, was not in this case what Trollope wanted.

In the *Autobiography*, Trollope returns to this event in the course of a more complete discussion of the issues involved and

23  Trollope, *Letters*, p. 587.          24  Trollope, *Letters*, p. 1012.
25  Trollope, *Letters*, p. 563.          26  Trollope, *Letters*, p. 1013.
27  Trollope, *Letters*, pp. 562–3.          28  Trollope, *Letters*, p. 563.
29  R. H. Super, *The Chronicler of Barsetshire* (Ann Arbor, University of Michigan Press, 1988), p. 310.
30  Quoted in Super, *Chronicler of Barsetshire*, p. 310.

Reade's habits become the occasion for a lengthy meditation on honesty and ownership:

Of all the writers of my day he has seemed to me to understand literary honesty the least. On one occasion, as he tells us in this book [*The Eighth Commandment*], he bought for a certain sum from a French author the right of using a plot taken from a play, – which he probably might have used without such purchase, and also without infringing on any international copyright act ... The plot was used by Reade in a novel; and a critic, discovering the adaptation, made known his discovery to the public. Whereupon the novelist became very angry, called his critic a pseudonymuncle, and defended himself by stating the fact of his own purchase. (p. 254)

Like Lizzie Eustace, Reade seems to think that owning a good gives him the right to lie about it. Although the law here, as in *The Eustace Diamonds*, did not regulate the problem, Trollope himself finds terms with which to castigate his fellow writer:

In all this he [Reade] seems to me to ignore what we all mean when we talk of literary plagiarism and literary honesty. The sin of which the author is accused is not that of taking another man's property, but of passing off as his own creation that which he did not himself create. When an author puts his name to a book he claims to have written all that there is therein, unless he makes direct signification to the contrary. (p. 254)

Again, "some years subsequently," Trollope writes,

there arose another similar question, in which Mr. Reade's opinion was declared even more plainly, and certainly very much more publicly. In a tale which he wrote he inserted a dialogue which he took from Swift, and took without any acknowledgement. As might have been expected, one of the critics of the day fell foul of him for this barefaced plagiarism. The author, however, defended himself, with very much abuse of the critic, by asserting that whereas Swift had found the jewel, he had supplied the setting; – an argument in which there was some little wit, and would have been much excellent truth, had he given the words as belonging to Swift and not to himself. (pp. 254–5)

Literary jewels, like the Eustace Diamonds themselves but unlike heirlooms, are vulnerable to modification and change; they can be set and reset in new arrangements. Although fictional goods, unlike fictitious objects, should not be subject to the annihilation which comes with plagiarism and theft, determining to whom the words belong, like determining the legal status of the diamonds, is a matter not subject to absolute determination.

To maintain an adequate attribution of the ownership of literary commodities, then, a regular monitoring of self and others appears required. "I have never," he writes in his *Autobiography*, "printed as my own a word that has been written by others" (p. 116). To do so, obviously, would be to violate the canons of literary honesty which he has devised across the course of his career; it would be to steal the words of another and dishonestly present them as his own. He does, however, admit to one exception in a footnote to the *Autobiography*: "The legal opinion as to heirlooms in *The Eustace Diamond* was written for me by Charles Mereweather, the present Member for Northampton. I am told that it has become the ruling authority on the subject" (p. 116). The *Autobiography*, as is only proper, serves here as a sort of final keeping of accounts, a rendering of property, honesty, and language; and in it he writes, "I think that an author, when he uses either the words or the plot of another, should own as much" (p. 116).

ers of that hearth is analogous to the relationship between novels and their readers; the novelist of domestic realism is something of a household designer, shaping the morality and intelligence of his or her readers.

We will return to the novelist's role as educator below; for the moment, it is enough to stress again the importance Eliot gave domestic design: "The subtle relation between all kinds of truth and fitness in our life forbids that bad taste [in domestic ornamentation] should ever be harmless to our moral sensibility or our intellectual discernment."[7] In spite of this importance, however, Eliot's involuted and defensive phrasing – "forbids that bad taste should ever be harmless" – suggests that the association between taste in ornamentation, morals, and intellect is cryptic at best. To understand this relation, Eliot constructs a series of descriptive metaphors, the most significant of which is appropriately familial and domestic. Innovators in design, she writes, are "modifying opinions, for they are modifying men's moods and habits, which are the mothers of opinions, having quite as much to do with their formation as the responsible father–Reason."[8] As I have suggested, domestic habit often rests beneath reflective consideration, as *doxa*, an unconsidered base silently shaping both activity and opinion.[9] Eliot conventionally genders domestic concerns, linking material culture with mood, habit and women, but it is the very obscurity of the power exercised by material culture which most completely associates it with the feminine. As Nancy Armstrong has convincingly argued, the distribution of power effected by domestic ideology means that women hold sway over those realms which are least visible – "the hidden mechanism of the heart" as Fredric Rowton had it.[10] *Middlemarch* is explicit about this obscured power, and attempts to revalue its realms: "the growing good of the world," as the novel famously claims, "is partly dependent on unhistoric acts."[11] Eliot's re-evaluation of taste in ornamentation partici-

---

7  George Eliot, "Grammar of Ornament," *Fortnightly Review* 1 (1865), p. 124.

8  Eliot, "Grammar," p. 124.

9  For a discussion of *doxa*, see Bourdieu, *Outline of a Theory of Practice*, p. 164.

10  Quoted in Nancy Armstrong, *Desire and Domestic Fiction: A Political History of the Novel* (New York, Oxford University Press, 1987), p. 40.

11  George Eliot, *Middlemarch* (London, Penguin, 1965), p. 896. All further references will be given parenthetically in the text.

pates in this larger re-evaluation of the unhistoric acts of those living hidden lives.

At the same time, Eliot is clearly devaluing feminine material culture – it opposes "responsible" reason. Her discomfort with material culture arises from the ability, associated with the feminine, to operate beneath the notice of reason. While material culture can be associated with wider thoughts and cares, the connection is suspect. When Eliot does focus on material culture – training the light of responsible reason on that unconsidered source of moods and habits – her concern is that which occupied us most fully in the first chapter: the alienation of people from the goods around them. In discussing Thackeray I argued that he finally understood no way to represent the relation of people to things other than by the estranged relation of the commodity form. This estrangement, while continually producing frustration, also allowed Thackeray to maintain his sense of a perceiving subject which desired and potentially might possess the things of the world. One sign of Eliot's shared concern is her use in *Middlemarch* of the same institutions and practices which figured prominently in Thackeray's narrative – auctions, pawnshops, and gambling. But Eliot's central representation of estrangement comes through her depiction of female attire. Women's dress is the paradigmatic instance of material culture in *Middlemarch*, the emblem of its structural importance for Eliot's understanding of subjectivity and social relations. What Slavoj Žižek would call "external custom," the material support for unconscious dispositions, finds its clearest expression in the clothing of the novel: *Middlemarch* opens, after the "Prelude," with a description of Dorothea Brooke's ornamentation, its successive chapters develop this initial concern, and its climax is, remarkably, presented as a recognition of the proper attitude towards adornment.

# I

Dorothea disdains the kind of attention to dress that *Middlemarch* openly displays: "Miss Brooke had that kind of beauty which seems to be thrown into relief by poor dress" (p. 29). She dresses plainly and scorns attempts at achieving "mere effect" (p. 114); Eliot, however, is keenly aware of the effects and importance of

Dorothea's apparel. Class pride and "well-bred economy" are two reasons Eliot gives for Dorothea's "plain dressing" (p. 29), but these social factors are quickly and firmly subordinated to a personal cause:

> she could not reconcile the anxieties of a spiritual life, involving eternal consequences, with a keen interest in guimp and artificial protrusions of drapery. Her mind was theoretic, and yearned by its nature after some lofty conception of the world which might frankly include the parish of Tipton and her own rule of conduct there. (p. 30)

There are alternative ways to consider dress: as Eliot indicates, it can be an indicator of class habits, but it can also be seen as an object of desire or need, the product of labor, an index of modesty, or an alienated commodity. But for Eliot dress primarily expresses character. Dorothea's scorn of the "solicitudes of feminine fashion" (p. 30) is an expression of her "theoretic" and abstract mind.

The contrast between Dorothea's austere clothing and the attention paid it by the narrator is characteristic of a more wide-spread mid-Victorian pattern. Although Eliot is describing dress from the thirties, the attention she pays it is characteristic of later decades. After the "raffish splendour" and individual flamboyance of the Regency, two trends came to shape mid-Victorian dress: the development of *haute couture* brought an exclusivity felt more broadly through society and the increasing power of mass manufacture encouraged the standardization of fashion. Charles Worth's great success, the continuing importance of widely circulated fashion news and plates, and the increasing use of paper patterns made fashionable clothing more broadly influential. The invention of the sewing machine and the development of large retail stores selling goods to be shipped throughout the Empire and making their money on quick sales, large volume, and a small margin of profit, indicated an increasing flattening of fashion distinctions.[12]

---

12 See Madeleine Ginsburg, "Clothing Manufacture 1860–1890," in *High Victorian Costume 1860–1890* (London, Victoria and Albert Museum, 1969), pp. 2–4; Janet Arnold, "The Cut and Construction of Women's Dresses," also in *High Victorian Costume*, pp. 21–9; Levitt, *Victorians Unbuttoned*, pp. 11–13; Geoffrey Squire, "Men and Angels; Fashion 1830–1860," in *Early Victorian Costume 1830–1860* (London, Victoria and Albert Museum, 1969), p. 5; and, finally, Marion Sichel, *Costume Reference 6: The Victorians* (London, B. T. Batsford, 1978).

Along with these developments in fashion, technology, and marketing, there emerges both a standardization in fashion and an obsession with discovering increasingly fine distinctions: "The dissection will be rapid but complete; it will extend to every detail – hands, feet, hair, and undergarments, will each receive a scrutinising glance, and opinion will be formed on the assemblage of them all, not on any single element."[13] The very obscurity of sartorial significance fuels scrutiny; the more plain dress is, the more one must study it to discover its significance. There was no monolithic sumptuary regulator in the culture – many writers established their own principles of dress – and this meant that interpretation of dress was more energetically insecure. As elsewhere, indeterminate codes encourage the overdetermination of meaning.

At the same time, as Richard Sennett asserts, "people began to take [appearances] more seriously, as signs of the personality of the wearer."[14] Dress was, as one writer in the 1870s had it, "a most eloquent expositor of the person";[15] in 1868, Caroline Stephen put this common view even more forcibly: "It is as hard to draw the line between person and dress as between mind and matter, and there is, perhaps, no form of matter into which, and by which, mind can infuse a more subtle and incalculably radiating influence than it does by and into dress."[16] Although mind's influence on matter is incalculable, Stephen provides her readers with a grammar of color and character: cold colors (steel grey, black) expressing severe natures, primary and delicate colors (pure blue, white, soft grey) expressing simplicity, and deep full colors (violet, deep blue, maroon) representing a self-controlled character. Without this scholastic precision, Anne Mozley notes that even the clothes of a man will "declare what he is in spite of himself."[17] This subtle infusion of character into clothing provides the basis for perhaps the most characteristic Victorian term

13 [Fredric Marshall], "French Home Life," *Blackwood's Magazine* 112 (August 1872), p. 167.
14 Sennett, *Public Man*, p. 164.
15 Quoted in Valerie Steele, *Fashion and Eroticism: Ideals of Feminine Beauty from the Victorian Era to the Jazz Age* (New York, Oxford University Press, 1985), p. 132.
16 [Caroline Stephen], "Thoughtfulness in Dress," *Cornhill* 18 (1868), p. 286.
17 [Anne Mozley], "Dress," *Blackwood's Magazine* 97 (April 1865), p. 429.

of sartorial praise: "honesty." Honest clothing generally meant dress which used no deceptive materials and which accurately represented the age and station of the wearer; but this anthropo-morphic figure of praise could only be used because the infusion of personality into adornment was complete. Clothing assumed a human, moral nature.

Dress represents personality, but this does not remove it from social concerns. One early critic of *Middlemarch* adopted Eliot's use of dress as the central emblem of feminine nature, and imag-ined "our young ladies" becoming "Dorotheas, with a vow to dress differently from other women, and to regulate their own conduct on the system of a general disapproval of the state of things into which they are born."[18] The attitudes of women were public issues, needing surveillance, and dress, as an indicator of such attitudes, thus became an important sign of social well-being. Personality, as Sennett has it, enters into society, and dress, as one conduit for its entrance, becomes of great importance to public discourse, worthy of the most intense dissection, scrutiny and evaluation.[19] While Eliot explains that the reasons for Dorothea's choice in dress are personal, her character's attire also sets into relief the "meanness of opportunity," and the "hin-drances" of a world without "coherent social faith," laid out in the novel's Prelude (pp. 25–6). Dorothea's clothing is immedi-ately likened to a "paragraph of to-day's newspaper" (p. 29), against which Dorothea's "stature" and "bearing" stand out like a biblical quotation. Eliot in this way has dress represent both Dorothea's "general disapproval of the state of things" and the state of things itself. Ground and background at the same time, dress is Dorothea and that against which she stands in relief. The division within women's subjectivity which I have been noting through the previous chapters – as both consumers and things consumed – recurs here. Gaskell negotiated this division by reconceiving subjectivity altogether, presenting it as tactical and everyday; but in the other texts considered, female subjectivity has been uneasily divided: Becky Sharp simultaneously was the emblem of commodified personality and the most skillful manip-ulator of commodities; the women at the Exhibition were both

18  Unsigned review of *Middlemarch*, in David Carroll, *Critical Heritage*, p. 315.
19  Sennett, *Public Man*, p. 193.

ideal viewers and objects viewed; and female characters in *Our Mutual Friend* were treated as objects by Dickens' reifying will while they were also agents of redemption.

In *Middlemarch*, the mechanism which negotiates the logical slippage between the two rhetorical functions of Dorothea's plain dress is, of course, repression: Dorothea represents herself in her dress by renunciation or negation, her vibrant mind expressing itself not in vibrant colors but, typically, in black or white. This repression does not belittle the importance of dress; it supports that importance while containing it. Clothing harmonizes what John Kucich calls "the essential contradiction in Dorothea," which, "might be said to lie between two kinds of desire – one appetitive and sensuous, the other self-renouncing and ascetic."[20]

In this regard, Dorothea is explicitly contrasted to her sister, Celia, and then, more fully, to Rosamond Vincy, whose desires express no equivalent asceticism. When Rosamond first appears at length, the description, like the initial depiction of Dorothea, attends closely to her attire, but sharply distinguishes between the two women:

> Much the same sort of movement and mixture went on in old England as we find in older Herodotus, who also, in telling what had been, thought it well to take a woman's lot for his starting-point; though Io, as a maiden apparently beguiled by attractive merchandise, was the reverse of Miss Brooke, and in this respect perhaps bore more resemblance to Rosamond Vincy, who had excellent taste in costume, with that nymph-like figure and pure blondness which gave the largest range to choice in the flow and colour of drapery. (pp. 122–3)

Herodotus opens *The History* by relating the Persian account of the abduction of Io, daughter of the Argive king, by Phoenician traders: along with many other women, Io descended to the harbor where the Phoenicians were selling exotic goods and these women bought "from among the wares whatever they had most set their hearts on"; while they were among the merchandise, the Phoenicians seized Io and fled.[21] Another version of this story in Herodotus has Io not being abducted but leaving freely to avoid the shame of exposure after having become pregnant with the child of the Phoenician captain. These stories present different

20 Kucich, *Repression*, p. 141.
21 Herodotus, *The History*, trans. David Greene (University of Chicago Press, 1987), p. 33.

views of Phoenician guilt, obviously, but they also suggest the ease with which female agency, if represented as obscure, can be used to justify opposing actions: Io was either raped, or she befriended the captain freely, or she was stolen like a piece of the merchandise she was admiring. Each of these versions, however, institutes historical narration with strangers entering town and exchanging goods for women, trafficking in doubled desires.

Beginning with this allusion, Rosamond is fully associated with commodified goods, and with dress in particular. The fascinating power of commodities–"beguiled by attractive merchandise" – causes Rosamond to lose her independence. While Dorothea maintains a tension between herself and her dress, Rosamond continually attends to her clothes and their effects and thus loses herself among the commodities that adorn her. In describing Rosamond, Eliot had no truck with the idea that the variety of fashion and intensity with which women attended to it were measures of the limitation of the female sphere of action. "With most women," said one contemporary commentator on feminine attire, "dress is their one tenement and holding," the only thing "to which they can ever in strict truth apply the potent, influential, entrancing words, 'my' and 'mine.'"[22] In contrast, Eliot's representation of Rosamond, like her satire of the "mind and millinery" novels written by "lady novelists," urges women to turn from this paraphernalia to concerns she sees as more substantial.[23] Girls are "accustomed to think of dress as the main ground of vanity," wrote Eliot in *The Mill on the Floss*, and the responsible novelist must work against this tendency.[24]

The commodities with which Rosamond surrounds herself are synecdoches for the other commodified elements of her life. Products of an education at Mrs. Lemon's, her manners, talents, and, especially, her "propriety of speech" reflect the class attitudes of that education rather than independence of mind (p. 123). Rosamond is keenly aware of the ways language, like taste in clothing, creates and maintains a social elite, and she carefully polices the borders of elite status. When her mother describes the young men Rosamond has refused as "superior"

---

22 [Mozley], "Dress," p. 426.
23 George Eliot, "Silly Novels by Lady Novelists," in *Essays*, pp. 300–24.
24 George Eliot, *Mill on the Floss*, p. 301.

Rosamond replies, "Oh, there are so many superior teas and sugars now. Superior is getting to be shopkeepers' slang" (p. 126).

Rosamond implies that scarcity contributes to social value in both verbal and sartorial economies. Eliot's representation of dress operates according to a similar principle, but to Rosamond's disadvantage. Dorothea's dress has a kind of Berkeleyan ontology, existing only when it is perceived, and then only when it is perceived by certain viewers; Rosamond's dress, in contrast, is continually attended to and therefore continually represented. Because dress is seen as an expression of character, Rosamond's character is implicitly understood as more accessible and less profound than Dorothea's. Thus, in the following incidental description of the two women, Rosamond is known by her dress and Dorothea by her thoughts:

> The servant-maid, their sole house-servant now, noticed her [Rosamond] coming down-stairs in her walking dress, and thought "there never did anybody look so pretty in a bonnet, poor thing".
> Meanwhile Dorothea's mind was filled with the project of going to Rosamond, and with the many thoughts, both of the past and the probable future, which gathered round the idea of that visit. (p. 828)

Servants enter into Eliot's imagination less than Dickens', Gaskell's, or Thackeray's. Eliot concluded her essay on "servant's logic" by suggesting that masters simply not attempt to understand their servants, as the two classes share no habits of mind; and, by and large, her representation of servants in *Middlemarch* follows this advice. But Rosamond, a more Thackerayan character than Dorothea, is more accessible to her servants; since her character is defined significantly by her dress, and as that dress can be apprehended by anyone (indeed, is constructed as a public good), her servant's knowledge of her is fairly thorough. Dorothea is understood in very different ways by different characters, but everyone sees the same things in Rosamond. In this way, Rosamond superficially resembles that commodified product of the Miss Pinkertons' school, Amelia Sedley. But Eliot's character may be compared more profitably with Becky Sharp. The emotional investments of the two authors in these characters conflict: Eliot is more completely critical of Rosamond than Thackeray is of Becky, who seduces her creator while she appalls him. But both characters engage in relentless, erotic self-commodification (encouraged by an education noted but not fully described by the authors) in the service of class aspirations; and both strategically emerge from that commodification to perform actions which are felt to be threatening and duplicitous.

Contrast, then, Rosamond's accessibility to her house-servant with Eliot's description of Dorothea's maid, Tantrip, on the day Dorothea decides to take off her heavy mourning dress:

Tantrip went away wondering at this strange contrariness in her young mistress – that just the morning when she had more of a widow's face than ever, she should have asked for her lighter mourning which she had waived before. Tantrip would never have found the clue to this mystery. (p. 847)

Eliot goes on to solve the "mystery" – clothes do express character, and the narrator is able to explain the relationship between dress and subjectivity – but the relationship between the clothing and character of Dorothea is too labyrinthine for the comprehension of most viewers. A servant can understand Rosamond, but Dorothea requires an omniscient narrator.

This implied contrast is made explicit when Dorothea, concerned about her husband's health, goes for the first time to the Lydgates' house. "It was about four o'clock," we are told,

when she drove to Lydgate's house in Lowick Gate, wishing, in her immediate doubt of finding him at home, that she had written beforehand. And he was not at home.

"Is Mrs. Lydgate at home?" said Dorothea ... Yes, Mrs. Lydgate was at home.

"I will go in and speak to her, if she will allow me. Will you ask her if she can see me – see Mrs. Casaubon, for a few minutes?" (p. 469)

While Dorothea is in her carriage and at the Lydgates' door, her dress is not mentioned. We do not see her, just as we neither see the servant nor have his or her speech quoted. After the invisible, silent servant lets Dorothea into the house, however, Dorothea's clothes suddenly appear:

When the drawing-room door opened and Dorothea entered, there was a sort of contrast, not infrequent in country life when the habits of different ranks were less blent than now. Let those who know, tell us exactly what stuff it was that Dorothea wore in those days of mild autumn – that thin white woollen stuff soft to the touch and soft to the eye. It always seemed to have been lately washed, and to smell of the sweet hedges – was always in the shape of a pelisse with sleeves hanging all out of the fashion. (p. 470)

The unusual appeal to "those who know" appears to set a limit on the narrator's authority and knowledge, suggesting that she does not recognize exactly what "stuff" Dorothea wore. Dorothea's dress, even when it is described, is recondite. Eliot seems to create a stage on which Dorothea is viewed by the narrator, "those who know," and the reader, in addition to the characters who are in the room just entered. This theatrical effect is then made explicit:

> Yet if she had entered before a still audience as Imogene or Cato's daughter, the dress might have seemed right enough: the grace and dignity were in her limbs and neck; and about her simply parted hair and candid eyes the large round poke which was then in the fate of women, seemed no more odd as a head-dress than the trencher we call a halo. By the present audience of two persons, no dramatic heroine could have been expected with more interest than Mrs. Casaubon. (p. 470)

Now that Eliot wants to emphasize the rightness of this dress and the beauty of her heroine, she turns from the dress to Dorothea's body; the plainness of this dress brings out the dignity and grace of her limbs and neck, the "candid" nature of her eyes. As in the novel's opening, dress is significant as it sets off Dorothea's physical beauty.

Dorothea, in historically accurate costume, is on stage though unconscious of the fact, and, on stage, is being herself. The dramatization of the scene appears to contradict Eliot's insistence that we are receiving a true representation of Dorothea; theater is not reality. But the gesture towards the theater, by faintly acknowledging the fictionality of the scene, makes it, in fact, seem more real. Dramatic presentation elides the narrator's presence and suggests to us that we are receiving Dorothea directly. The appeal to the stage strengthens the reader's impression that Dorothea has an existence independent of the narrator's imagination (and thus indirectly strengthens the narrator's authority). Equally important, the nineteenth-century stage (particularly the melodramatic stage) could be conceived, as it is here, not only as presenting an illusion, but as presenting the truth of a person otherwise inaccessible. By figuring Dorothea as an actress absorbed in her role, Eliot is not suggesting that she is artificial, but is presenting her in her most authentic guise. "What these people tried to find in the theater," Sennett argues, "was a world where you could indeed be absolutely sure that the people you saw were genuine."[25]

In the embedded narrative of Lydgate's love for Laure, *Middlemarch* presents us with a lesson on the correct viewing of effective theatrical representation. One evening, while in Paris studying galvanism, "tired with his experimenting, and not being able to elicit the facts he needed, he [Lydgate] left his frogs and rabbits to some repose under their trying and mysterious dispensation of unexplained shocks," and goes to the theater to see a melodrama (p. 180). He has already been to the play many times and has fallen in love with its leading actress, known to us only as Laure. That evening, however, Laure appears to slip, stab and kill her actor-husband, and the initial horror of the scene comes from our discovery that what has appeared theatrical has become "real." A play has had dreadful consequences: "a shriek and a swoon were demanded by the play, but [Laure's] swooning too was real this time" (p. 180). When the subsequent legal investigation absolves Laure of any guilt in the death, Lydgate follows her to Avignon, more besotted with her for her suffering, and prepares to propose. There, however, we receive the final shock of the scene: not that the theatrical became real, but that it was real all along. "'I will tell you something,'" Laure says, "'My foot really slipped.'"

"I know, I know," said Lydgate, deprecatingly. "It was a fatal accident – a dreadful stroke of calamity that bound me to you the more."

Again Laure paused a little and then said, slowly, "*I meant to do it* ... I did not plan: it came to me in the play – *I meant to do it.*" (p. 182)

Laure is careful to note that she did not use the (false) play as an instrument of her (real) designs: "I did not plan." And yet she meant to do it: her designs emerged out of the play itself. Drama produces the real.

Lydgate twice misunderstands the relation of theater and reality, and he will suffer again from this inability to read this relationship accurately when he meets Rosamond. Initially, "Lydgate was in love with this actress, as a man is in love with a woman

25 Sennett, *Public Man*, p. 176. In *Private Theatricals* (Cambridge, Harvard University Press, 1990), Nina Auerbach traces the volatile exchange in Victorian theater between the destabilizing multiplicity of the self (associated with dishonesty) and the drive towards the unity, coherence and truth of the self.

whom he never expects to speak to" (p. 180). This spectator's love need not have developed into anything more; "the remote impersonal passion for her beauty" only passes into "personal devotion, and tender thought of her lot" when he believes that a dreadful stroke of calamity has fallen upon her; the apparent entrance of the real into the theater transforms his affections for Laure. When he "leaped and climbed, he hardly knew how, on to the stage, and was active in help, making the acquaintance of his heroine," he moved from a spectator's role to that of an actor (p. 181). Now, free from the illusions of the stage, he thinks, a real affective relationship can begin.

But Laure remains a "heroine" and, without knowing it, Lydgate never descends from the stage. Laure's acting continues throughout the events after her husband's murder culminating with her performance for the proposing Lydgate: "Laure looked at him in silence with a melancholy radiance from under her grand eyelids, until he was full of rapturous certainty, and knelt close to her knees" (p. 182). Just as the first theatrical moment was in fact one that enacted Laure's real feelings, so, inversely, the second moment of revelation (when she tells Lydgate the truth) is richly theatrical. Attentive to the affects of each action, the manipulation of emotions by gesture, Laure and Eliot carefully construct this as yet another stage. Lydgate, however, swollen with rapturous certainty, does not notice the footlights. When Laure announces her mundane reasons for murdering her husband – "he wearied me; he was too fond: he would live in Paris" – Lydgate finally believes himself in possession of the truth (p. 182). Returning to dispense mysterious shocks to his rabbits and frogs, Lydgate believes "that illusions were at an end for him" (p. 183), not recognizing that he has just played a part in a grand drama, a rabbit among the frogs, the unknowing subject of a sensational experiment with bodily effects. For Eliot's reader, however, Lydgate's participation in the illusionistic French drama created by Eliot and her character anticipates his participation in the British drama that will be staged for him. By drily framing this melodramatic tale with Lydgate's experiments, Eliot is making the larger point that truth emerges from art as well as from science; when great actresses – like Laure or Dorothea – appear on the stage, the theatrical and the true are indistinguishable.

Rosamond, like Laure or Dorothea, is an actress on the stage – but, in Eliot's eyes, she is an inept performer. When Dorothea enters the room in Lowick Gate, Rosamond remains self-conscious and artificial:

To Rosamond she [Mrs. Casaubon] was one of those county divinities not mixing with Middlemarch mortality, whose slightest marks of manner or appearance were worthy of her study; moreover, Rosamond was not without satisfaction that Mrs. Casaubon should have an opportunity of studying *her*. What is the use of being exquisite if you are not seen by the best judges? (p. 470)

Rosamond errs in thinking to take Dorothea as an model for fashion: Dorothea's dress, as we have been told, is not quite typical of her class – Celia would be a better choice. But this class distinction, like that made at the passage's beginning, is in any case discarded for a more abstract, moral one; the emulative appetites of Eliot's characters have little of the class menace of those in *Vanity Fair*. Though Eliot tells us that the scene is characteristic of a particular moment in social relations, that class history is forgotten under the weight of the subsequent analysis of individual response. Rosamond's scrutiny of Dorothea's "slightest marks" is in the service of her own pavonine self-fascination. Her understanding of herself is articulated through her appearance to others, defined by her identification with the place from which she is viewed.[26]

With Rosamond in the room is Ladislaw, but Dorothea does not initially notice him:

Dorothea put out her hand with her usual simple kindness, and looked admiringly at Lydgate's lovely young bride – aware that there was a gentleman standing at a distance, but seeing him merely as a coated figure at a wide angle. The gentleman was too much occupied with the presence of the one woman to reflect on the contrast between the two – a contrast that would certainly have been striking to a calm observer. (p. 470)

The selectivity of perception operating in the representation of Dorothea's dress is represented again by the fact that Ladislaw only sees Dorothea, and she does not see him. His dress is noted only in order to make the point that Dorothea does not attend to him; the women gaze at each other and the man chooses between them. If Rosamond feels that Dorothea is an especially valued perceiver of her dress, Ladislaw has certainly become understood by the narrator as an especially valued perceiver of Dorothea's.

26  See Žižek, *Sublime Object*, pp. 105–7.

Describing Dorothea's dress when Ladislaw is present – whether or not that dress is described from his perspective – helps Eliot establish their erotic relationship. The flaccid Casaubon, by contrast, has not been a significant perceiver: when he first meets Dorothea at the Grange, when they tour Lowick, when they meet after their engagement, and throughout their marriage generally, Dorothea's dress is not described.

When Dorothea does recognize this coated figure, Ladislaw's own dress is only minimally pictured: he takes up his hat, but we are not told whether it was silk or beaver, fawn or black. Dorothea's myopia reinforces a more widespread social habit: although the dress of men was publicly scrutinized for signs of character, clothing did not have the singular importance for men that it had for women. The attire of responsible reason was secondary. Lydgate is perhaps extreme in despising "a man who calculated his effects of his costume" (p. 634), but others would at least be indifferent.

Eliot concludes this scene by returning to Rosamond's mixture of vanity and alienation: she and Dorothea

> were both tall, and their eyes were on a level; but imagine Rosamond's infantine blondness and wondrous crown of hair-plaits, with her pale-blue dress of a fit and fashion so perfect that no dressmaker could look at it without emotion, a large embroidered collar which it was to be hoped all beholders would know the price of, her small hands duly set off with rings, and that controlled self-consciousness of manner which is the expensive substitute for simplicity. (pp. 470–1)

From Imogene, Cato's daughter, and an appreciative, knowledgeable audience we move to an audience of dressmakers. Having become beguiled by attractive merchandise, Rosamond becomes merchandise herself, her expensive manner, like her clothes, evaluated only in terms of price; retroactively, we again appreciate the contrasting plainness of Dorothea's dress. Like Becky Sharp and the women who attended the Great Exhibition, Rosamond is unable to escape the divided, paradoxical situation of being a consumer of material culture and material itself.

Because this interpellation of women in the world of self-admiring commodities was a general social phenomenon, Rosamond's attention to dress makes her fundamentally indistinguishable from the mass. Even in striving for distinction she is merely a provincial version of what Eliot elsewhere calls "one of

the ordinary crowd in silk and gems."[27] Distinguishing oneself
from the masses was then (as it remains) an acute problem: "As
society is now constituted," writes Fredric Marshall, "we rarely
seek to form any tastes whatever for ourselves; we generally take
them ready-made from the upholster, the dress-maker, the tailor,
and the *modiste* who naturally keep on modifying them as rapidly
as possible, because it is in their interest to do so."[28] The dress-
maker who provides his clients with their tastes – through fash-
ion-plates like those in the *Keepsake*, for instance – has become the
best audience (other than the consumer herself) for the packaged
woman. Like Marshall, Eliot is complaining that the logic of
mass-produced fashion excludes individual agency, restricting
the possibility of considered choice. Avoiding the solicitudes of
feminine fashion, Dorothea avoids commodification.

Only Eliot's continuing use of dress to define the contradictions of character can explain the extraordinarily odd exclama-
tion Dorothea makes at the novel's climax when she accepts
Ladislaw: "'We could live quite well on my own fortune,'"
Dorothea cries, "'it is too much – seven-hundred-a-year – I want
so little – no new clothes – and I will learn what everything
costs'" (p. 870). The novel's highest pitch of intensity is capped
with a reference to clothing; if Herodotus began his narrative by
placing a woman among goods, Eliot brings hers to its crisis by
having her heroine renounce dress. The oscillating movement of
this dynamic – wherein dress is brought to attention, its costs figured, and then is rejected – defines Eliot's understanding of material culture more generally.

Wanting little in the way of clothes is affirmed; the austerity of
the novel's opening continues, but now is determined by reference to economic necessity and (implicitly) the fear of commodification rather religious fervor. To "learn what everything costs"
resonates, of course, beyond the expense of clothing, but the sustained interest in dress makes this phrase particularly effective.

27 George Eliot, *Daniel Deronda* (Harmondsworth, Penguin, 1967), p. 617. On the
  demand that one distinguish oneself from the mass, see Bowlby, *Just Looking*,
  pp. 18–34 and Igor Kopytoff, "The Cultural Biography of Things:
  Commodities as Process," in Arjun Appadurai, ed., *The Social Life of Things:
  Commodities in Cultural Perspective* (Cambridge University Press, 1986),
  pp. 64–91.
28 [Fredric Marshall], "French Home Life," *Blackwood's Magazine* 111 (January
  1872), p. 32.

Eliot recommends responsible consumerism to her women readers, an appreciation of what one needs, and a determination to avoid involvement in adornment beyond that point; only restraint can prevent clothing and subjectivity from descent into the commodified world of dressmakers and *modistes*.

## II

Conventionally, the careful consumption of household goods was the responsibility of women: Dorothea is educated into the domestic management of the hearth, the economy which Victorian conduct books urged on women. As Nancy Armstrong argues, speaking of a process she sees continuing from the eighteenth-century, "the female character and that of the home became one and the same as she translated her husband's income into the objects and personnel comprising his household."[29] Dorothea's affirmation of love for Ladislaw is couched in terms which underscore her identity with domestic economy and the character of the home.

In the Lydgate household, unlike that of the Ladislaws, however, the husband both brings in the income and manages the domestic economy. Rosamond is concerned with the preparations for her marriage, and has handkerchiefs made and a *trousseau* supplied; but the money for these comes from her father, Mr. Vincy. Lydgate himself must buy the plate and furniture, all "the requisite things" (p. 389). And, after she is married to Lydgate, Rosamond is said to believe that good housekeeping "consisted simply in ordering the best of everything"; the problems of domestic economy are seen as "his difficulties" (p. 635), not hers or theirs.

Domestic economy then becomes a problem for the couple because of Lydgate's habits of thought:

That distinction of mind which belonged to his intellectual ardor, did not penetrate his feeling and judgement about furniture, or women, or the desirability of its being known (without his telling) that he was better born than other country surgeons. He did not mean to think of furniture at present; but whenever he did so, it was to be feared that neither biology nor schemes of reform would lift him above the vulgarity of feeling that there would be an incompatibility in his furniture not being of the best. (pp. 179–80)

29 Nancy Armstrong, *Domestic Novel*, p. 83.

Eliot is depicting the difficulty we saw in her letters: Lydgate assumes material culture is beneath his notice, unconnected with his wider thoughts and cares. And this intellectual and social pride creates the silent assumption that his surroundings will automatically be tasteful and expensive. "He could not imagine" pursuing his work

in such a home as Wrench had – the doors all open, the oil-cloth worn, the children in soiled pinafores, and lunch lingering in the form of bones, black-handled knives, and willow pattern. But Wrench had a wretched lymphatic wife who made a mummy of herself indoors in a large shawl; and he must have begun altogether with an ill-chosen domestic apparatus. (p. 389)

By giving to Lydgate the responsibility for their "domestic apparatus" – the abstract phrasing suggests Lydgate's inexperience in thinking concretely about the home – Eliot arranges her narrative material so that one dramatic focal point of her description of the marriage is the moment Lydgate first tells his wife of their trouble. He assumes that she must know they are in debt, and thinks it is wise now to discuss the matter with her. Their conversation, then, becomes a call to Rosamond for sacrifice. But her response is the "silvery neutrality" of narrow, injured propriety: "what can *I* do?" (p. 640). The answer to this question, which, as we saw, Dorothea will give, is to restrain domestic needs, buy no new dresses, and discover "what everything costs." Rosamond, however, fully interpellated in the things of her world, cannot conceive of this reply. Instead of her sacrificing private luxury for the public benefit of her husband's work, his work is, at the novel's end, sacrificed, so that her desires can be met. The couple enters a world reminiscent of *Vanity Fair*, with carriages, continental bathing sites, and gouty wealth, where Rosamond, "exquisite ornament to the drawing-room" (p. 632), circulates, upon Lydgate's death, out of his home and into the carriage of an "elderly and wealthy physician" (p. 893). Eliot's summary of Lydgate's position is precise: "Alas! the scientific conscience had got into the debasing company of money obligation and selfish respects" (p. 795). His efforts in his work to avoid being implicated in trade – perhaps most fully shown by his determination to prescribe and not dispense drugs – have come to nothing because of his domestic inattention and the "selfish respects" of his wife.

Given this descent, the next consistent step is for Lydgate to begin to gamble; that gambling initially appears out of character for Lydgate suggests that the logic of his fall has taken over from Eliot's concern with sustaining a coherent representation of character. Just as he loses his autonomy when he enters into "money obligation," so his character becomes more determined by the narrative conventions of economic decline. As I argued in the first chapter, gambling appears to take place outside of the determined circulation of commodities. Something may be had for nothing; it is an "easy way of getting money" (p. 721). But, as Lydgate comes to believe that talent is not predictably rewarded, he begins to conceive of gambling as the figure for all economic activity: "I don't see that there's any money-getting without chance ... if a man gets it in a profession, it's pretty sure to come by chance" (p. 695). By making income depend on chance, gambling makes it independent of individuals, and creates for Lydgate a form of alienation as crippling as that which affects Rosamond.

Eliot does not endorse Lydgate's belief that all money is chance-gotten, but she does argue that the relationship between talent and rewards is sufficiently attenuated for the two to be thought of as separate. Bills must be limited so that the mind does not expend itself in narrow anxieties. Daniel Cottom notes that Eliot fully enters into the ideology of the liberal intellectual, independent not only of the antiquated, aristocratic ties of literary patronage, but also of the economic world of commodity exchange. And this independence is created and maintained by a careful calibration of the relations between public and private: "What is negotiated in the balancing act maintained in Eliot's writing is a division between private and public worlds that would submit the private to the public and yet would preserve within that submission an impression of the sacrifice it entailed."[30] One of the recurrent names for this enduring impression of sacrifice is, of course, "wife"; through their self-sacrifice, women have central importance in establishing a break between domestic economy and intellectual labor. Rosamond's discontent with this role, as Eliot notes, "was due to the conditions of mar-

---

30 Daniel Cottom, *Social Figures: George Eliot, Social History, and Literary Representation* (Minneapolis, University of Minnesota Press, 1987), p. 187.

riage itself, to its demand for self-suppression and tolerance, and not to the nature of her husband" (p. 810). As the proper manager of the domestic apparatus, the wife must exercise restraint and sacrifice so that the intellectual energy of the husband could be freed up: "In the British climate there is no incompatibility between scientific insight and furnished lodgings: the incompatibility is chiefly between scientific ambition and a wife who objects to that kind of residence" (p. 732).

The material culture of the house occupies an important but suspect position in Eliot's balancing act. Material culture must be attended to by the wife so that its importance can be minimized. It must neither be ignored, nor allowed to engage her vanity, as this can lead her into excess and her husband into "money-obligation." The consequences of the alienation resulting from vain involvement in goods are graphically represented in the pages following our discovery of the Lydgate's financial problems, where Eliot associates the alienation of goods with two institutions now familiar to us: the auction and the pawnshop.

Auctions, like gambling and vanity itself, register the alienation of people from objects; as we saw in *Vanity Fair* and *Cranford*, they can cause objects to circulate without relation to the individuals around them. When we are told that Lydgate has decided to stave off his creditors by having a bill of sale drawn up on the furniture of his house, readers recognize the possibility of an approaching sale. And, as we expect, a sale is almost immediately described – but not one of the Lydgates' goods. Instead, we are given a displaced and comic version of that possibility: "The public," we are told,

> if it chose, was to have the advantage of buying, under the distinguished auspices of Mr. Borthrop Trumbull, the furniture, books, and pictures, which anybody might see by the handbills to be the best in every kind, belonging to Edwin Larcher, Esq. This was not one of the sales indicating the depression of trade; on the contrary, it is due to Mr. Larcher's great success in the carrying business, which warranted his purchase of a mansion near Riverston. (p. 649)

We have anticipated the sale of Lydgate's goods, but we get the sale of Larcher's; and, when Dorothea lends Lydgate 1,000 pounds, it appears that the threat of an auction is averted for Lydgate, that this auction of Larcher's goods will not anticipate an unhappy auction of the young doctor's. But, in an unexpected fashion, it does. The mansion into which Larcher is moving is that of "an illustrious Spa physician" such as Lydgate will become at the novel's end. Lydgate will sever his relations to the goods of his past not through the failure we anticipate here, but through the financial success that will provide for Rosamond's desires.

The auction of Larcher's possessions, as a public institution devoted to the display and distribution of private objects, recycles not merely wealth but significance: in the neatly defined and resonant narrative space formed for the competing desires of the public, the meanings of objects are developed and reinforced as their purely monetary value is recreated and calculated anew. This combination of the economic and the semiotic – which Baudrillard has analyzed as the "code of political economy" – has been laid out neatly by Featherstone's brother Solomon: "'Auctioneer's talk wild … Not but what Trumbull has made money'" (p. 348).

Thus, when a Mrs. Mawmsy worries that the fender currently on the auction block is dangerous, its edge like a knife, Mr. Trumbull straightaway replies:

Quite true … and most uncommonly useful to have a fender at hand that will cut, if you have a leather shoetie or bit of string that wants cutting and no knife at hand: many a man has been left hanging because there was no knife to cut him down. Gentlemen, here's a fender that if you had the misfortune to hang yourselves would cut you down in no time – with astonishing celerity – four-and-sixpence – five – five-and-sixpence – an appropriate thing for a spare bedroom where there was a four poster and a guest a little out of his mind – six shillings – thank you Mr. Clintup. (p. 652)

Worried that his neighbors will think his purchase rash, Mr Clintup, whose bid is not raised, says the fender was worth having just to tell Trumbull's joke. It is Trumbull's joke, then, produced in the "warming rivalry" of competitive sale (p. 653), and not the fender that is most valuable. The fender becomes merely a prop for the discourse of value produced around it. Barthes similarly described the relationship between advertisement and commodities in his discussion of dress:

This unavoidable presence of human speech is clearly not an innocent one. Why does Fashion utter clothing so abundantly? Why does it interpose, between the object and its user, such a luxury of words … such a network of meaning? The reason is, of course, an economic one.

Calculating, industrial society is obliged to form consumers who don't calculate.[31]

Clintup does not calculate the value of the good he is buying; instead he attends to the luxury of words that Trumbull so abundantly utters.

The pressure of Trumbull's language is inclusive, translating dissimilar objects into a homogeneous, monetary spectrum of value: "Surely among all men whose vocation requires them to exhibit their powers of speech," writes Eliot,

the happiest is a prosperous provincial auctioneer keenly alive to his own jokes and sensible of his encyclopedic knowledge. Some saturnine, sour-blooded persons might object to be constantly insisting on the merits of all articles from bootjacks to "Berghems"; but Mr. Borthrop Trumbull had a kindly liquid in his veins; he was an admirer by nature, and would have liked to have the universe under his hammer, feeling that it would go at a higher figure for his recommendation. (pp. 651–2)

The institution of the auction, supported by the nature of the auctioneer, determines the value of the articles for sale; the articles themselves, bootjacks and paintings by Berghem alike, are only distantly connected with the process. Eliot notes that Trumbull's job is one depending on his linguistic facility; and her implicit criticisms of that job, humorously made, include the violation of the normative relation of language (and value) to its objects.

By presenting this image of Trumbull, Eliot preemptively, implicitly defends herself from the criticism she makes of him; her profession requires writing as his requires speech, and, as we saw with Thackeray, one current criticism of writers was that they were merely representing money, their words serving as abstract tokens of exchange. In this light, novels would themselves become auctions, spaces where, under economic pressure, language is severed from the universe under the hammer, becoming merely a sign of spiralling exchange value. Eliot's principal argument against this claim, at which I will look more carefully in a moment, is that her profession distances her from objects not into the abstraction of money but into the abstraction of the aesthetic. This response is anticipated in the emergence of art at the auction itself. Ladislaw, as one understood to be knowledgeable

31 Roland Barthes, *The Fashion System*, trans. Matthew Ward and Richard Howard (New York, Hill and Wang, 1983), p. xi.

about such things, has been asked by Mrs. Bulstrode to attend the auction and to buy for her a painting by Guido Reni. When the painting comes up for sale, Ladislaw proudly registers his scorn for the crass identification of aesthetic value with economic value by bidding a mere five pounds – much below what Trumbull thinks it is worth. Trumbull chidingly comments: """Full many a gem," as the poet says, has been allowed to go at a nominal price because the public knew no better, because it was offered in circles where there was – I was going to say a low feeling, but no! – Six pounds – six guineas'" (p. 656). Under the force of Trumbull's expansive appreciation, Gray's "Elegy," like the Guido itself, is pressed into economic service. But Eliot, in turn, coopts this cooptation by using Gray's poem for the aesthetic structure of her own text: the image of hidden wealth, if rightly recalled from Gray's "Elegy," ramifies beyond this particular scene. Its widest application, of course, is to the larger themes of the book as a whole, from the cygnet among the swans of the Prelude to the hidden lives and unvisited tombs of the Finale. But, more locally, in the country yard where the auction takes place, the hidden lives of Ladislaw's ancestors are revealed to him by the blackmailer Raffles.

If Trumbull uses language to inflate the worth of the objects he sells, Raffles commodifies language – in the form of narratives about the past – in order to sell it to interested parties. We saw, in the last chapter, the anxiety of Eliot's friend Trollope regarding the economic circulation of his reputation as an author, the money which could be made from stories with his name on their paper. "A *name*," Eliot understood, "is precisely the highest-priced thing in literature."[32] In *Middlemarch*, names again are turned to money, and stories of previous days, real or fictional, are circulated for profit. "Reputation and accountability," writes Alexander Welsh of Eliot's work, "have become so impersonal that third parties are able to make a commodity of such stories which might be given away free as gossip."[33] The auctioneer, blackmailer, and the novelist share a verbal facility, entering private lives, making public and economically valuable what was

---

32  Eliot, *Letters*, vol. IV, p. 25.
33  Alexander Welsh, *George Eliot and Blackmail* (Cambridge, Harvard University Press, 1985), p. 216.

private and outside of the circuit of exchange. With something of Trumbull's jovial interest in others, Raffles describes Ladislaw's family history: "'Lord bless you, I knew all about 'em – a little in what you may call the respectable thieving line – the high style of receiving-house – none of your holes and corners – first rate, Slap-up shop, high profits and no mistake'" (p. 658). Auctions are commercial scenes, sites of the circulation of commodities and the production of value, with which Ladislaw is uncomfortable; this pawnshop is even more distasteful. The auction marks a point of transition in one person's life – here Edwin Larcher – by describing the circulation of his goods out of his hands; the receiving-house is a less legitimate version of this same process.

The pawnshop run by Ladislaw's ancestors is at the bottom of what Eliot called "the plot about Bulstrode." This line of the narrative, as Henry James complained, is melodramatic, incorporating elements of the sensation novels which had been popular in the decade prior to the appearance of *Middlemarch*. Peter Brooks notes that the melodramatic mode is bound to the "possibility, and necessity, of saying everything."[34] At the largest level of the plot in *Middlemarch*, this means the recuperation and enunciation of the past, of Ladislaw's ancestral history and Bulstrode's actions; and the agent of this recuperation is the loquacious Raffles. Trumbull's expansive language – his desire to recommend the entire universe – is also, surprisingly, aligned with this melodramatic mode; and the uncomplicated understanding of value which his speech embodies comically duplicates the clarity of the moral universe in melodrama. When, in the midst of Trumbull's unbridled comic patter, the startling image of a man hung amid the quotidian furnishings of the household rises, the submerged connection to melodrama becomes visible.

Pawnshops tend to strip narratives of the past from objects, to insist that value resides in the mobility and the power of exchange. That the plot of *The Moonstone*, for instance, should depend on the stolen jewel appearing to pass through a pawnshop is easily understood: the operative tension in mysteries, the source of their narrative interest, is between the assumption that the significance of the past can be recuperated and those forces,

---

34 Peter Brooks, *The Melodramatic Imagination: Balzac, Henry James, Melodrama, and the Mode of Excess* (New York, Columbia University Press, 1985), p. 42.

human, natural, and institutional, that oppose such recuperation. Similarly, when the prostitute Esther, in *Mary Barton*, goes to visit the Bartons, she changes her "finery" for plain clothes in a pawn-shop, borrowing clothes from those in hock, transforming herself into a woman without a history.[35] Bulstrode's determined attempt to obliterate his past – by ignoring his step-daughter, and, once his fortune is established, by repressing his life as a receiver of stolen goods – only repeats the effects of the pawn-shop itself. As a receiver of goods, Bulstrode occluded the moral history of objects in order to profit from them; in his later life he just as conveniently occluded the narratives of his own dubious past. To the degree that Eliot saw her task as the weaving of lots and the tracing of webs, the pawnshop hidden beneath the Bulstrode plot and the auction at its surface are images of an entropic process she attempts to counter; and the alienation of Rosamond and Lydgate from their goods is on a continuum with the auction of Larcher's goods and the pawnshop run by Bulstrode. The force of this entropic process is contained by her modes of representation: the pawnshop, though central to "the plot regarding Bulstrode," is described only perfunctorily; and the auction of the goods belonging to the insignificant Edwin Larcher is rendered comic. Thus, while Lydgate ignores material culture, Eliot warily recognizes its power and attempts to contain it.

# III

The crucial clue in the reconstruction of Bulstrode's past appears on the small slip of paper Raffles discovers on his visit to Rigg Featherstone:

[Raffles] jerked forward the flask and ... reminded himself by his move-ment with the flask that it had become dangerously loose from its leather covering, and catching sight of a folded paper which had fallen within the fender, he took it up and shoved it under the leather so as to make the glass firm. (p. 452)

Eliot's description of the paper and its use is empirical and direct, and the narrative quickly passes on to other concerns. The paper could be simply a demonstration of what Barthes calls "l'effet du réel," a detail signifying, by its irrelevance to

---

35  Gaskell, *Mary Barton*, p. 292.

any larger aesthetic design, the verisimilitude of the representation.[36]

But Eliot's wary attitude towards material culture encourages her to state the significance of this object more explicitly; even incidental goods in her text must be incorporated into a conscious, positive system of value. The scrap of paper does more than merely grant authority to the narrative's claim of referential accuracy; it operates within the plot as a clue. We are told, at chapter's end, that the paper "was a letter signed *Nicholas Bulstrode*" (p. 453). From this note, Raffles will later discover where Bulstrode lives and will return to blackmail him. So it is the writing on the paper, rather than the paper itself, that actually forwards the plot of the text; the paper is only a vehicle for signs. As Elizabeth Ermarth argues, throughout Eliot's writing "the objects with which human beings must contend are intentional objects: not inert objects like rocks and stones and trees, but ones informed by consciousness."[37] Material culture in *Middlemarch* is more culture than material.

Eliot has anticipated the discovery of Bulstrode's letter at the beginning of this particular chapter and, in doing so, added yet another layer of intention to the physical object:

Who shall tell what may be the effect of writing? If it happens to have been cut in stone, though it lie face downmost for ages on a forsaken beach, or "rest quietly under the drums and tramplings of many conquests," it may end by letting us into the secret of usurpations and other scandals gossiped about long empires ago: – this world being apparently a huge whispering-gallery. Such conditions are often minutely represented in our petty lifetime. As the stone which has been kicked by generations of clowns may come by curious links of effect under the eyes of a scholar, through whose labors it may at last fix the date of invasions and unlock religions, so a bit of ink and paper which has long been an innocent wrapping or stop-gap may at last be laid open under the one pair of eyes which have knowledge enough to turn it into the opening of a catastrophe. (p. 448)

The "bit of ink and paper," a simple physical object, can be converted into an intentional object, a piece of knowledge, through the agency of time, chance, and the attention of "one pair

36 Roland Barthes, "The Reality Effect," in *The Rustle of Language*, trans. Richard Howard (New York, Hill and Wang, 1986).

37 Elizabeth Deeds Ermarth, *Realism and Consensus in the English Novel* (Princeton University Press, 1985), p. 225.

of eyes." Like Dorothea's dress when admired by Ladislaw, this writing must be seen by the right perceivers, by "those who know." Writing might "happen" to be cut in stone, or written on a bit of paper, used as "an innocent wrapping or stop-gap," but these physical circumstances are less important than the dissemination of knowledge. The paper thus becomes not simply a gesture towards verisimilitude, nor the carrier of signs with consequence for this particular plot, but an instance of a more general understanding of the wayward consequence of writing and the reconstruction of the past.

"Obsessive reference to the 'concrete,'" writes Barthes, rather impishly, "is always brandished like a weapon against meaning."[38] Reference to semiotic codes expands and develops meaning, widening the range of significance; reference to the concrete constricts significance, tethering it to a univocal meaning. Thackeray's insistent reference to objects, for instance, slides into congruence with the nihilism of his allegories: the more faithful the representation of material bric-a-brac, the more attenuated the meaning extracted. Furthermore, the repeated gesture towards the "real" and away from the implicating structures of cultural codes retards narrative propulsion: "the signified," Barthes writes, "is expelled from the sign, and with it, of course, the possibility of developing a *form of the signified*, i.e. narrative structure itself." [39] As I noted in the first chapter, narrative structure is only recuperated for Thackeray at the level of the commodity, and we saw Gaskell's narrative characterized as being "held by the trimming of a bonnet."[40]

Eliot, by contrast, situates her objects in *Middlemarch* on an aesthetic and semiotic plane, and refers not to things but to their significance. Like the auction and the pawnshop, *Middlemarch* moves away from a narrowly material understanding of goods; instead of translating goods into their exchange value, however, she rewrites them as aesthetic objects. Trumbull presses objects (including aesthetic objects like Gray's "Elegy") into economic service; but Eliot takes those objects and puts them to aesthetic use, developing her own novelistic form. Aesthetic reference

---

38  Barthes, "Reality Effect," p. 146.
39  Barthes, "Reality Effect," p. 147.
40  Dodsworth, "Women Without Men," p. 132.

distances her writing from the "real," and provides a system of significance other than that of the commodity by which she and her readers can understand her prose. Henry James famously complains that *Middlemarch* suffers from the distance of its reference to "the concrete": "We feel in her, always, that she proceeds from the abstract to the concrete; that her figures and situations are evolved, as the phrase is, from her moral consciousness, and are only indirectly the products of observation."[41] James is contrasting Eliot here with Balzac; not for Eliot was Balzac's attention to "things," about which James elsewhere wrote:

There is nothing in all imaginative literature that in the least resembles his mighty passion for *things* – for material objects, for furniture, upholstery, bricks and mortar. The world that contained these things filled his consciousness, and *being*, at its intensest, meant simply being thoroughly at home among them ... To get on in this world, to succeed, to live greatly in all one's senses, to have plenty of *things* – this was Balzac's infinite; it was here that his heart expanded.[42]

By attempting to create, in the aesthetic structure of her text, a source of value and significance other than that of commodified things, Eliot replicates Lydgate's attempt to keep his mind free from the "money-obligation" which material culture can compel. As we saw at the beginning of this chapter, Eliot suggests that a consciousness filled with things, carpets and upholstery, is not a passion but a burden, and the narratives she published similarly move more comfortably among "wider thoughts and cares" than among objects.

Eliot's wary distance from material culture was not simply a matter of the representation of character or the fabrication of aesthetic form, but also a matter of professional obligation: "An author who would keep a pure and noble conscience, and with that a developing instead of degenerating intellect and taste, must cast out of his aims the aim to be rich. And therefore he must keep his expenditure low – he must make for himself no dire necessity to earn sums in order to pay bills."[43] Unlike Thackeray, who understood the "trading determination" as the

41 Henry James, Review of John Walter Cross, *George Eliot's Life as Related in her Letters and Journals*, available in David Carroll, *Critical Heritage*, p. 498.
42 Henry James, *Literary Criticism: French Writers, Other European Writers, the Prefaces to the New York Edition* (New York, Library of America, 1984), p. 48.
43 Eliot, *Essays*, pp. 440–1.

primary motivation of writers, Eliot understood art as ideally existing apart from trade. Lydgate's failure is analogous to the failure of the author entangled by the "dire necessity" of debt. By constructing aesthetic codes through the goods she represents, Eliot attempted to contain their threat and free herself from the constraints of economic practice. But this divided maneuver does not expel material culture from her consideration; instead, by making it an occasion for conflict, Eliot assures its place in the center of her aesthetic.

consequences of this vampiric process do not end there: Rosamond – who would be a fitting prey for Stoker's fiend – having entered into the world of goods, then causes the ruin of her husband. Like Lucy in *Dracula*, Rosamond's departure from the animate world of the realistic novel is most significant when she endangers the men around her.

But the threat of a spectral, menacing material culture does not remain confined to characters in novels; it extends to the authors of those novels as well. As we saw in *Middlemarch*, writing must submit to the same rigorous scrutiny as the domestic activity of wives if it is to avoid being caught up in commodification: expenditure must be watched and kept low, consumption thoughtfully restrained, the cost of clothing learned and its purchase regulated. Mid-Victorian novels in this way anticipate the *fin-de-siècle* not on the level of content but, more significantly, on the level of authorial practice: the writers of these texts scrupulously must resist the possibility that, as producers of material culture, they themselves might become the vassals of a representational system that threatens to use them in a levelling economy of undifferentiated reproduction.

Rather than closing this study of Victorian material culture with the wallpaper incinerated at Waterbath, then, perhaps it is better to recall Oscar Wilde's combat with the interior decoration of his final sickroom: "My wallpaper and I are fighting a duel to the death," Wilde said. "One or the other of us has to go."[6] The relationship between the writer and the surrounding appurtenances he or she represents is a mortal one – and, as we first saw in *Vanity Fair*, the appurtenances tend to survive their owner. At the same time, however, this fatal relationship is constitutive, helping to produce the culture which serves as an occasion for the forms and figures constructing subjectivity and social practices.

6 Richard Ellman, *Oscar Wilde* (New York, Vintage, 1988), p. 581.

# Works cited

Adorno, Theodor. "Letters to Walter Benjamin," trans. Harry
   Zohn. *New Left Review* 81 (1973), 55–80.
   *Minima Moralia: Reflections from Damaged Life*, trans. E. F. N.
   Jephcott. London: Verso, 1978.
   *Philosophy of Modern Music*, trans. Anne Mitchell and Wesley
   Blomster. New York: The Seabury Press, 1973.
"Aleph." *London Scenes and London People*. London: W. H. &
   L. Collingridge, 1880.
Allingham, William. *By the Way: Verses, Fragments, and Notes*.
   London: Longman's Green, & Co., 1912.
Anderson, Perry. "The Figures of Descent," *New Left Review* 161
   (January/February 1987), 20–77.
Appadurai, Arjun, ed. *The Social Life of Things: Commodities in
   Cultural Perspective*. Cambridge University Press, 1986.
Armstrong, Meg. "'A Jumble of Foreignness': The Sublime
   Musayums of Nineteenth-Century Fairs and Exhibitions,"
   *Cultural Critique* 23 (Winter 1992–3), 199–250.
Armstrong, Nancy. *Desire and Domestic Fiction: A Political History
   of the Novel*. New York: Oxford University Press, 1987.
Arnold, Janet. "The Cut and Construction of Women's Dresses,"
   in Costume Society, *High Victorian Costume 1860–1890*.
   London: Victoria and Albert Museum, 1969. 21–9.
Auerbach, Nina. *Communities of Women: An Idea in Fiction*.
   Cambridge, MA: Harvard University Press, 1978.
   *Private Theatricals*. Cambridge, MA: Harvard University Press,
   1990.
Babbage, Charles. *The Exposition of 1851*, in *The Works of Charles
   Babbage*, vol. x, ed. Martin Campbell-Kelly. London: William
   Pickering, 1989 (1851).
Bachelard, Gaston. *The Poetics of Space*, trans. Maria Jolas. Boston:
   Beacon Press, 1969.

# Works cited

Bagehot, Walter. "Charles Dickens," in *The Collected Works of Walter Bagehot*, ed. Norman St. John-Stevas. 15 vols. Cambridge, MA: Harvard University Press, 1965. II, 76–107.

"Sterne and Thackeray," in *Collected Works*. II, 279–311.

Barthes, Roland. *The Fashion System*, trans. Matthew Ward and Richard Howard. New York: Hill and Wang, 1983.

"The Reality Effect," in *The Rustle of Language*, trans. Richard Howard. New York: Hill and Wang, 1986. 141–8.

Bataille, Georges. *The Accursed Share: An Essay on General Economy*, trans. Robert Hurley. 3 vols. New York: Zone Books, 1988.

Baudrillard, Jean. *For a Critique of the Political Economy of the Sign*. St. Louis: Telos Press, 1981.

Benjamin, Walter. *Charles Baudelaire: A Lyric Poet in the Era of High Capitalism*. London: New Left Books, 1979.

*Illuminations*, trans. Harry Zohn. New York: Schocken Books, 1969.

*Moscow Diary*, ed. Gary Smith, trans. Richard Sieburth. Cambridge, MA: Harvard University Press, 1986.

*On the Origin of German Tragic Drama*, trans. John Osborne. London: New Left Books, 1977.

*Reflections: Essays, Aphorisms, Autobiographical Writings*, trans. Edmund Jephcott. New York: Schocken, 1986.

Bennett, Tony. "The Exhibitionary Complex," *New Formations* 4 (Spring 1988), 73–102.

Benson, Susan Porter. *Counter Cultures: Saleswomen, Managers, and Customers in American Department Stores, 1890–1940*. Urbana: University of Illinois Press, 1986.

Berman, Marshall. *All That Is Solid Melts into Air: The Experience of Modernity*. New York: Simon and Schuster, 1982.

Bhabha, Homi K. "The Other Question: Difference, Discrimination, and the Discourse of Colonialism" in *Out There: Marginalization and Contemporary Cultures*, ed. Russell Ferguson et al. Cambridge, MA: MIT Press, 1990. 71–87.

Boone, Joseph Allen. *Tradition Counter Tradition: Love and the Form of Fiction*. University of Chicago Press, 1987.

Bourdieu, Pierre. *Distinction: A Social Critique of the Judgement of Taste*, trans. Richard Nice. Cambridge, MA: Harvard University Press, 1984.

*Outline of a Theory of Practice*, trans. Richard Nice. Cambridge University Press, 1977.

Bowlby, Rachel. *Just Looking: Consumer Culture in Dreiser, Gissing, and Zola*. New York: Methuen, 1985.

Brantlinger, Patrick. *The Rule of Darkness: British Culture and Imperialism, 1830–1914*. Ithaca: Cornell University Press, 1988.

*Spirit of Reform: British Literature and Politics, 1832–1867*. Cambridge, MA: Harvard University Press, 1977

[Brewster, David]. Rev. of *Exposition of 1851*, by Charles Babbage. *North British Review* 15:30 (August 1851), 529–68.

Briggs, Asa. *Victorian Things*. University of Chicago Press, 1989.

Brooks, Peter. *The Melodramatic Imagination: Balzac, Henry James, Melodrama, and the Mode of Excess*. New York: Columbia, 1985.

Brown, Alice. "Later-Day Cranford," *The Atlantic Monthly* 77 (April 1896), 526–34.

Buck-Morss, Susan. *The Dialectics of Seeing: Walter Benjamin and the Arcades Project*. Cambridge, MA: MIT Press, 1989.

Carey, John. *Thackeray: Prodigal Genius*. London: Faber and Faber, 1977.

*The Violent Effigy: A Study of Dickens' Imagination*. London: Faber and Faber, 1973.

Carroll, David. *George Eliot: The Critical Heritage*. New York: Barnes & Noble, 1971.

Carroll, Lewis. *The Letters of Lewis Carroll*, ed. Morton Cohen. 2 vols. New York: Oxford University Press, 1979.

Chadwick, George F. *The Works of Sir Joseph Paxton*. London: The Architectural Press, 1961.

Clifford, James. "On Collecting Art and Culture," in *Out There: Marginalization and Contemporary Cultures*, ed. Russell Ferguson, et al. Cambridge, MA: MIT Press, 1990. 141–69.

Collins, Philip. *Dickens and Crime*. London: Macmillan & Co., 1962.

ed. *Dickens, Interviews and Recollections*. 2 vols. London: Macmillan, 1981.

Cottom, Daniel. *Social Figures: George Eliot, Social History, and Literary Representation*. Minneapolis: University of Minnesota Press, 1987.

*The Crystal Palace Exhibition; Illustrated Catalogue*. New York: Dover Publications, 1970.

*The Crystal Palace that Fox Built*, illus. John Gilbert. London: David Bogue, 1851.

Culver, Stuart. "What Manikins Want: The Wonderful Wizard of

Oz and The Art of Decorating Dry Goods Windows,"
  *Representations* 21 (Winter 1988), 97–116.

Dalzell, Robert Jr. *American Participation in the Great Exhibition of
  1851*. Amherst College Press, 1960.

De Man, Paul. *The Rhetoric of Romanticism*. New York: Columbia
  University Press, 1984.
  "Wordsworth and Hölderlin," in *Romanticism*, 46–65.
  "Wordsworth and the Victorians," in *Romanticism*, 83–92.

de Certeau, Michel. *The Practice of Everyday Life*, trans. Steven F.
  Rendall. Berkeley: University of California Press, 1984.

de Lauretis, Teresa. "Eccentric Subjects: Feminist Theory and
  Historical Consciousness," *Feminist Studies* 16:1 (Spring
  1990), 115–50.

Dennis, Barbara, and David Skilton, eds. *Reform and Intellectual
  Debate in Victorian England*. Beckenham: Croom Helm, 1987.

Derrida, Jacques. *Given Time I: Counterfeit Money*, trans. Peggy
  Kamuf. University of Chicago Press, 1992.

Dickens, Charles. *Charles Dickens' Book of Memoranda*, transcribed
  by Fred Kaplan. New York: New York Public Library, 1981.
  *The Letters of Charles Dickens*, ed. Madelaine House, Graham
  Storey, et al. 7 vols. Oxford: Clarendon, 1965–.
  *Great Expectations*. Oxford: Oxford Illustrated Press, 1953.
  *Our Mutual Friend*. London: Penguin, 1971.
  *Uncommercial Traveller and Reprinted Pieces*. Oxford University
  Press, 1958.
  and Horne, R. H. "The Great Exhibition and the Little One," in
  Harry Stone, ed., *Charles Dickens Uncollected Writings from
  Household Words*. Bloomington: Indiana University Press,
  1968. 319–30.
  and Wills, W. H. "The Metropolitan Protectives," in Stone, 253–74.

Dickens, Mamie. *My Father as I Recall Him*. New York: E. P.
  Dutton & Co., 1898.

Dodd, G. "London Shops and Bazaars," in Charles Knight, ed.,
  *London*. London: Henry G. Bohn, 1851.

Dodsworth, Martin. "Women Without Men at Cranford," *Essays
  in Criticism* 13:2 (April 1963), 132–45.

Drew, William A. *Glimpses and Gatherings During a Voyage and
  Visit to London and the Great Exhibition in the Summer of 1851*.
  Augusta, ME: Homan & Manley, 1852.

Dyer, Gary. "The 'Vanity Fair' of Nineteenth-Century England:

Commerce, Women, and the East in the Ladies Bazaar," *Nineteenth-Century Fiction* 46:2 (September 1991), 181–95.

Eliot, George. *Daniel Deronda*. Harmondsworth: Penguin, 1967.

*Essays*, ed. Thomas Pinney. New York: Columbia University Press, 1963.

*George Eliot Letters*, ed. Gordon Haight. 9 vols. New Haven: Yale University Press, 1954–78.

"Grammer of Ornament," *Fortnightly Review* 1 (1865), 124–5.

*Middlemarch*. London: Penguin, 1965.

*The Mill on the Floss*. New York: Oxford University Press, 1980.

Ellman, Richard. *Oscar Wilde*. New York: Vintage, 1988.

Engels, Friedrich. *The Condition of the Working Class in England*, trans. W. O. Henderson and W. H. Chaloner. Stanford University Press, 1968.

Ermarth, Elizabeth Deeds. *Realism and Consensus in the English Novel*. Princeton University Press, 1985.

*Exhibition Catalogue Advertiser*. London: Spicer and Clowes, 1851.

Fay, C. R. *The Palace of Industry, 1851*. Cambridge University Press, 1951.

Feltes, N. N. *Modes of Production of Victorian Novels*. University of Chicago Press, 1986.

Fisher, Philip. "City Matters: City Minds," in J. H. Buckley, ed. *The Worlds of Victorian Fiction*. Cambridge, MA: Harvard University Press, 1975. 371–89.

Ford, George. *Dickens and His Readers: Aspects of Novel Criticism since 1836*. Princeton University Press, 1955.

Forster, John. *The Life of Charles Dickens*. 3 vols. London: Chapman and Hall, 1874.

Forty, Adrian. *Objects of Desire: Design and Society from Wedgwood to IBM*. New York: Pantheon, 1984.

Foucault, Michel. *The Order of Things: An Archaeology of the Human Sciences*. New York: Vintage, 1973.

Francis, J. *A History of the English Railways. Its Social Relations and Revelations*. 2 vols. London: Longman, Brown, Green, and Longman's, 1851.

Freud, Sigmund. "Fragment of an Analysis of a Case of Hysteria," in *Dora: An Analysis of a Case of Hysteria*. New York: Macmillan, 1963. 21–144.

"Fetishism," in *Collected Papers*, ed. James Strachey. 5 vols. New York: Basic Books, 1959. V, 198–204.

"Negation," in *The Standard Edition of the Complete Psychological Works of Sigmund Freud*. 24 vols. London: Hogarth Press, 1953–74. XIX, 235–9.

"The Uncanny," In *Collected Papers*, ed. James Strachey. 5 vols. New York: Basic Books, 1959. IV, 368–407.

Gallagher, Catherine. *The Industrial Reformation of English Fiction: Social Discourse and Narrative Fiction, 1832–1867*. University of Chicago Press, 1985.

Garbor, Marjorie. *Vested Interests: Cross-dressing and Cultural Anxiety*. New York: Routledge, 1992.

Gaskell, Elizabeth. *Cranford*. London: Oxford University Press, 1972.

*The Letters of Mrs. Gaskell*, ed. J. A. V. Chapple and Arthur Pollard. Cambridge, MA: Harvard University Press, 1967.

*Mary Barton*. Harmondsworth: Penguin, 1970.

Geertz, Clifford. *The Interpretation of Cultures*. New York: Basic Books, 1973.

Giddens, Anthony. *Consequences of Modernity*. Stanford University Press, 1990.

Giedion, Sigfried. *Space, Time, and Architecture*. Cambridge, MA: Harvard University Press, 1954.

Ginsburg, Madeleine. "Clothing Manufacture 1860–1890," in Costume Society, *High Victorian Costume 1860–1890*. London: Victoria and Albert Museum, 1969. 2–9.

Graham, Wendy. "A Narrative History of Class Consciousness," *Boundary* 2 15: 1/2 (Fall 1986, Winter 1987), 41–68.

Greenhalgh, Paul. *Ephemeral Vistas: Expositions Universelles, Great Exhibitions and World Fairs, 1851–1939*. Manchester University Press, 1988.

Hamer, Mary. *Writing by Numbers: Trollope's Serial Fiction*. Cambridge University Press, 1987.

Hardy, Barbara. *The Exposure of Luxury: Radical Themes in Thackeray*. University of Pittsburgh Press, 1972.

"Objects in Novels," *Genre* 10 (Winter 1977), 485–500.

Harvey, David. *The Urbanization of Capital: Studies in the History and Theory of Capitalist Urbanization*. Baltimore: The Johns Hopkins Press, 1985.

Haug, Wolfgang. *Critique of Commodity Aesthetics: Appearance, Sexuality, and Advertising in Capitalist Society*, trans. Robert Bock. Cambridge: Polity Press, 1986.

# Works cited

Herbert, Christopher. *Trollope and Comic Pleasure*. University of Chicago Press, 1987.

Herodotus. *The History*, trans. David Greene. University of Chicago Press, 1987.

Hippolyte, Jean. "A Spoken Commentary on Freud's *Verneinung*," in Jacques Lacan, *The Seminar of Jacques Lacan: Freud's Papers on Technique, 1953–4*, trans. John Forrester, ed. Jacques-Alain Miller. New York: Norton, 1988. 289–97.

Hobsbawm, Eric. *The Age of Capital: 1848–1875*. New York: Meridian, 1984.

Horkheimer Max, and Theodor Adorno. *The Dialectic of Enlightenment*, trans. John Cumming. New York: Continuum, 1988.

House, Humphry. *The Dickens World*. London: Oxford University Press, 1942.

"The House that Paxton Built." London: Darton & Co., [1851].

Howes, Craig. "*Pendennis* and the Controversy on the 'Dignity of Literature,'" *Nineteenth-Century Fiction* 41 (1986), 269–98. Rpt. in *William Makepeace Thackeray*, ed. Harold Bloom. New York: Chelsea House Publishers, 1987. 233–53.

Irigaray, Luce. *This Sex Which Is Not One*, trans. Catherine Porter. Ithaca: Cornell University Press, 1985.

James, Henry. *European Writers and the Prefaces*, ed. Leon Edel and Mark Wilson. New York: Library of America, 1984.

    *Spoils of Poynton*. New York: Penguin, 1963.

    *Literary Criticism: French Writers, Other European Writers, the Prefaces to the New York Edition*. New York: Library of America, 1984.

Jameson, Fredric. "Cognitive Mapping," in *Marxism and the Interpretation of Culture*, ed. Cary Nelson and Lawrence Grossberg. Urbana: University of Illinois Press, 1988. 347–57.

    *Ideologies of Theory: Essays 1971–1986*. 2 vols. Minneapolis: University of Minnesota Press, 1988.

    *Marxism and Form: Twentieth Century Dialectical Theories of Literature*. Princeton University Press, 1971.

    *The Political Unconscious: Narrative as a Socially Symbolic Act*. Ithaca: Cornell University Press, 1981.

Jones, Gareth Stedman. *Outcast London: A Study in the Relationship Between Classes in Victorian Society*. New York: Pantheon, 1984.

Kendrick, Walter M. *The Novel Machine: The Theory and Fiction of Anthony Trollope.* Baltimore: Johns Hopkins University Press, 1980.

*Knight's Cyclopedia of the Industry of all Nations.* London: Charles Knight, 1851.

Knoepflmacher, U. C. *Laughter and Despair: Readings in Ten Novels of the Victorian Era.* Berkeley: University of California Press, 1971.

Kopytoff, Igor. "The Cultural Biography of Things: Commodities as Process," in Arjun Appadurai, ed., *The Social Life of Things: Commodities in Cultural Perspective.* Cambridge University Press, 1986, 64–91.

Kristeva, Julia. *The Kristeva Reader,* ed. Toril Moi. New York: Columbia University Press, 1986

Kucich John. *Excess and Restraint in Charles Dickens.* Athens: University of Georgia Press, 1981.

*Repression in Victorian Fiction: Charlotte Brontë, George Eliot, and Charles Dickens.* Berkeley: University of California Press, 1987.

Lacan, Jacques. *Ecrits: A Selection,* trans. Alan Sheridan. New York: Norton, 1977.

"The Meaning of Phallus," in Juliet Mitchell and Jacqueline Rose, eds., *Feminine Sexuality.* New York: Norton, 1982. 74–85.

Lefebvre, Henri. *Everyday Life in the Modern World,* trans. Sach Rabinowitch. London: Allan Lane, Penguin, 1971.

Levine, George. *The Realistic Imagination: English Fiction from Frankenstein to Lady Chatterley.* University of Chicago Press, 1981.

Levitt, Sarah. *Victorians Unbuttoned: Registered Designs for Clothing, their Makers and Wearers, 1839–1900.* London: George Allen & Unwin, 1986.

Lewin, Henry Grote. *The Railway Mania and its Aftermath, 1845–1852.* Newton Abbot: David and Charles, 1968 (1936).

Loofbourow, John. *Thackeray and the Form of Fiction.* Princeton University Press, 1964.

Lukács, Georg. *History and Class Consciousness: Studies in Marxist Dialectics,* trans. Rodney Livingstone. Cambridge: The MIT Press, 1968.

Macpherson, C. B. "Human Rights as Property Rights," *Dissent* 24 (Winter 1977), 72–7.

*The Political Theory of Possessive Individualism: Hobbes to Locke*.
Oxford: Clarendon Press, 1962.

Madden, R. R. *The Literary Life and Correspondence of the Countess of Blessington*. 2 vols. New York: Harper and Brothers, 1855.

Marcus, Steven. "Language into Structure: Pickwick Revisited," *Daedalus* 101: 1 (Winter 1972), 183–202.

[Marshall, Fredric]. "French Home Life," *Blackwood's Magazine* 111 (January 1872), 30–46; 112 (August 1872), 154–69.

Marx, Karl. *Capital*, trans. Ben Fowkes. New York: Vintage, 1977.
*Grundrisse*, trans. Martin Nicolaus. New York: Vintage, 1973.
*The Holy Family*, in *The Marx–Engels Reader*, trans. and ed. Robert Tucker. New York: W. W. Norton, 1978.

Masson, David. "Thackeray and Dickens," *North British Review* 20: 29 (May 1851), 30–47. Rpt. in Geoffrey Tillotson, ed., *Thackeray: The Critical Heritage*. London: Routledge & Kegan Paul, 1968. 111–26.

Mauss, Marcel. *The Gift: Forms and Functions of Exchange in Archaic Societies*, trans. Ian Cunnison. London: Cohen, 1954.

Mayhew, Henry. *London Labour and the London Poor*. 4 vols. New York: Dover Publications, 1968.

Mill, J. S. *On Liberty*. Harmondsworth: Penguin, 1982.

Miller, Andrew H. "Subjectivity Ltd: The Discourse of Liability in the Joint-Stock Companies Act of 1856 and Gaskell's *Cranford*," *ELH* 61 (1994), 139–57.
"Epistemological Claustrophobia and Critical Transcendence" *Yale Journal of Criticism* 7: 2 (Fall 1994), 131–49.

Miller, D. A. *Novel and the Police*. Berkeley: University of California Press, 1988.

Miller, Michael. *The Bon Marché: Bourgeois Culture and the Department Store, 1869–1920*. Princeton University Press, 1981.

Miller, William. *Humiliation*. Ithaca: Cornell University Press, 1993.

Mitchell, Timothy. *Colonizing Egypt*. Cambridge University Press, 1988.

Modleski, Tania. *Feminism Without Women, Culture and Criticism in a "Postfeminist" Age*. New York: Routledge, 1991.

Morris, R. J. "Leeds and the Crystal Palace," *Victorian Studies* 13:3 (March 1970), 283–300.

[Mozley, Anne]. "Dress," *Blackwood's Magazine* 97 (April 1865), 425–38.

# Works cited

Newman, Karen. "City Talk: Women and Commodification in Jonson's *Epicoene*," *ELH* 56: 3 (Fall 1987), 503–18.

Nord, Deborah. "The Urban Peripatetic: Spectator, Streetwalker, Woman Writer," *Nineteenth-Century Fiction* 46:3 (December 1991), 351–75.

Nunokowa, Jeff. *The Afterlife of Property: Domestic Security and the Victorian Novel.* Princeton University Press, 1994.

Olsen, Donald J. "Victorian London: Specialization, Segregation, and Privacy," *Victorian Studies* 17:3 (March 1974), 265–78.

Orwell, George. "Oysters and Brown Stout," *The Collected Essays of George Orwell.* 4 vols. Vol. III, ed. Sonia Orwell and Ian Angus. New York: Harcourt Brace Jovanovich, 1968. 299–302

*The Palace of Glass and the Gathering of People.* London: The Religious Tract Society, 1851.

Pollins, Harold. "Railway Contractors and the Finance of Railway Development in Britain," in M. C. Reed, ed. *Railways in the Victorian Economy: Studies in Finance and Economic Growth.* Newton Abbot: David and Charles, 1969. 212–28.

Poovey, Mary. *Uneven Developments: The Ideological Work of Gender in Mid-Victorian England.* University of Chicago Press, 1989.

Ray, Gordon, ed. *The Letters and Private Papers of William Makepeace Thackeray.* 4 vols. Cambridge, MA: Harvard University Press, 1945–6.

*The Uses of Adversity.* New York: McGraw Hill, 1955.

Richards, Thomas. *The Commodity Culture of Victorian England: Advertising and Spectacle, 1851–1914.* Stanford University Press, 1990.

Saunders, David. *Authorship and Copyright.* London: Routledge, 1992.

Schivelbusch, Wolfgang. *The Railway Journey: The Industrialization of Time and Space in the Nineteenth Century.* Berkeley: University of California Press, 1986.

*Disenchanted Light: The Industrialization of Light in the Nineteenth Century.* Berkeley: University of California Press, 1988.

Schor, Hilary. "Affairs of the Alphabet: Reading, Writing, and Narrating in Cranford," *Novel* 22: 3 (Spring 1989), 288–304.

*Scheherezade in the Marketplace: Elizabeth Gaskell and the Victorian Novel.* New York: Oxford University Press, 1992.

Sedgwick, Eve Kosofsky. *Between Men: English Literature and Male*

Works cited

*Homosocial Desire*. New York: Columbia University Press, 1985.

Sennett, Richard. *The Fall of Public Man: On the Social Psychology of Capitalism*. New York: Vintage, 1978.

"Plate Glass," *Raritan* 6:4 (1987), 1–15.

Shannon, H. A. "The Coming of the General Limited Liability," in E. M. Carus Wilson, ed., *Essays in Economic History*, 3 vols. London: E. Arnold, 1954. I, 358–99.

Short, Audrey. "Workers Under Glass in 1851," *Victorian Studies* 10:2 (Dec. 1966), 193–202.

Sichel, Marion. *Costume Reference 6: The Victorians*. London: B. T. Batsford. 1978.

Simmel, Georg. "The Berlin Trade Exhibition," trans. Sam Whimster. *Theory, Culture & Society*. 8 (1991), 119–23.

"The Metropolis and Mental Life," in *The Sociology of Georg Simmel*, trans. Kurt H. Wolff. Glencoe, Illinois: The Free Press, 1950.

Slater, Michael. "The Bachelor's Pocket Book for 1851," in Don Richard Cox, ed., *Sexuality and Victorian Literature*. Knoxville: University of Tennessee Press, 1984. 128–40.

Sloterdijk, Peter. *Critique of Cynical Reason*. Minneapolis: University of Minnesota Press, 1987.

Smith, Charles Manby. *The Little World of London*. London: Arthur Hall, Virtue & Co., 1857.

Smith, Dorothy. *Everyday Life as Problematic: A Feminist Sociology*. Boston: Northeastern University Press, 1987.

Squire, Geoffrey. "Men and Angels; Fashion 1830–1860," in Costume Society, *Early Victorian Costume 1830–1860*. London: Victoria and Albert Museum, 1969. 2–11.

Steele, Valerie. *Fashion and Eroticism: Ideals of Feminine Beauty from the Victorian Era to the Jazz Age*. New York: Oxford University Press, 1985.

[Stephen, Caroline]. "Thoughtfulness in Dress," *Cornhill* 18 (1868), 281–98.

Stone, Harry, ed. *Charles Dickens Uncollected Writings from Household Words*. Bloomington: Indiana University Press, 1968.

Super, R. H. *The Chronicler of Barsetshire*. Ann Arbor: University of Michigan Press, 1988.

Tafuri, Manfredo. *Architecture and Utopia: Design and Capitalist*

*Development*, trans. Barbara Luigia La Penta. Cambridge, MA: MIT Press, 1976.

Tennyson, Alfred. "Ode Sung at the Opening of the International Exhibition," in *Tennyson: Poems and Plays*. Oxford University Press, 1965. 207.

Thackeray, William. "A Brother of the Press on the History of a Literary Man, Laman Blanchard, and the Chances of the Literary Profession," in *Works*. XXV, 465–79.

*The Complete Works of William Makepeace Thackeray*, 25 vols. New York: Harper & Brothers, 1904.

*The History of Pendennis*. Harmondsworth: Penguin, 1972.

"Mr. Moloney's Account of the Crystal Palace," *Punch* 20 (1851) 1.

*Novels By Eminent Hands*, in *Works*. XII, 467–540.

*Philip*, in *Works*. XX–XXI.

*Sketches and Travels in London*, in *Works*. XII, 541–74.

*Vanity Fair*. London: Oxford University Press, 1983.

Thompson, E. P. "Time, Work, Discipline, and Industrial Capitalism," *Past and Present* 38 (December 1967), 56–97.

Thompson, Michael. *Rubbish Theory: The Creation and Destruction of Value*. Oxford University Press, 1979.

Tollemache, Beatrix L. "Cranford Souvenirs," *Temple Bar* 105 (August 1895), 536–9

Trollope, Anthony. *An Autobiography*. Oxford University Press, 1950

*The Eustace Diamonds*. 2 vols. Oxford University Press, 1983.

*The Letters of Anthony Trollope*, ed. N. John Hall. 2 vols. Stanford University Press, 1983.

*Phineas Finn*. Harmondsworth: Penguin, 1972.

Tupper, Martin. "The Great Exhibition," in *Three Hundred Sonnets*. London: Arthur Hall, Virtue & Co., 1860.

Valverde, Mariana. "The Love of Finery: Fashion and the Fallen Woman in Nineteenth-Century Social Discourse," *Victorian Studies* 32:2 (Winter 1989), 168–88.

Vanden Bossche, Chris R. "Cookery, not Rookery: Family and Class in *David Copperfield*," *Dickens Studies Annual* 15 (1986), 87–110.

Van Ghent, Dorothy. "The Dickens World: the View from Todgers," in Martin Price, ed., *Dickens*. Englewood Cliffs: Prentice Hall, 1967. 24–38.

Works cited

Van Zanten, David. "Architectural Polychromy: Life in Architecture," in Robin Middleton, ed., *The Beaux-Arts and Nineteenth Century Architecture*. Cambridge, MA: MIT Press, 1982.

  *The Architectural Polychromy of the 1830's*. New York: Garland Press, 1977.

Veblen, Thorstein. *The Theory of the Leisure Class: An Economic Study in the Evolution of Institutions*. New York: NAL–Penguin, 1953.

Walzer, Michael. *Spheres of Justice*. New York: Basic Books, 1983.

Ward, James. *The World in its Workshops*. London: W^m. S. Orr & Co., 1851.

Warren, Samuel. *The Lily and the Bee*. Leipzig: Tauchnitz, 1851.

Watt, Ian. *Conrad in the Nineteenth Century*. London: Chatto and Windus, 1980.

Weber, Max, *General Economic History*. New Brunswick: Transaction Books, 1981.

Welsh, Alexander. *The City of Dickens*. Cambridge, MA: Harvard University Press, 1986.

  *George Eliot and Blackmail*. Cambridge, MA: Harvard University Press, 1985.

Whewell, William. "The General Bearing of the Great Exhibition on the Progress of Art and Science," in *Lectures on the Results of the Great Exhibition*. London: David Bogue, 1852. 3–25.

Wicke, Jennifer. *Advertising Fictions: Literature, Advertisement, and Social Reading*. New York: Columbia University Press, 1988.

Williams, Raymond. *The Country and City*. New York: Oxford University Press, 1973.

  *The English Novel: From Dickens to Lawrence*. London: Hogarth, 1984.

  *Marxism and Literature*. Oxford University Press, 1977.

Williams, Rosalind. *Dream Worlds: Mass Consumption in Late Nineteeenth-century France*. Berkeley: University of California Press, 1982.

Wilson, J. F., ed. *A Memorial to the North of London Working Classes' Industrial Exhibition*. London: Petter and Galpin, n.d.

Wise, Thomas James, ed., *The Brontës: their Lives, Friendships, and Correspondence*. 4 vols. Philadelphia: Porcupine Press, 1980.

Wolfe, Patricia. "Structure and Movement in *Cranford*," *Nineteenth-Century Fiction* 33:2 (September 1968), 161–76.

# Works cited

Wordsworth, William. *The Prelude*, ed. J. C. Maxwell. New York: Oxford University Press, 1971.

Wornum, Ralph. "Prize Essay: The Exhibition as a Lesson in Taste," in *The Crystal Palace Exhibition*. New York: Dover Publications, 1970. i–xxii

Žižek, Slavoj. *The Sublime Object of Ideology*. London: Verso, 1989.

# Index

# Index

commodification 6–7
  and death 19–21, 36–7, 91–2, 123, 210
  of Great Exhibition and Crystal Palace
    90
  of language 48, 197–8
  of novel 8–9, 12–13, 44–9, 182–8
  of subjectivity 12, 15, 38
  of women 25, 31, 64–70, 136–38, 170–3,
    196–9, 204–6
  see also commodity culture, commodity
    exchange, commodity form
commodity culture 6–7, 14–15, 91
  see also commodification, commodity
    exchange, commodity form
commodity exchange
  in Cranford 98–100
  and death 92
  in Dickens 133–4
  in Eliot 208–14
  and Great Exhibition 53, 86–90, 57n23
  Lukács on 28–9, 124–5
  Marx on 33–4
  in Thackeray 30–4, 38, 41, 44, 47–9, 217
  in Trollope 159–63, 170–1, 180–1
  see also commodification, commodity
    culture, commodity form
commodity form 159, 162
  and death 18–23, 36, 37
  and narrative form 7–9, 12–13, 38, 160,
    167–8
  Thackeray and 14–16, 18–25, 29–30, 49,
    192
  see also commodification, commodity
    culture, commodity exchange
community 11, 119
  absence of in Thackeray 38, 40–4
  in Cranford 99–100, 114–18
  see also atomization and fragmentation,
    social
Conrad, Joseph 156
consumption 1–2, 10, 206–7
  and Great Exhibition 57, 64–8, 86
  in Thackeray 24–5, 31, 37
  women as consumers 64–8, 206–7
Cook, John Douglas 44n62
copyright 8–9, 44, 78
  Trollope and 162, 184–8
Cottom, Daniel 208
Crystal Palace 10, 50–90, 91, 109, 116, 189
  see also Great Exhibition
The Crystal Palace that Fox Built 62
Culver, Stuart 66, 69n56

Dalzell, Robert 73n73
dandy 16–18, 133–4

death
  and commodification 18–22, 36, 37,
    91–3, 123, 210
  in Cranford 100, 103, 114
  in Eliot 201–2, 210, 213
  narrative form and 93–5, 145
  Thackeray and 18–22, 37, 50–1
debt and credit
  in Thackeray 30, 40
  see also bankruptcy
de Certeau, Michel 99, 101, 118
de Lauretis, Teresa 66
de Man, Paul 156
Dennis, Barbara 122n10
department stores 6, 57–8, 88
  see also shops and shopping
Derrida, Jacques 115, 165, 169
desire 26–7, 36–7
  for commodities 1–6, 10, 14–25, 30, 34–7,
    64–7, 82–3, 86, 93, 136–8, 196, 205
  in Dickens 136–8
  in Eliot 196, 205
  female 10, 64–7, 82, 93, 196
  at Great Exhibition 10, 64–70, 82–3, 86
  male 10, 66–70, 93, 136–8
  servant's 14–19, 30, 31n35, 42, 66, 83
  in Thackeray 9, 14–26, 30, 34–7
detectives and detection
  in Cranford 103–8, 110
  in The Eustace Diamonds 170, 179
  in Our Mutual Friend 120, 126–32, 156
  in Middlemarch 199, 201–2, 214
  see also police
Dicey, A. V. 38n54
Dickens, Catherine 119–20, 137, 158
Dickens, Charles
  alienation in 128–37, 144–5
  and the body 129, 150–2
  commodity exchange in 133–4
  David Copperfield 139, 157n71
  desire in 136–8
  detection and police in 120, 126–31, 156
  domesticity and 11, 119–20, 123, 139n50,
    139n52, 157n71
  and Gaskell 101, 105–6, 110–11, 130–1,
    135, 138, 142, 176–7
  and Great Exhibition 50, 74–5, 79, 86
  Great Expectations 137
  and housekeeping 119–21, 138–9,189
  Little Dorrit 134
  Memoranda Book 121
  "The Metropolitan Protectives" 80n93,
    130
  Our Mutual Friend 119–58, 196, 219
  Pickwick Papers 105–6, 111, 177

# Index

# Index

# Index

Richards, Thomas 52n5, 60n30, 61, 72, 89n122
Richardson, Coke 194
Rowton, Fredric 192
Ruskin, John 123, 127n22

Sala, G. A. 129n26
satire 18–21, 66, 100
Saunders, David 9n18
Schivelbusch, Wolfgang 53–4, 58n27, 58n28, 127n22
Schor, Hilary 95, 101, 176–7
Sedgwick, Eve Kosofsky 136
Sennett, Richard 4, 57n24, 195, 200–1
servants
  in Thackeray 14–18, 21–2, 28–30, 35, 42–4, 47, 50, 66, 79, 83
  in *Middlemarch* 198–9
Shannon, H. A. 8n15
shops and shopping 1–6, 23, 32, 68n53, 91–2, 137
  in *Cranford* 99–100, 116–17
  curiosity shops 22n13
  generating narratives 22n13, 24n19
  Great Exhibition and 51–2, 63–8, 87–90
  in Thackeray 23, 31, 42–3, 45–6, 53
  *see* department stores, shop-windows
shop-windows 62n37
  in London 1–6, 22n14, 51–2, 71, 88–90, 122
  "shop-window quality" 84
  in Thackeray 23, 42–3, 49, 147–8
  women behind 66–70
  *see* shops and shopping, department stores, glass
Short, Audrey 79n90, 83n104
Sichel, Marion 193n12
Simmel, Georg 34, 61n31, 65, 84, 130
Skilton, David 122n10
Slater, Michael 70n59
Sloterdijk, Peter 29n33
Smith, Charles Manby 2–5, 22n15, 90
Smith, Dorothy 104–5, 118
Smith, George 185
Smith, Southwood 158
Southey, Robert 95, 101–2, 111
space
  in Dickens' novels 11, 50, 137–8, 147–9, 157–8
  of exchange 50–64, 82, 88–90, 116, 219
  in Great Exhibition 10, 51–3, 66, 88–90, 116
  and railways 53–7, 58–60
  snug 50, 137, 148–9, 159
  in Thackeray's novels 9–10, 50

Squire, Geoffrey 193n12
Steele, Valerie 194n15
Stephen, Caroline 194
subjectivity
  in Dickens 131–3, 142, 152–3, 155, 195
  in Eliot 13, 195, 204–6
  female 11, 46–7, 66–70, 93, 115–18, 142, 204–7
  in Gaskell 93, 114–18, 142, 195
  and Great Exhibition 61, 66–70, 93, 195, 204
  ownership of 12, 161–3
  split 131–2, 152–3, 201n25
  in Thackeray 9, 29–30, 34, 38–44, 93, 195, 204
  in Trollope 161–3, 170, 173–7
Super, R. H. 186

Tafuri, Manfredo 60–1
taste 84–6, 98–9, 122–3, 197, 202–6
Tennyson, Alfred, Lord 62
Thackeray, William
  alienation in 15, 26, 28–30, 47, 192
  auctions in 19–22, 35–6, 38
  bankruptcy and 22–3, 27–8, 34, 36
  *The Book of Snobs* 35
  "A Brother of the Press" 44–5
  *Catherine* 46
  commodity exchange and 30–4, 38, 41, 44, 47–9, 217
  commodity form and 14–16, 18–25, 29–30, 49, 192
  community, absence of 38, 40–4
  consumption 24–5, 31, 37
  and *Cranford* 99–100, 116, 117
  debt and credit 30, 40
  desire in 9, 14–15, 30, 34–7
  and Dickens 34–5, 48, 145–8
  and dress 16–19
  and Eliot 12, 37, 192, 193, 209, 211, 216
  fetishism and 9, 19, 21, 25–6, 46, 52
  gambling in 39
  "George de Barnwell" 45–6
  gift exchange in 40–3
  and Great Exhibition 50–3, 64, 68, 79, 83
  *Henry Esmond* 37
  *The History of Pendennis* 17–18, 26, 48, 116
  jewelry in 16
  "Mr. Moloney's Account of the Crystal Palace" 62
  and narrative form 33, 42–5, 52
  *The Newcombes* 42n61
  ownership and property in 17–18, 27
  pawnshops in 23–4, 31, 36, 49

241

# Index

Thackeray, William (*cont.*)
  *Philip* 48–9
  servants in 14–18, 21–2, 28–30, 35, 42–4,
    47, 50, 66, 79, 83
  shops and shopping in 23, 31, 42–3,
    45–6, 53
  shop-windows in 23, 42–3, 49, 147–8
  *Sketches and Travels in London* 23–5, 49, 66
  space in 9–10, 50
  subjectivity in 9, 29–30, 34, 38–44, 93,
    195, 204
  and Trollope 160, 162, 173, 178, 182
  and utopia 16–17, 29–30, 35–8, 40, 42
  *Vanity Fair* 14–49, 50–3, 64–8, 93,
    99–100, 117, 147–8, 160, 203, 207, 209,
    219, 221
  *Virginians* 27
  walking in 23, 32, 43, 48
theaters 71, 200–2
theft 6, 12, 21, 134, 197
  in Trollope 163–4, 168–71, 178–81, 183,
    187–8
  *see also* police, detectives and detection
Thompson, E. P. 54n11
Thompson, Michael 125n17
Tollemache, Beatrix L. 101n27
trash 124–5, 125n17
Trollope, Anthony
  *Autobiography* 159–60, 168n12, 173–7,
    180n18, 181–3, 186–8
  commodity exchange and 159–62, 170–1,
    181
  and Dickens 159
  *The Eustace Diamonds* 11–12, 30, 159–88
  jewelry in 12, 159–68, 169–71, 187
  and narrative form 160, 164–5, 167–8
  *Phineas Finn* 183
  and the Post Office 169, 173, 174–5, 176
  and property 12, 161–73, 185–8
  subjectivity in 161–3, 170, 173–7
  and Thackeray 160, 162, 173, 178, 182
  *The Way We Live Now* 180n18
  and theft 163–4, 168–71, 178–81, 183,
    187–8
Tupper, Martin 63n38
Turner, J. M. W. 58–9

United States 73–4, 174
utopia 5, 9–10, 65, 99, 126–7

Crystal Palace as 60–1, 65
  in *Vanity Fair* 16–17, 29–30, 35–8, 40, 42

value
  exchange 211–13, 216–17
Valverde, Mariana 31n35
Vanden Bossche, Chris R. 139n52, 157n71
Van Ghent, Dorothy 123n13, 152
Van Zanten, David 57n23
Veblen, Thorstein 14n3
*Verneinung* 124
Vincent, Henry 79

walking
  in Dickens 134, 135, 141
  through Great Exhibition 53, 57
  through London 1–6, 23, 32, 134, 135,
    141
  in Thackeray 23, 32, 43, 48, 50
Walzer, Michael 34n43
Ward, James 58
Warren, Samuel 58
Watt, Ian 156
Weber, Max 130, 141, 159
Welsh, Alexander 138, 212
Whewell, William 54, 72–3, 84
Whiteley, William 57n24
Wicke, Jennifer 2n4
Wilde, Oscar 221
Williams, Raymond 121–2, 153n67
Williams, Rosalind 57n24
Wills, W. H. 80n93, 128n25
Wilson, J. F. 83–4
Wolfe, Patricia 111
Wordsworth, William 154–6
working classes
  at Great Exhibition 10, 76–84
Wornum, Ralph 84–6
Worth, Charles 193
writing
  and domesticity 11, 119–20, 139–41,
    157–8
  as enclave 157–8
  materiality of 97–104, 172–3, 181
  as play 140–5
  *see also* language, narrative form

Žižek, Slavoj 148–9, 203

242